INCREMENTAL CONCEPTUALIZATION FOR LANGUAGE PRODUCTION

Markus Guhe

Routledge
Taylor & Francis Group

LONDON AND NEW YORK

First published 2007 by Lawrence Erlbaum Associates, Inc.

Published 2018 by Routledge
2 Park Square, Milton Park, Abingdon, Oxon OX14 4RN
52 Vanderbilt Avenue, New York, NY 10017

First issued in paperback 2018

Routledge is an imprint of the Taylor & Francis Group, an informa business

Copyright © 2007 by Taylor & Francis

CIP information for this volume can be obtained
from the Library of Congress

This thesis was accepted as doctoral dissertation by the Department of Informatics, University of Hamburg, and based on this work the author was granted the academic degree Dr. rer. nat.
Date of the oral examination: December 19, 2003
Review committee:
Prof. Dr. Christopher Habel
Prof. Dr. Wolfgang Menzel
Prof. Dr. Dietrich Dörner

Cover Design: Kathryn Houghtaling-Lacey

ISBN 13: 978-1-138-97250-6 (pbk)
ISBN 13: 978-0-8058-5624-8 (hbk)

∼ CONTENTS ∼

W HEN WE HUMANS talk, a lot of things happen simultaneously: We move our tongue, we listen to what we say, we think about what to say next, we watch the person we are talking to, we feel an itch and scratch, we notice that it is lunch time and we are hungry … In other words, we are occupied with a plethora of tasks. Nevertheless, we are capable of observing what is happening around us and simultaneously talking more or less fluently. This book is about, on the one hand, this simultaneity of thinking and speaking and, on the other hand, the piecemeal way in which we construct an internal representation of the external world and use this internal representation for speaking. Although these two observations are not new, in this book I present the first computational model that captures them in a cognitively adequate fashion. That is, I present a computational model of the cognitive process of conceptualization, which is the mind's process that produces the semantic representations that can be transformed into language. Apart from discussing the theoretical foundations of such a model, in this book I present INC (the incremental conceptualizer), the first model of its kind.

In the past 7 years, when I explained what this book is about at scientific conferences, via e-mail, or in informal discussions, I received mainly two reactions: great interest and a sense that I was a bit mad trying to tackle this open-ended problem. The scepticism is mainly due to the fact that the investigation of conceptualization faces a difficult problem: It is not directly observable but only via other modalities, mainly language. (This, incidentally, leads to a lot of confusion about the topics involved.) It is also hardly definable what belongs to conceptualization and what to other areas of cognition. The great interest is due to the fact that although it is obvious that thinking and speaking take place simultaneously, it is also something difficult to grasp, so that most explanations are rather vague. This is the point where a computational model provides new insights, and this is the main contribution of this book. However, it is also clear (without 7 years of research) that such a model must be more than incomplete. My hope, therefore, is that my model INC inspires new thoughts; it certainly is no complete model of the thinking needed for language or even thinking in general.

In this book I pursue an interdisciplinary approach in the spirit of cognitive science. Even though I think this is the best way to do science, it faces a hard problem: I will probably not be able to satisfy the readers of all contributing disciplines. I cannot think of a better way to defend myself than by citing Peter Gärdenfors (2000):

> While writing the text, I felt like a centaur, standing on four legs ...: philosophy, computer science, psychology, and linguistics ... Since these disciplines pull in difference directions—in particular when it comes to methodological questions—there is a considerable risk that my centaur has ended up in a four-legged split.
>
> A consequence of this split is that I will satisfy no one. Philosophers will complain that my arguments are weak; psychologists will point to a wealth of evidence ... that I have not accounted for; linguistics will indict me for glossing over the intricacies of language ...; and computer scientists will ridicule me for developing algorithms for the various processes that I describe.
>
> I plead guilty to all four charges. My aim is to unify ideas from different disciplines into a general theory ... . This is a work within cognitive science and not one in philosophy, psychology, linguistics, or computer science. My ambition here is to present a coherent research program that others will find attractive and use as a basis for more detailed investigations. (p. ix)

The only charge I think I am not really guilty of is the one of computer science—after all, I managed to obtain a PhD in this discipline with this work. Most likely this means I am even more guilty of the other three charges. The value of this book lies in its integration of its two major topics: incrementality and conceptualization.

I don't have time; what do I read?

If you do not wish to read the whole text, I recommend that you start with §2, which illustrates the issue of incremental conceptualization with an example. §13 describes conceptualization in more detail, §20 the corresponding representations. §23 treats the issue of incrementality, and §24 provides a blueprint of an incremental architecture. Chapter 8 lays out the overall architecture of the model INC (incremental conceptualizer), which brings together the ideas of incrementality and conceptualization. Chapter 13 describes simulations carried out with the implementation of INC, and chapter 16 summarizes the theses that I develop in this book.

I give a short overview of each chapter's main points at their beginnings, which should make it easier to find the parts that interest you.

Acknowledgments

I want to thank my PhD supervisors for discussions and comments: Christopher Habel, Wolfgang Menzel, and Dietrich Dörner.

Most of the research described in this book was carried out as part of my PhD in the project *ConcEv* (Conceptualizing Events; pronounce like the work *conceive*) at the University of Hamburg. ConcEv was funded by the DFG (Deutsche Forschungsgemeinschaft) in the priority program *Language Production* under grant Ha-1237/10 to Christopher Habel. Without Christopher's help and support, this book would never have been written.

Heike Tappe and Ladina Tschander (and Christopher of course), my project colaborators, inspired many ideas and compelled me to explain and defend them. Thanks also to all the students that worked for *ConcEv* over the years and contributed their time and ideas: Andy Adiwidjaja, Christian Gerhard, Steffen Huber, Nadine Jochims, Bärbel Rieckmann, Jorgen Schaefer, Heidi Schmolck, Anni-Yasmin Turhan, and Jette Viethen.

Thomas Barkowsky, Carola Eschenbach, Ralf Klabunde, and Frank Schilder commented on parts of this text without being obliged to do so. I am obliged to them. Lars Kulik unfortunately left Hamburg before the text had matured enough so that I could bother him with it, but we discussed some tricky problems, which I understand much better now. Koenraad de Smedt, Dick Hudson, and Gerard Kempen clarified issues regarding their own work. Robert Dale asked some seemingly innocent questions, which led to some important changes in the text. Frank Ritter and seven anonymous reviewers provided me with important feedback.

Although the text is essentially my PhD thesis, it required considerable time to convert it into a book. Wayne Gray, Ellen Bard, and Mark Steedman provided me the freedom to pursue this project although I should have spent my time working on our common projects.

Wayne Gray also initiated the contact to Lawrence Erlbaum and supported this book. Frank Ritter played a crucial role in finally convincing Lawrence Erlbaum to publish it.

At Lawrence Erlbaum, Bill Webber immediately liked the idea to make this book. I am all the more grateful for this as it is an unusual thing to do for Lawrence Erlbaum. After Bill left, Lori Handelman seamlessly continued where Bill left off and provided me with every support I needed. And after Lori left, Steve Rutter did the same. Thanks also to the production and marketing teams for the professional and uncomplicated collaboration.

I especially thank Cordula Klein. Mainly for putting up with me and leaving me alone when I brooded over something intricate while always offering me her indispensable moral support. All the more, as she had not only to endure this project as my PhD thesis but also as a "proper" publication project. She also read much of the text, suggested many improvements, and helped in preparing the final manuscript.

Last but not least I thank my parents, who made me curious about the world and supported and encouraged me not only during the last years while I worked on this thesis/book. They always provided a quiet retreat with a warm fire and excellent food. To them I dedicate this work.

INTRODUCTION

*H*UMANS ARE THINKING while they are speaking without any great effort. Although this observation is not new, up to now there has been no attempt to capture it in a computational model, in particular in a model that operates in a cognitively adequate manner. In this book, I describe such a model for a comparatively simple task (which already is complex, nonetheless) that not only produces verbal output adequate for a given situation, but whose computations simulate the cognitive processes of humans.

In this chapter, I first give a general introduction (§1) and then present a motivating example that will demonstrate the main points of this book (§2). Furthermore, I ask the questions that I want to answer (§3) and the questions that I consider relevant for the issue of conceptualization but that I cannot treat in depth, because they would require another text of at least the length of this one (§4). Then, I lay out my methodology by describing the scientific disciplines I draw on (§5). Because the issues of conceptualization and incrementality are usually treated in different disciplines (psycholinguistics and computer science) and to facilitate seeing the connections between both issues, I give an example of how the issues of incrementality and conceptualization are interrelated (§6). Concluding this chapter, I present an outline of the remainder of the book (§7).

§1   *Thinking while speaking*

This book is about the fact that humans think while they speak. Although this observation may sound trivial, it involves highly complex tasks. In fact, it is one of the issues where two new problems crop up each time one believes to have found a partial answer to one aspect of the original question. The observation that thinking and speaking go hand in hand is not new. For example, in his famous essay "Über die allmähliche Verfertigung der Gedanken beim Reden" Heinrich von von Kleist (1985) observes the following:*

---

* The English translation is roughly this: "I believe that many a great orator in the moment that he opened his mouth did not know what he would say. But the certainty that he would scoop the necessary fullness of thought from the circumstances and from the arousal of his mind resulting from this made him bold enough to set the beginning on good luck."

Ich glaube, daß mancher große Redner, in dem Augenblick, da er den Mund aufmachte, noch nicht wußte, was er sagen würde. Aber die Überzeugung, daß er die ihm nötige Gedankenfülle schon aus den Umständen, und der daraus resultierenden Erregung seines Gemüts schöpfen würde, machte ihn dreist genug, den Anfang, auf gutes Glück hin, zu setzen. (p. 309)

Nowadays one would probably cast this in different, more sober terms: Utterance production commences as soon as the communicative intention is conceived, although the utterance plan is not complete. Von von Kleist goes on:*

Ein solches Reden ist wahrhaft lautes Denken. Die Reihen der Vorstellungen und ihrer Bezeichnungen gehen nebeneinander fort, und die Gemütsakte, für eins und das andere, kongruieren. Die Sprache ist alsdann keine Fessel, etwa wie ein Hemmschuh an dem Rade des Geistes, sondern wie ein zweites mit ihm parallel fortlaufendes, Rad an seiner Achse. (p. 311)

Thus, after a speaker has started an utterance on an incomplete utterance plan, planning and speaking go on like "two wheels on one axis." In other words, thinking and speaking are tightly connected, and they are temporally closely linked. Accordingly, speaking cannot be seen isolated from thinking.

There is a long tradition, originating with Aristotle (384–322 BC), of viewing speaking and thinking as the capabilities that make humans human and set them aside from all other living beings. Perhaps the passion with which the discussion whether both are essentially the same or whether they are different is a consequence of this. Johann Gottfried Herder (1744–1803), for example, takes one of the extreme positions: *Speaking is thinking aloud*. Noam Chomsky's *language organs* are the other extreme, because their genetic predetermination and specialization on language processing set them apart from a notion of thinking that encompasses speaking (N. Smith, 1999). Wilhelm von Humboldt (1767–1835) and Wilhelm Wundt (1832–1920), to mention just two influential scientists of the 19th century commenting on this question, take intermediary positions, in which they acknowledge the strong interrelation between thinking and speaking but take them to be separate. Today, the discussion of the relation between thinking and speaking is often led by arguing for or against the hypothesis proposed by Benjamin Lee Whorf (1897–1941), which says that humans can only think what they can talk about. Thus, it is a form of the first extreme position. The general problem of the influence of language on thinking is called *linguistic determinism*, and the problem of how different languages

---

* In English: "Such speaking truly is thinking aloud. The sequences of notions and their relations proceed next to each other, and the acts of mind for the one and the other are congruent. Language is, then, no chain, like a drag at the wheel of the mind, but like a second wheel going in parallel on the mind's axis."

cause people to think differently is called *linguistic relativity* (Harley, 2001, p. 81). Exploring the relation between thinking and speaking is the first major theme of this book. However, instead of discussing the issues of linguistic determinism and linguistic relativity, I focus on how a *thinking for speaking* (Slobin, 1996) can be realized in a computational model. Thinking for speaking means that when humans speak, they think in a particular way.

This book's second major theme is the temporal interleaving of thinking and speaking put forward so eloquently by von Kleist. The temporal dimension has also been commented on previously. Hermann Paul (1846–1921) understood the production of utterances (*sentences* in his terminology) in a holistic way: There is a complete conceptualization, which is then expressed sequentially. Wilhelm Wundt argued that a sentence has a twofold nature, a simultaneous one and a sequential one:

> From a psychological point of view, the sentence is both a simultaneous and a sequential structure. It is simultaneous because at each moment it is present in consciousness as a totality even though individual subordinate elements may occasionally disappear from it. It is sequential because the configuration changes from moment to moment in its cognitive condition as individual constituents move into the focus of attention and out again one after the other.   (Wundt, 1900, translated by Blumenthal, 1970, p. 21)

This shows that utterances have a dual nature: They can be seen as a whole as well as a sequence of "subordinate elements." In other words, a communicative intention is a high-level verbalization goal that is realized by generating a sequence of increments or concepts. But let us start with an example.

§ 2   *Incremental conceptualization: An example*

Imagine you are sitting at an airport, look out of the window while you are waiting to board, and watch what is happening in the maneuvering area. Imagine further that you describe what you see to another person, who cannot see what you are seeing, say, a person you are talking to on the telephone. How do you accomplish this? What mental capabilities do you need, and what mental operations do you perform? Assume you observe the scene depicted in figure 1.1.* In this scene, a plane docks onto a gate. Four phases can be identified and described verbally:

---

* When looking out of the window, you will usually not have a bird's-eye perspective on a maneuvering area. The actual task I use in this book is that such scenes as in figure 1.1 are presented on a monitor.

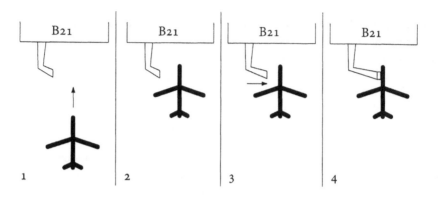

Figure 1.1: Example scene: Docking of a plane

(1) a. *Ein Flugzeug fährt auf ein Gate zu.**
         'A plane is moving toward a gate.'†
     b. *Es stoppt beim Gate.*
         'It stops at the gate.'
     c. *Der Laufgang bewegt sich auf das Flugzeug zu.*
         'The walkway is moving toward the plane.'
     d. *Er erreicht das Flugzeug.*
         'It reaches the plane.'

I illuminate the cognitive task that produces verbal output for the visual input *while* the described events take place (not afterward). Because I focus on conceptualization, I do not treat visual perception in detail. Instead, I assume the existence of a *perceptual preprocessing unit* (PPU) preceding conceptualization. The PPU provides the input to conceptualization, which consists of simple concepts, called *perceived entities*.

The task is a case of what I call *incremental conceptualization*. Conceptualization is the task that produces prelinguistic, semantic representations‡ from nonlinguistic

---

* The examples given throughout the text are mostly in German, because the model INC, which I develop in this book, is compared to German verbalization data.

† There is no English word that directly translates the German *fahren*. *Drive* comes closest but has a different usage. For this reason, *fahren* always is translated as *move*, although *move* is more general (German: *bewegen*).

‡ Opinions differ on what semantic representations are. Because I follow the approach by Levelt (1989), I also adopt his notion of semantic representation, which is similar to Jackendoff's (1990, 1997, 2002). These semantic representations are special conceptual representations, namely linear conceptual representations that can be encoded linguistically. They are, therefore, more abstract than, for example, the semantic representations by Bierwisch and Schreuder (1992).

input. The nonlinguistic input comes from various sources, in particular from outside the system, that is, from sensory input (visual, auditory, etc.), but also from other cognitive systems, for example, long-term memory or components performing inferences and deductions. Put differently, conceptualization is the cognitive task that produces *prelinguistic* output from *non*linguistic input. In this book, I focus on perceptual input.

The attribute *incremental* means that conceptualization and its subtasks are performed in a *piecemeal* and *parallel* fashion. *Piecemeal* characterizes two facts. First, you need not see the whole scene before you can start describing it. Instead, you can start talking and describe a part of the scene before the scene ends. Second, utterances are not produced as wholes but piece by piece: You start with one concept, then add another, then another, and so on. Similarly, on the linguistic level you plan and produce one word at a time. *Parallel* means that you perform multiple things at the same time, for example, processing the visual input, linking this input to your memories of similar scenes, and producing a verbal description for it.* This enables you to describe what you see while you are observing.

The overwhelming complexity of conceptualization can be reduced by focusing on the *data-driven* aspects of the task. This allows you to concentrate on studying

1. How a newly perceived event is integrated into the internal conceptual representation of the scene,
2. Which events are verbalized,
3. The order in which they are verbalized, and
4. How a semantic expression describing an event is generated.

These are the four main tasks of conceptualization. The first one, *construction*, builds up an internal representation of the external state of affairs from the perceived input by using knowledge about how the world is structured. *Selection* decides on the content to be verbalized with respect to the current verbalization goal. In this book, I consider only a fixed verbalization goal: describing the scene that is currently observed. *Linearization* brings the selected content into an appropriate order; for example, it decides whether two phases of the scene are described in the temporal order in which they occurred or whether the order is changed. *PVM-generation* (*generation of preverbal messages*), finally, generates a prelinguistic (semantic) representation for the content to be verbalized. The term *preverbal messages* for semantic representations was proposed by Levelt (1989).

---

* *Parallel processing* can mean two things: simultaneous processing of multiple instances of the same problem, e.g. when a search problem is split up recursively into multiple instances, or simultaneous processing of different problems. I always use parallelism in the second sense, except when I discuss it explicitly in chapter 5.

These four tasks use two auxiliary ones. The first one is the aforementioned mentioned *PPU*, which takes perceptual input data and forms simple concepts that are the input to conceptualization. The distinction between perception and conceptualization is not as clear-cut as this, because the influences are mutual, but this simplification is a useful and common assumption for the purpose at hand. The second additional task is the *concept matcher*. It enables the construction task to access long-term knowledge, that is, the knowledge that is present independently of the conceptualization of an observed scene. It serves, in particular, to access knowledge of how to build complex concepts from simpler ones.

Focusing on the data-drivenness emphasizes the need for incremental processing: As soon as a new piece of information (increment) is available, it is processed with respect to the current conceptual representation. Processing the scene in figure 1.1 in an incremental fashion means, therefore, to use an approach in which not the whole scene is observed before conceptual processing commences, for example, before boundaries between the phases are identified, but input is processed as it becomes available.* In the *online* setting, language production starts before the scene has ended. In contrast, in an *offline* setting, the scene did end before verbalization commences, which means that all information required for a verbal description of the scene is available beforehand. The temporal proximity of stimulus material and verbalization in the online setting makes it possible to correlate what is happening to its verbal description. This is a major advantage, because investigating conceptualization suffers from the problem that it is not directly observable. Therefore, a surface modality must be employed to infer what takes place on the conceptual level. And because most often the surface modality is language, effects of conceptualization are often mistakenly taken to be effects of language (§12).

Describing the example scene by giving verbal descriptions of its four phases already illustrates two important points. First, a human observer of this scene is capable of segmenting the input stream into subscenes (phases)—a prerequisite for piecemeal processing. Second, the subscenes are part of the overall scene; that is, the representation is hierarchically structured. The hierarchy is the reason that a human observer can recognize the succession of the four phases as a DOCKING† scene. In addition to the *part-of* hierarchy, there is another, equally important one, the *subsumption* hierarchy (figure 1.2). The former establishes the relations between an entity and its parts; for example, a COCKPIT is part of a PLANE; the latter relates kinds of entities, for which reason it is also called *is-a* hierarchy, because, for example,

* I will make an even stronger claim by extending this to the production of output; that is, output is produced as soon as possible. I call this *Extended Wundt's Principle* (cf. term 6, p. 70).
† When I refer to concepts in an informal sense, I will use intuitively plausible names, like DOCKING or PLANE. However, these labels are not used in the formal conceptual representations, which are introduced in §6 and described more extensively in appendix A.

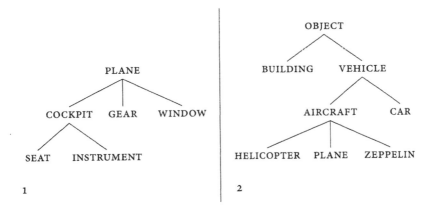

Figure 1.2: A part-of hierarchy (1) and subsumption hierarchy (2)

a HELICOPTER *is a* kind of AIRCRAFT.

The two hierarchies establish relations between *concepts*, the building blocks of conceptual representations. A concept is a system-internal representation of a concrete or abstract entity or a set of entities. (This notion of concept differs from the one used in psychology; see p. 52.) To show which concepts are involved in the example scene, I first need to make a refinement. Up to now, I regarded scenes and phases as unanalyzed wholes. However, they are actually organized in different, interrelated substructures. Three major substructures are required to represent scenes like the example scene: *object*, *spatial structure*, and *situation*. This is a subdivision within the subsumption hierarchy, because these substructures contain different kinds of concepts.

Concrete *objects* in the world (vehicles, buildings, etc.) are the most obvious kinds of concepts. In our scene we have three objects: PLANE, GATE, and WALK-WAY. A small subsumption hierarchy representing knowledge about how objects are hierarchically organized is given in the right half of figure 1.2.

Objects are related by *spatial entities*, which provide information about where an object is located or about the path of motion it is following. Examples for the DOCK-ING scene are TOWARD(PLANE, GATE) and AT(PLANE, GATE). The most important spatial entities in examples like this are *paths* (the trajectory an object is following) and *locations* (the position of an object).

Each phase of the scene is represented by a *situation*, which comprises notions like *event*, *process*, and *state* (Bach, 1986; Davidson, 1967). In short, states are situations without changes (the gate being on the maneuvering area), processes are situations involving a constant change (a plane moving across the maneuvering

area), and events are processes with an endpoint (a plane moving to the runway).*
However, these situation types are based on linguistic analyzes, and distinguishing
them on the conceptual level proves difficult. Consider the first phase of the scene.
As the PLANE is moving steadily, the situation is a process. Yet, the observer could
infer that the movement had a starting point, which he or she did not observe, for
example, the moment when the plane touched down on the runway or when it
turned off from the runway onto the taxiway. This would classify the same situation
as event. Furthermore, after phase 2 the movement is an event in any case, because
then it has an endpoint. But then again, if the movement itself is described after
phase 2, it can be described as a process: *The plane was moving toward the gate.* Thus,
when describing the movement, different aspects of the situation can be highlighted,
depending on whether the starting point and/or endpoint are taken into account.
In other words, the same situation can be described from different perspectives.
Consequently, the movement is a process as well as an event, depending on the
knowledge that is highlighted. The problem with this duality of the situation is that
representing both, event and process, is no satisfactory solution, because computing
all possibilities of all aspects of the observed situations complicates conceptualization significantly. The simpler solution is to use an integrated representation on the
conceptual level that captures the common properties of all views on the situation
and to determine the situation type only when a situation is actually verbalized.
Therefore, I will just use SITUATION concepts that are further specified by attributes. The most important attributes (1) distinguish instantaneous from extended
situations and (2) specify whether the situation is completed. Having made this
distinction, I will use *event* and *situation* synonymously most of the time, because
most of the situations in scenarios like the one in the example would indeed be
classified as events.

The sequence of the situations representing the example's four phases are represented in the part-of hierarchy in figure 1.3. The left-to-right ordering indicates
temporal precedence. Here, two types of situations are used: one for a change of
position (MOVE) and one for the transition of motion to standstill (STOP). (The
transition from standstill to motion is captured by a START concept, which I leave
implicit for the time being, but see §20.) Concepts are entities internal to the cog-
nizer. This is of interest for situations, because it is debatable whether they are
internal (mental) or external (abstract) entities. I consider them internal for two
reasons. First, a situation can be represented in different ways. Second, Avrahami
and Kareev (1994) show that it depends on an individual's experience as to what
constitutes a situation.

---

* When the plane arrives at the runway, the situation ends (event); however the plane could—in
principle—move forever across the maneuvering area, for example, by moving in a circle (process).

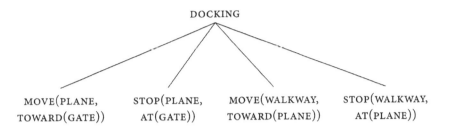

Figure 1.3: Example scene: Representation of the situation structure

Apart from representing temporal information, the main function of situations is to link objects and spatial entities. For example, the situation in phase 1 can be represented as MOVE(PLANE, TOWARD(GATE)), where the MOVE concept relates the PLANE and the TOWARD path. Furthermore, the situation structure of the docking scene warrants the generalization that in phases 1 and 3 an object changes its position, whereas in the other two a moving object ceases to move (the movement reaches its endpoint). Using the concepts introduced earlier the underlying conceptual representation of the verbalizations (1a–1d) can be described by propositions such as the following:

(2) S1 : MOVE(PLANE, TOWARD(GATE))

(3) S2 : STOP(PLANE, AT(GATE))

(4) S3 : MOVE(WALKWAY, TOWARD(PLANE))

(5) S4 : STOP(WALKWAY, AT(PLANE))

The two predicates represent two different kinds of events: MOVE and STOP. The former describes a movement along a path, the latter the cessation of such a movement. The terms S1–S4 stand for the four situations and make it possible to refer to them, for example, to represent relations between situations. The first argument of the predicates is an object, which is the *bearer of motion*, that is, the moving object. The second argument is a proposition describing the corresponding path for a MOVE and the location for a STOP predicate.

A disadvantage of this representation is that it does not explicitly state that PLANE, GATE, and WALKWAY always refer to the same entity. One way to mark this is to give them subscripts, for example, $PLANE_1$.* In other words, the representational formalism should allow to capture the identity of entities without requiring additional inferences. This means it must provide means that do not require creating

---

* This corresponds to defining a term—in the sense of formal logic—that is a label in the representation for the entity. The referential nets formalism is based on this idea (see § 6 and appendix A).

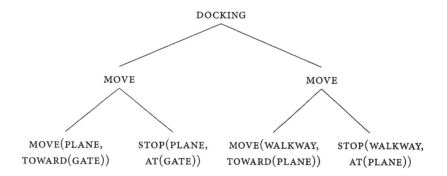

Figure 1.4: Example scene: More elaborated representation of the hierarchical event structure

a new representation for each phase of a scene and then explicitly computing the relations to the previous one. Furthermore, it must allow to represent changes, for example, the fact that the PLANE is at different locations. So, incremental processing requires *dynamic representations*, that is, representations that can be modified and extended.

The four conceptualization tasks execute the following operations on such a dynamic conceptual representation of the scene. Construction builds up the hierarchical structure and determines that the sequence of the four phases constitute a DOCKING situation. Selection chooses which of the situations are described verbally; for example, it may decide to verbalize phases 1 and 2 and the overall DOCKING situation. Linearization can, for example, invert the verbalization of phases 1 and 2, leading to utterances like *The plane stopped after it moved toward the gate*. PVM-generation, finally, generates semantic representations that describe the situations and that are similar to the ones given in (2)–(5).

Concluding the introductory discussion of this example, observe that the first two motion events are performed by the PLANE, the last two by the WALKWAY. Each pair of movements can be represented by a more complex and abstract motion concept, labeled MOVE in figure 1.4. Considering the flexibility of cognition, it is likely that both kinds of representations can be used. I will, however, focus on representations that have this intermediary level, because it will prove useful.

§ 3   Research questions

In this book I address a number of research questions, which result in a number of theses, which are given in detail in chapter 16. Part A of this book illuminates the task of conceptualization. Because conceptualization is too wide a topic, I restrict it in three ways. First, no modalities other than language are considered. Second, I consider only the production of language; that is, the direction of conceptualization is fixed: from perceptual input to semantic structures. Third, I address only the conceptualization of events (situations); objects and other entities are used only to complement event structures. Put concisely, my first research question is *What constitutes event conceptualization for language production?* Complementing these major restrictions are two minor ones. First, I consider no reasoning over elements retrieved from long-term memory. The knowledge stored in the simple long-term memory model only serves to construct hierarchical structures in the conceptual representation. Second, I do not address learning issues; apart from the perceptual information about the scene, all knowledge is present from the start.

The second major topic of this book, discussed in part B, is incrementality. Hence, the second research question is *What is incrementality?* This means, in particular, the incrementality of conceptualization, because incrementality is an important aspect of conceptualization. However, incrementality itself is just a mode of processing and, therefore, a wide topic. My account of it is accordingly broad, while, at the same time, it establishes the connections to conceptualization. These connections focus on two more special issues. First *Which dynamic representations can be used for incremental processing?* Incremental processing requires dynamic representations (§ 2), which means it requires particular conceptual representations. Second *How does incrementality save resources?* The main motivation for using incremental processing is to save resources by evaluating new information in relation to the existing information. Thus, when only some of the information changes, it is advantageous to update only those pieces of information that are affected by the change.

So, conceptualization and incrementality are the two central notions. Until I flesh them out, it is helpful to keep two formulations in mind: *Conceptualization comprises the computations of a speaker to generate preverbal messages,* and *incrementality is the piecemeal and parallel processing of information.*

After exploring both issues in their own right in the first two parts, I integrate them in the model INC (*incremental conceptualizer*, pronounce *ink*) in part C. The discussion in this part focuses on the question *How does INC integrate incrementality and conceptualization?* This question addresses the issue of how a model of a conceptualizer (a computational device carrying out the conceptualization task) is shaped by the incremental processing method. This is no limitation; rather, it is a way to learn something about human language production, because humans produce language incrementally and nonincremental accounts are limited in their cognitive adequacy. So, this is the point to ask: *Can INC account for the empirical data?* In other words, does INC reproduce empirically observed behavior? Simulations carried out by an implementation of INC allow us to compare the model to the empirical data; more specifically, the output generated by INC's implementation is compared to the transcriptions of human verbalizations. INC can indeed account for a range of data, in particular for default verbalizations that capture the majority of cases, but also for unusual verbalizations, such as very detailed or superficial descriptions of a scene. However, in this book, I am mainly concerned with modeling issues, so the amount of empirical research is limited, especially compared to full-fledged psychological experiments.

§ 4   *What this book is not about*

Conceptualization touches on or encompasses many other issues, and to keep this book to a manageable size, I cannot talk about them here. I assume that this does not substantially change the way conceptualization is to be modeled but would merely enhance the picture that I develop.

Intentionality and *consciousness* are difficult notions. Take the task of selecting the content to be verbalized. It is quite natural to describe this as *The speaker decides to verbalize this concept*. Such formulations resort to conscious or volitional decisions. I take a different perspective here, laying the focus on the data-drivenness and incrementality of conceptualization and show that this yields valuable insights. This includes that I assume volitional decisions to describe a scene are made in an area of cognition that is not covered by INC. However, it is not unlikely that such decisions are necessary for the proper functioning of INC's selection process. Thus, I do not address "the big question" but concentrate on how communicative intentions that serve the overall communicative goal, which is to generate a verbalization of an observed scene in an online fashion, can be determined.

Dialogue is an important issue for conceptualization, because a speaker is really an interlocutor. Therefore, the speaker may have information he obtained earlier from interlocutors that now are hearers. Focusing on the data-driven aspects of language production allows for reducing the dialogue to a monologue: No information coming from other interlocutors needs to be taken into account. Additionally, other interlocutors need not be explicitly modeled. This is tantamount to assuming a default hearer. Bard et al. (2000) and Bard and Aylett (2004) furthermore show that a speaker maintains a much less detailed model of the listener than is often assumed, which makes the need for addressing this issue less urgent. Similarly, only some aspects of *discourse* have to be considered, whereas others, such as detailed information about the hearer, can be neglected.

Conceptual representations are *multimodal* in principle. One aspect of their multimodality is that they should be general enough so that they can be used not only for speaking but also for other tasks in other modalities, such as navigating through space in the taxiing scenario. Navigating through space would, however, require either another processing component operating on the same representation or a conceptualizer that is also capable of a *thinking for navigating* in addition to Slobin's *thinking for speaking*. I do consider multimodality in one respect, namely in that the input of the conceptualizer is nonlinguistic but comes from the visual system, and the overall task of conceptualization is to translate it into propositional semantic representations. Thus, conceptualization is rather independent from linguistic considerations; instead, it is a mediator between language and other modalities (§ 9).

Gestures, finally, offer additional possibilities for investigating conceptualization, because they are nonlinguistic while at the same time closely tied to language production. The language production model by Levelt (1989), which is my starting point (see chap. 3), has been extended to speech accompanying gestures by Krauss, Chen, and Gottesman (2000) and De Ruiter (2000). (Both models are not implemented and take a somewhat different approach than IN C does. Yet, De Ruiter's model is much closer, because it also takes Levelt's model as framework.) For the production of an utterance, the verbal and the gestural output originate from a common source, termed *growth point* by McNeill (1992). Although McNeill rejects the information processing approach, something like growth points must be located within the conceptualizer, because otherwise gesture and utterance could not be about the same content, and they could not be generated in a coordinated fashion, for example, with respect to time. Experimental results reported by Melinger and Levelt (2004) support this view. Although gestures provide additional means of expressing content, they do not lie at the core of the conceptualizer model on which I concentrate here. This is backed up by the fact that, as Levelt (1989) points out, his language production model is not particular to speaking but can also be used for writing, and for successful written communication, no gestures are required.

§ 5   *Disciplines and methods*

I draw on methods and results from different disciplines: cognitive science, artificial intelligence (AI), linguistics, natural language generation (NLG), and natural language production. In this section, I briefly explain what each contributes to the overall undertaking.

The aim of *cognitive science* is to build models and systems that mimic (simulate) human cognition and behavior as closely as possible. Its emphasis lies on explaining the way processing is done, not just to build models that match input to output in order to reproduce empirical data. I will use the terms *model* and *system* as follows.

TERM 1: MODEL
A model is a textual and/or formal description of tasks and representations.

TERM 2: SYSTEM
A system is an implemented model. To build an implementation (an executable program), additional assumptions have to be made, whereas other issues can only be realized in a reduced version due to complexity.

(Throughout the book, I provide short characterizations of central terms. You could call them definitions, but I want to avoid the mathematical connotation. Despite this, I also use *define* and *definition* in the text. These characterizations are repeated as part of the glossary given in the appendix.) Cognitive science is more concerned with creating models than systems, because its main aim is to understand *how the mind works* (as Steven Pinker formulates it) and not simply to construct running programs. INC is designed to account for human cognitive processing mechanisms when humans perform the task described in §2. Hence, it is primarily a model. There are two reasons for also implementingINC, that is, for building a system for the model. First, with the implementation, it is possible to compare the model's behavior with verbalizations produced by humans. Second, because implementing always means to make further decisions in order to make the model detailed enough to be executable, it is necessary to make modifications of the model, which improve its quality and accuracy. However, building a system also means that not all issues can be realized in detail because this would make the system too complex. For example, although there are sophisticated models of human memory, INC only contains a simple memory model. Making it more detailed would make INC more complex, while not contributing to the core ideas for whose exploration it is built.

INC realizes a part of the model of language production by Levelt (1989, 1999). This model comes from the field of *natural language production*, which is a subfield of *psycholinguistics*, a discipline contributing to cognitive science.

Because the output of conceptualization consists of semantic representations of utterances, I draw on results from *linguistics* to check whether the representations are adequate not only under a processing perspective but also under a descriptive–structural one. This is necessary for two reasons. First, the body of linguistic data investigated in linguistics is considerably larger than in psycholinguistics, and psycholinguistic data about semantic or conceptual phenomena are even scarcer. Second, psycholinguistic data are rather different from linguistic data. Psycholinguistics uses mainly reaction time experiments or other psychological methods, whereas linguistics is concerned with explaining differences in the structure of language and languages. A model, however, should account for both kinds of data.

From *artificial intelligence* (AI) in general and *natural language generation* (NLG) in particular—seen as a sub-field of AI—come techniques for building a model that conforms to cognitive constraints and for refining the cognitive model when implementing the system. Gaps in the model can be filled with technical solutions, which is justified by the fact that natural and technical solutions more often than not resemble each other. So, even though there are differences in the goals of cognitive science and NLG/AI, the disciplines are far from being incompatible. On the contrary, there is considerable overlap, which can be seen by the fact that AI is one of the mainstays of cognitive science. Systems for generating natural language built with and without cognitive considerations have a lot more commonalities than differences, as a comparison by E. Reiter (1994) shows (see also de Smedt, Horacek, & Zock, 1996; E. Reiter & Dale, 2000). (For this reason, I use the "cognitive" term *production* and the "technical" *generation* interchangeably. Where the distinction is relevant, I point it out.) Nevertheless, one must be very cautious with transfers from NLG/AI to cognitive science, because they must not limit the cognitive adequacy of the resulting model or system.

I first take a cognitive science, then an NLG/AI perspective on the task described in §2. After that, I outline what can be learned from bringing the two perspectives together.

🎙 THE COGNITIVE SCIENCE PERSPECTIVE.   My major aim is to account for the way humans accomplish the verbalization task described in §2, the *online description of events*. I provide explanations by building INC, which is designed to be as cognitively adequate as possible. Thus, not only the overall behavior of the model should be cognitively adequate but also the way in which it carries out computations, that is, the way in which it performs the subtasks of conceptualization.

As already pointed out in §2, the overall task can be subdivided into two major parts: a perceptual preprocessing and the conceptualization proper. I treat the perceptual preprocessing as a subsidiary task to get from the input of the overall system to simple concepts (perceived entities). As mentioned earlier conceptualization consists of four main tasks: construction of a conceptual representation, selection of events to be verbalized, linearization of the selected events, and the generation of preverbal messages (PVM-generation) describing the events. Construction takes perceived entities as input and constructs more complex as well as simpler concepts by *grouping* and *segmentation* operations, respectively. In the docking example, the simpler motion concepts are taken together to form the complexMOVE and DOCK-ING concepts. Selection decides which events of the conceptual representation are verbalized. Because I consider the conceptualization of events, the selection task only examines the event (situation) structure. Thus, it decides, for example, whether the complexDOCKING event is verbalized but not the simpler events. Other concepts, for example, objects, are not considered for verbalization. Linearization brings the selected events into an appropriate order. This makes it possible to generate utterances that do not reflect the chronological order of events, for example,

(6)   *Das Flugzeug hat angedockt, nachdem es gelandet ist.*
      'The plane docked after it landed.'

PVM-generation, finally, generates preverbal messages (semantic representations) for the selected and linearized events. This is necessary, because an event concept like DOCKING is not a semantic representation: It must still be determined how it is verbalized. For example, describing events usually involves generating referring expressions for the bearer of motion, for example, *das Flugzug* 'the plane', *das große Flugzeug* 'the big plane', or *es* 'it' for a PLANE concept. The decision of what constitutes an adequate description of the PLANE is not made by selecting the event.

The execution of these tasks, as well as the performance of humans and systems in general, depends very much on the available resources. As most resources, cognitive resources are limited. Therefore, a cognitive model must account for these limitations. From the cognitive science perspective, the limitations of resources is not a technical consideration (Does the computer have enough memory?) but a cognitive consideration (What happens if human memory is exceeded?) INC allows us to vary the available resources by assigning values to parameters like the number of events that can be held in memory after being selected for verbalization but that have not yet been verbalized. Although conceptualization is mainly about how an individual human conceptualizes the world, there is also intersubjective consistency in humans' performance. Resource parameters are a useful mechanism for this: The majority of human verbalizations of a scene are captured by setting the parameters to default values, whereas more unusual verbalizations need different settings.

❧ THE NLG/AI PERSPECTIVE.   Although my overall goal is to build a cognitively adequate model of an incremental conceptualizer, I employ many techniques from AI and NLG. The aim of NLG/AI is to build systems that behave in an intelligent way (AI) or that generate natural language (NLG). The issue of cognitive adequacy is not one of its major concerns.

Because conceptualization can be observed only indirectly, the empirical data inevitably have big gaps, exacerbated by the small number of empirical studies on conceptualization. Thus, although INC integrates many results from empirical studies, white spaces remain. When filling the gaps in the model, one has to approximate how humans solve the problem. These estimates guide further empirical investigations. When the data show that the model is wrong, a new, better model can be built.

I draw on results from different areas of AI: first, the processing of sensory input, second, knowledge representation, third—lying at the core of this book—dynamic representations, that is, questions of how knowledge can change over time. Fourth, as a subdiscipline of computer science, AI provides means for dealing with all issues of computational modeling, system-building, and embedding a model in an environment.

My approach also differs significantly from the standard NLG /AI approach. The four tasks of conceptualization have no real counterparts in NLG systems. The most important reason for this is that such systems are typically built for text generation, not speaking. One consequence is that incremental systems (i.e. systems where subsequent planning stages are carried out in parallel, output is generated while input is read in, and which usually operate without feedback) are rare. Typical NLG systems perform four different tasks to generate semantic representations: content determination, document structuring, aggregation,* and generation of referring expressions (E. Reiter & Dale, 2000). Sometimes, lexicalization is included in this list. This division of labor is quite different compared to the one taking place in conceptualization, where, for example, the generation of referring expressions is an integral part of PVM-generation, not a separate task.

INC also differs from typical NLG approaches in that it is embedded in an environment to which it reacts and does not generate texts over an unchanging knowledge base. From the ensuing data-drivenness follows that the time it can spend on its computations is limited, which means that INC has some similarities to *anytime* approaches, because it is capable of generating output in (almost) any time (§31).

❧ BRINGING THE VIEWS TOGETHER.   To sum up, I employ AI techniques in order to achieve the overall goal of cognitive science, which is explaining human cognition. I do this by building a cognitively adequate model, an approach best described as *cognitive modeling*. Cognitive modeling goes back to the works by Allen Newell and Herbert Simon, described, for example, in Newell and Simon (1963, 1972). The most important contribution that models of cognition make to cognitive science is that they generate hypotheses of how the mind works. Corroborations as well as falsifications of the hypotheses serve to gain new insights. Simon (1996) called this "understanding by simulating" (p. 13).

Vice versa, cognitive modeling can fulfill a similar role for AI as bionics does for engineering, although this is not the standard view in AI. Russell and Norvig (2003), for example, bring forward that aircraft could be constructed only after their

---

* *Aggregation* is a contraction of information. An example is that instead of *A man crosses the street* and *The man has an umbrella*, only one utterance is generated: *A man with an umbrella crosses the street.*

builders abandoned the idea of building artificial birds. Analogously, AI should not bother with trying to build artificial humans. Yet, the air streaming along the surface of a wing works according to the same physical principle in birds and aircraft. So, although in the early days of aviation nobody spoke of bionics, the transfer of ideas is similar. Furthermore, as even Russell and Norvig admit, in the fields concerned with the processing of natural language, a colaboration between cognitive and noncognitive approaches proved fruitful. There is good reason for this: For language—in contrast to flying—humans set the standard; that is, humans define, for example, what counts as an adequate description of a scene.

Put concisely, from cognitive science I take the goal to produce a model/system that is as cognitively adequate as possible; from NLG/AI I take methods to refine the model and methods to build a system, which can then be tested against empirical data. The results can be used to refine the model, and the circle starts anew.

§ 6   *Effects of incrementality on representations*

In the context of conceptualization, it is a stark abstraction to talk about representations without accounting for the fact that they change over time. Neglecting this is an abstraction that leads to artefacts. I demonstrate this for the case of the perspectivization of utterances. Nondynamic accounts of cognitive representations must assume a process that performs the perspectivization. In an incremental model this is not necessary. Instead, perspectivization is just an effect of the time course of utterance production (de Smedt, 1990a, 1990b). Before making this argument in more detail, I give a short account of INC's representational formalism, *referential nets*. A more detailed description is given in appendix A.

❧ SHORT OVERVIEW OF REFERENTIAL NETS.   *Referential nets* (*refNets*) consist of interrelated *referential objects* (*refOs*; Eschenbach, 1988; Habel, 1982, 1986). A refO represents an entity. Formally, a refO is a term ($r_1, r_2, r_3, \ldots$). A refO can have *attributes* and *designations* associated with it, for example,

(7)
$$
\begin{array}{l}
\text{human} \longrightarrow \\
\text{male} \nearrow
\end{array}
\;\; r_1 \;\;
\begin{array}{l}
\longleftarrow \text{'DAVID'} \\
\nwarrow \text{father\_of('RUTH')} \\
\nwarrow \iota x\, \text{wife('SARAH', }x)
\end{array}
$$

Attributes are written to the left, designations to the right. Attributes represent conceptual knowledge like the refO's *sort*, which is mandatory and always stands in first position, here human. Other attributes contain essential, defining properties of the entity that can be used for conceptual inferences. Designations are meaning-related expressions of one of three kinds: *names* ('DAVID'), *functional expressions* (father_of('RUTH')), or *descriptions*. Descriptions are of the form: op var pred, where op $\in \{\iota, \eta, \text{all\_t}, \text{some\_t}\}$ is the operator, var $\in \{x, y, z, \ldots\}$ a variable, and pred a predicate–argument structure. The operators reflect the cardinality of the refO and the definiteness of the predicate (Habel, 1986, p. 137; see table 1.1). Thus, ιx wife('SARAH', x) can be read as *the entity whose wife is Sarah*. Correspondingly, ηx wife('SARAH', x) stands for *Sarah is a wife of this entity*,—in which case the entity represented by r1 (David) could have more than one wife.

	DEFINITE	INDEFINITE
cardinality $= 1$	ι	η
cardinality > 1	some_t	all_t

Table 1.1: Operators in referential nets

RefOs, attributes, and designations can be added, deleted, or modified. Thus, referential nets are dynamic representations. In addition, they are well-suited for representing conceptual and meaning-related knowledge and can be extended in order to represent multimodal knowledge. For example, Habel (1987) extends them by introducing *depictions* to represent pictorial knowledge about refOs. Similarly, it would be possible to extend the formalism by knowledge in other modalities.

❧ PERSPECTIVIZATION AS AN EFFECT OF INCREMENTALITY.   All utterances have a perspective. Consider a typical example:

(8) a. *Mary hits John.*
     b. *John is hit by Mary.*

Both utterances describe the same state of affairs but have a different perspective. In other words, both are statements about the world that describe the same proposition: hit(mary, john). Yet, (8a) is a statement about Mary, whereas (8b) is a statement about John. Nonincremental accounts of language production usually assume a two-stage process for this. In the first stage, it is decided to verbalize a certain state of affairs, that is, a proposition is chosen, and only then the perspective is computed by a separate *perspectivization* task (Ziesche, 1997).

There are, however, two explanations for how utterances with different perspectives can be produced. The first is that (8a) and (8b) are generated from different conceptualizations; that is, there are different propositions on the conceptual level: hit(mary, john) and hit_by(john, mary). In this case, the perspective taken depends on perceptual factors, for example, whether the observer focuses on John or

Mary during the scene. It is reasonable to assume that the situations are conceptualized differently, because hitting and being hit are quite different things.

The second explanation is based on processing considerations and is therefore the interesting possibility with respect to incremental processing (de Smedt, 1990b). The proposition hit(mary, john) can be represented in a referential net as follows:

(9)

$$
\begin{array}{lll}
\text{human} \longrightarrow & r1 & \longleftarrow \text{'MARY'} \\
\text{female} \nearrow & & \searrow \eta x \, hit(r2, x, r3) \\[2ex]
\text{situation} \longrightarrow & r2 & \longrightarrow \eta x \, hit(x, r1, r3) \\[2ex]
\text{human} \longrightarrow & r3 & \longleftarrow \text{'JOHN'} \\
\text{male} \nearrow & & \searrow \eta x \, hit(r2, r1, x)
\end{array}
$$

This representation contains three refOs: one for each person and one for the situation. They are related via a description consisting of hit as predicate and three arguments: the situation in first, the "hitter" in second, and the "hittee" in third position. The latter two correspond to the thematic roles *agent* and *patient*. Thus, despite being conceptual representations, these expressions are already close to a semantic representation. On the basis of this representation, the perspective depends on the sequence in which the refOs are accessed. The speaker may start with one of the refOs representing Mary (r1) or John (r3). This determines the perspective, because the speaker now makes a statement about one of the persons involved, Mary or John. Alternatively, the situation refO (r2) can be chosen first. (But, again, the perspective depends on which of the other two refOs is accessed first.) Note that referential nets also allow different predicates for hit and hit_by, which means that it allows us to model different conceptualizations.

§7 *Outline of the book*

The book has three major parts. Part A addresses the issue of conceptualization. Chapter 2 draws the boundary between language production and other cognitive tasks and describes the language production model by Levelt (1989) of which INC models the first component. Chapter 3 discusses conceptualization and the subtasks that must be performed by a conceptualizer in order to generate online descriptions of events. These subtasks constitute INC's major division of labor. Chapter 4 describes the representations that are used for accomplishing the conceptualization task.

Part B gives a general account of incrementality. The first chapter of this part (chapter 5) presents a general account of incremental processing by discussing relevant literature, providing a blueprint of incremental models, and describing the dimensions along which incremental models can vary. Chapter 6 explores the issue of the representations needed for incremental processing (i.e. incremental representations) and describes how underspecification formalisms can be used for incremental processing. Chapter 7 wraps up the theoretical first two parts of the book by addressing some issues related to resources and the way in which incremental processing can save resources in a cognitively adequate manner.

Part C presents the INC model in detail. This part builds on the results of the first two theoretical ones and integrates their results into a coherent model. After chapter 8 describes INC's overall architecture, its representations and processes are the topic of the ensuing chapters. Chapter 13 reports simulations carried out with INC, and chapter 14 outlines how INC can be extended by a rudimentary monitoring component.

The book closes with some proposals of how to extend INC (chapter 15) and a chapter that summarizes the theses I am proposing (chapter 16).

There are two points about the structure of the text. First, part A abstracts away from incrementality, while part B abstracts away from conceptualization. Among other things, this leads to a rather rough transition between the two parts. Please bear with me at that point. The problem is ameliorated by the fact that I comment on the connections between the two issues throughout both parts. Second, chapter 16 is not truly meant to be read last. Indeed, it will be useful to consult it while reading the text. In a sense it fulfills a similar function as the glossary.

CONCEPTUALIZATION

LANGUAGE PRODUCTION

*L*ANGUAGE PRODUCTION IS only one of a plethora of cognitive tasks humans perform. This chapter has, therefore, two main topics: an outline of language production and the relation of language production to other cognitive tasks. This means I describe the boundary between language production and other cognitive faculties. Drawing such boundaries poses a common problem in cognitive science and AI, closely related to the problem of modularity. Therefore, I discuss the degree to which the human language production faculty is modular. Although language production is a task in its own right, separate from other cognitive tasks, it also intermingles with other tasks to a degree that makes it difficult to draw this boundary. This is particularly true of conceptualization. Nevertheless, language production and conceptualization possess traits of modules.

After motivating that it is worthwhile to investigate language production (§ 8), I elaborate on the mediator function of conceptualization (§ 9) and present Levelt's (1989) language production model (§ 10). Finally, I illuminate to which degree the human language production system is modular (§ 11). I first give some criteria for judging whether a component is a module and explain the idea of quasi-modules. I then argue that some problems in investigating conceptualization that are due to nonmodular properties can be overcome by using a setting in which conceptualization is data-driven, that is, reacting to input. Finally, I point out that conceptualization—being the least modular component of language production—is somewhere between being modular and being nonmodular by discussing the degree of its language specificity.

§ 8   *Investigating language production*

Compared to the number of models and systems for language comprehension, there are only few a for the production of language. The growing interest in automatized language processing in recent years has not changed this situation. Only about 10% of pages in textbooks on computational linguistics, for example, are about language generation (Carstensen et al., 2001; Jurafsky & Martin, 2000). In addition, most language production systems have very little to say about how *humans* produce language: Although they aim to generate language that is as natural as possible, they do not perform the computations in a cognitively adequate manner. (For an outline and an overview of such noncognitive systems, see E. Reiter & Dale, 2000.)

One reason for the small number of language production systems is that the task of generating language is often (albeit often implicitly) regarded as the inverse of language comprehension. The assumption is that once language comprehension is fully understood, one takes the inverse and gets a language production model. However, *parsing*, the basic technique used in language comprehension systems, plays only a minor role in language production, whereas very different techniques are important for language production. McDonald (1987) illustrates this point by characterizing the generation of natural language as being mainly a *choice task*: After the content to be verbalized has been determined, a sequence of choices must be made in order to find the linguistic means that express it. In contrast, language comprehension mainly consists of *hypothesis management*: Given a sequence of words, one must hypothesize what meaning fits the parsed material best. The initially infinite set of hypotheses is narrowed down step by step. Note that these characterizations only serve to motivate the overall point. They are not meant to define the two tasks.

The choices during language production are often regarded as less critical operations than removing a hypothesis in language comprehension, because this may have the effect that the system is not able to come up with the correct meaning of an utterance. However, choices in language production can make subsequent choices, which would be necessary for expressing the chosen content, impossible.

Another reason for the neglect of language production is that research motivated by practical considerations uses surrogates for most language generation tasks (e.g., prefabricated, "canned" text) when it is possible to define a set of possible expressions sufficient for the task. There are corresponding methods for language comprehension systems, for example, using *controlled languages*, that is, languages that are restricted in their expressive power. This drastically increases the performance of the system. Usually, however, such methods are deemed unacceptable, and the aim is to build language comprehension systems that can cope with the full complexity of natural language. Reasons—if any are given at all—typically are based on usability. However, it is not clear that a voice-operated navigation system actually needs such broad capabilities, and systems that are currently in practical use restrict the kinds of utterances they can comprehend.

Taken together with the arguments presented in chapter 1, there are three main reasons for investigating language production. First, compared to language comprehension and to noncognitive approaches to language production (NLG), there has been only little research. Second, language production viewed from a cognitive perspective offers the chance to learn from nature, providing additional methods, which can be used for improving NLG systems. Third, the problems of language production are different from the problems of language comprehension: Inverting comprehension will not yield models of language production. For building natural dialogue systems interacting with a human user, this has, for example, the consequence that it does not suffice to build a sophisticated language comprehension system; one must also build an adequate language production subsystem.

§ 9   *Conceptualization as mediator for language*

In the production of online descriptions of events, visual input and verbal output are correlated. As the visual world and the world of spoken language are different, it is straightforward to assume their representations are in different modalities. Thus, what happens in the one world must be translated before it can stimulate anything in the other. The translation is one of the tasks of conceptualization.

The opposite view, however, namely that all thinking takes place in only one (usually propositional) format, is very prominent. Two of a number of debates addressing this question are the *imagery debate* and the debate about whether there is a *language of thought*. The idea of a language of thought (Fodor, 1975) says that humans think with an inventory of symbols that can be combined with a limited set of rules. Fodor's main argument is that there is a strong similarity between linguistic representations and other mental representations. Additionally, propositional representations can easily represent abstract entities, which is difficult with other representational formats. If there is a language of thought then, most likely, all thinking is propositional.

However, the issues discussed in the imagery debate cast doubts on this view (Kosslyn, 1994, 1995). Results from empirical studies indicate that imagistic representations are different in nature from propositional ones. One of the main arguments for the existence of imagistic representations comes from experiments where participants have to rotate objects mentally. The rotation takes longer the greater the angle of rotation is, for example, rotating an object by 45° takes less time than rotating it by 225°. In a purely propositional account, the different angles cannot explain this difference, because processing a symbol representing 45° takes as long as processing a symbol representing 225°. Therefore, a different kind of representation must be used for such operations, imagistic representations.

Further evidence against a solely propositional account of cognition comes from Glenberg, Robertson, Jansen, and Johnson-Glenberg (1999), who show that

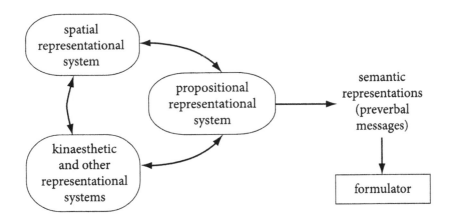

Figure 2.1: Representational systems involved in thought and language (Levelt, 1989, p. 73)

explanations traditionally given in propositional terms contradict empirical results. For example, in the processing of negations, an assertion A and its negation ¬A are processed equally fast, whereas in the propositional account, the negative version should require more time because first A must be evaluated and then, in a second step, its negation.

Thus, propositional representations alone do not suffice for a full account of thinking. Other types of knowledge include, most notably, spatial, imagery, and kinesthetic knowledge (Levelt, 1989, p. 73; see figure 2.1). On the semantic level, however, all representations must be propositional. Thus, conceptualization must convert nonpropositional knowledge into propositions. Because referential nets can represent knowledge in other modalities, I assume that adding modalities only enhances INC but does not alter it substantially.

An equally important issue is the domain-dependency of conceptualization. For example, Markman and Gentner (2001) state that "even in the seemingly abstract domain of mathematics cognitive performance is affected by domain content" (p. 224). INC was developed within two different domains; online descriptions of drawings of sketch maps (§ 53) and descriptions of motion events. This means that INC possesses at least some generality and is not just a model for a particular domain.

§ 10   *Levelt's tripartite architecture*

The most prominent model of language production that is based on cognitive and psycholinguistic considerations and that furthermore goes all the way from com-

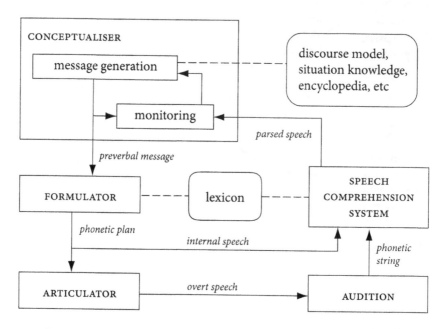

Figure 2.2: Levelt's (1989, p. 9) blueprint for the speaker (slightly coarsened)

municative intentions to articulatory output is the one by Willem Levelt, described
in Levelt (1989) and in modified versions in Levelt (1999) and Levelt, Roelofs, and
Meyer (1999). I mainly use the 1989 version as framework, because it makes the
most elaborate claims about the conceptualizer. Levelt concentrates on speaking
and assumes that writing or using sign language work along the same lines, despite
their different output modalities. Instead of an articulator (see below), a signing or
writing component would be required, of course.

The three main components of Levelt's architecture are the *conceptualizer*, the
formulator, and the *articulator* (figure 2.2). The two interfaces between these components are the *preverbal message* between conceptualizer and formulator and the
phonetic plan between formulator and articulator. The strict sequentiality of the
architecture allows no feedback between components but only within modules
(Levelt, 1989, pp. 15–16). Consequently, a component does not know how far its
output has already been processed by subsequent components. This is important
when output is erroneous or incomplete, because there is no possibility for a subsequent component to send back information about this to a preceding one. Such
cases are handled by the *monitoring* component that reads in the *parsed speech* of
the *speech comprehension system*. Besides component-internal feedback, this is the

only feedback in the model. It enables the conceptualizer to keep track of what of the planned utterance(s) is already produced, and it makes it possible to detect deviations. This is called *self-monitoring*, because it is not the monitoring of other interlocutors but of the speaker himself. Because this is only a model of the speaker, monitoring of another person speaking is not considered.

The *conceptualizer* consists of two subcomponents: *message generation*, which generates preverbal messages, and *monitoring*. INC is a model of the message generation component. Message generation performs the following four main tasks (Levelt's and my terms are given in parentheses):

1. Building up of an internal representation (bookkeeping, construction),
2. Selection of the content to be verbalized (macroplanning 1, selection),
3. Bringing the selected content into a linear order (macroplanning 2, linearization),
4. Generating a preverbal message for the content to be verbalized (microplanning, PVM-generation).

In INC, these tasks are realized as incrementally working processes. Using processes as means of structuring allows characterization of incremental processing as *parallel processing of a sequential information stream*. This means three things. First, there are multiple processes running in parallel. Second, these processes are arranged in a fixed sequence so that the output of one process is the input to its successor. Third, there is no feedback to previous processes in the sequence as specified by Levelt.

Besides an internal representation of the external states of affairs, the conceptualizer has access to other knowledge: the discourse model, long-term memory, which contains encyclopedic knowledge, and much more; in fact, the conceptualizer has access to all information that can be expressed verbally. However, knowledge represented in nonpropositional formats must be transformed into propositional knowledge in order to be verbalized, because at the end of conceptualization, knowledge must be present as *preverbal messages*, the characteristic input of the formulator. For the necessity of characteristic input, see § 11.

Preverbal messages are a special kind of conceptual representation. Mainly two properties set them apart from other conceptual representations. First, whereas conceptual representations are hierarchical, preverbal messages are sequential in the sense that they contain neither part-of nor subsumption relations. Second, preverbal messages are those conceptual representations that contain meaning to be conveyed (Jackendoff, 1987, 1990, 1997; Wiese, 2003b). They hold exactly the information that is necessary for the formulator to encode the intended meaning linguistically, that is, to generate a phonetic plan. This implies that the other two components have no access to the internal representations of the conceptualizer. This would be just another form of feedback. In this sense, preverbal messages can also be called *prelinguistic* or *semantic representations*. However, this view is not shared by all semantic theories (e.g., two-level semantics; Bierwisch & Schreuder, 1992).

The traditional view on preverbal messages as static semantic representations is too simple in the context of incremental processing. Instead, preverbal messages are representations that are generated and processed incrementally; that is, they are sequences of increments. Therefore, I will also call them *incremental preverbal messages* (Guhe, 2003; Guhe, Habel, & Tappe, 2000). Under the production perspective, this has two eminent consequences. First, for each increment of an incremental preverbal message, it must be ascertained that it fits to the increments already generated. This is the *consistency condition*. Second, all increments of an incremental preverbal message taken together must form a complete semantic representation as, for example, proposed by Jackendoff (1990). This is the *completeness condition*. A detailed account of incremental preverbal messages is given in §48.

Because I do not consider components of Levelt's model other than the conceptualizer, I only sketch out the remaining ones. The *formulator* takes preverbal messages and encodes them linguistically, resulting in the *phonetic plan*. The formulator (but not the conceptualizer) has access to the *lexicon*. Models of the formulator include IPG (Kempen & Hoenkamp, 1987), IPF (de Smedt, 1990a), SYNPHONICS (Günther, Schopp, & Ziesche, 1995), WEAVER (Roelofs, 1997), and Performance Grammar (Kempen, 1997). The phonetic plan is a program for articulation. It is also direct input to the speech comprehension system, in which case it is called *internal speech*. The *articulator* computes motor commands from the phonetic plan and executes them. The result is the production of *overt speech*, which is a succession of speech sounds. This is also the output of the articulator and input to the *audition* component.

Audition transforms overt speech (speech sounds) into *phonetic strings*. It not only takes overt speech from the speaker but also from other interlocutors, that is, when the speaker is in fact a hearer. The phonetic string is the counterpart of the phonetic plan. Like internal speech it serves as input to the *speech comprehension system*. The speech comprehension system analyzes the phonetic string and the internal speech phonologically and grammatically into *parsed speech*, which is the input to the monitoring component of the conceptualizer. Listening to one's own speech, be it internal or overt, is the prerequisite for self-monitoring.

So, in Levelt's model, production and comprehension of natural language take place in different components. The only shared components are the conceptualizer and the lexicon, and the differences of the tasks involved in production and comprehension corroborate this view. However, there are also proposals for *bi-directional* or *reversible* grammars, for example, Performance Grammar (Kempen, 1997; cf. E. Reiter & Dale, 2000, pp. 194–196, for a general overview). Such grammars can be used for production and comprehension alike. Results from empirical studies indicate that from some point onward the production and the comprehension systems come together. Levelt et al. (1999) argue that the lemma level* is this point (p. 7, assumption 3), which means that it is located within the formulator. Although this implies that the conceptualizer is a component that is exclusively used for language production, it must be noted that the parsed speech, which is input to the monitor, is coming from the speech comprehension system. In this sense, it is also a language comprehension component. (Chapter 14 gives an outline of how INC can be extended by a self-monitoring component.)

The knowledge representations depicted in figure 2.2 are special views on human knowledge that focus on the knowledge available for the production of language. Yet, they are static views. From a performance perspective, there are three memory structures. The first is *working memory*, where parsed speech and preverbal messages are stored. Working memory is used for other tasks as well, such as the selection and linearization of utterances. This is necessary for planning multiple utterances in advance, for example, when structuring a small speech according to the rules of rhetoric in advance. Limitations of working memory influence which utterances are generated. If, for example, its capacity is exceeded, utterances that were scheduled for verbalization may be forgotten, and they are either not verbalized at all, or they must be planned anew. INC possesses a parameter that corresponds to how much working memory is available for conceptualization. Varying the parameter leads to different verbalizations.† The other two memory structures are specialized buffers: The *syntactic buffer* stores the surface structure (an intermediary structure of the formulator), and the *articulatory buffer* stores the phonetic plan. Both buffers are limited in size; as in the case of working memory, errors arise when their capacity is exceeded.

Preverbal messages, as well as the other two interface representations, are never completely available at a given point in time—except for short utterances. However, the incremental mode of operation makes it (theoretically) possible to produce infinite utterances with limited storage capacity, which is not possible in a nonincremental mode of operation. Buffers are usually needed for incremental processing, because they serve to compensate differences in processing speed of the single components. Additionally, they allow a reordering of increments, which is required because of the rapid production of output. Chapter 5 provides more detail of the role of buffers in incremental processing.

---

* A *lemma* is that part of a lexical item that contains the nonphonological information (Levelt, 1989, pp. 188–198).
† Resource limitations are one of the main topics of chapter 7. How different values for parameters influence the behavior of INC is the topic of chapter 13. The parameter I am referring to here is the *length of traverse buffer* (LOTB).

§ 11   Conceptualization and other cognitive tasks

In the remainder of this chapter, I draw the boundary between conceptualization and other cognitive tasks.

❧ MODULARITY OF CONCEPTUALIZATION.   A central issue to every model of a cognitive faculty is its modularity. As modularity itself is not my topic, I will not retell the story of the *modularity debate*—the debate over whether modules can explain aspects of human cognition. This debate is still not settled. Two particularly prominent approaches to cognition that reject the idea of modularity are cognitive linguistics (Lakoff, 1987; Langacker, 1987/1991, 2000), which focuses on interrelations between different cognitive faculties instead of the interrelations within one cognitive faculty, and connectionism (Rumelhart & McClelland, 1986), which rejects the idea of symbols and representations.* A major motivation for doing so is the *symbol grounding problem*.† Because symbol, representation, and module are basic notions in my approach, let it be enough to say that I agree with the claims made by Levelt and Fodor on this issue (see below). Thus, my work is in the tradition of modular, symbolic approaches to cognition.

To which degree is the human language production faculty and, in particular, the conceptualizer modular? Fodor (1983) provides a set of nine criteria that are commonly used to distinguish modules from nonmodules:

1. Domain specificity
2. Mandatoriness
3. Limited central access to the mental representations
4. Fast speed
5. Informational encapsulation
6. "Shallow" outputs
7. Association with fixed neural architecture
8. Characteristic and specific breakdown patterns
9. Ontogeny that exhibits a characteristic pace and sequencing

---

* More precisely, both approaches do not explicitly reject modularity. They consider it irrelevant. The upshot is that all elements used for a task can be considered belonging to one module; for example, the neurons performing phonological encoding can be considered the phonological module. Yet, since all neurons are connected by the same type of links, there are no interfaces to other modules, say the morphological module. Furthermore, the distinction between modules is not defined by the builder of the model but emerges.

† The symbol grounding problem is the problem that symbol definitions are circular, because symbols are defined in terms of other symbols (Harnad, 1990). Symbols are not connected to extra-symbolic properties; they are not *grounded*. As I argue in §18, there are other ways of dealing with this problem than rejecting symbols.

Note that Fodor uses these criteria to argue for the modularity of input systems, which means they describe systems for automatic processing. Nevertheless, the criteria are usually taken to judge whether something is a module or not. Apart from input and output systems, Fodor argues for the existence of *transducers*, which translate the different kinds of input into neural signals (e.g., transducers that compute neural signals from light) and a *central system*, which is a nonmodular, general-purpose system for inference, deduction, and reasoning. The central system is the system in which executive control takes place, and it is the place of conscious, volitional processes.

What happens if not all nine criteria are met? The studies of the polyglot savant Christopher led Smith and Tsimpli (1995, 1996) to develop a "picture of language [that] crucially involves aspects of the central system as well, so the bald alternative of 'modular/non-modular' is simplistic, indeed false" (1996, p. 16). Agreeing with Fodor, they consider informational encapsulation and cognitive impenetrability (Fodor's limited central access to the mental representations) to be the most important aspects of modularity. Their findings reveal that "some system could be cognitively impenetrable but not informationally encapsulated, whilst the reverse relation is impossible" (p. 13). They capture this in the notion of *quasi-modules*: Although these "have the domain specificity of modules, they are not informationally encapsulated and they exploit a non-perceptual vocabulary" (p. 1).

This view is supported by Levelt's reluctance to speak of modules. He prefers to call the parts of his model *components*. Levelt (1989) characterizes components as relatively autonomous specialists that generate *characteristic output* from *characteristic input* (pp. 13–20). Besides its characteristic input, a component only has minimal access to other information and is influenced only minimally by other components. This makes input *characteristic* input. Characteristic output is output that serves as characteristic input to other components.

Levelt and Fodor agree in that the central system is the least modular component, and the more peripheral a cognitive component is the more modular it is. With regard to the language production system, this means that the closer a component is to overt speech, the more informationally encapsulated and the less cognitively penetrable it is. Consequently, the conceptualizer is the least modular component and the articulator the most modular. This view is supported by the fact that *automatic processes* can run in parallel (in different modules), whereas the *controlled processing* in the central system requires attention and is, therefore, sequential (Levelt, 1989, pp. 20–21). INC's parallel processes, which model the subtasks of conceptualization, show that the conceptualizer has these properties, because, on the one hand, their functionality can be separated and characteristic input and output can be defined, but, on the other hand they are not as independent from each other as automatic processes are. The main reason for this is that they use a shared memory (see chapter 9), similar to working memory. The shared memory has two main advantages: It simplifies the model by reducing processing and storage redundancies, and it allows *indirect feedback*, which can account for some phenomena that strictly unidirectional models have difficulty explaining. (See p. 87 and term 21 on p. 92 on indirect feedback.)

This indicates that the conceptualizer-internal components have some properties of modules but lack others: Due to the shared memory, the components are not fully informationally encapsulated. This does not mean that they also must be cognitively penetrable. These are exactly the properties of quasi-modules. Nevertheless, I continue to call them components. Furthermore, I use *process* and *component* almost synonymously, because INC's components are implemented as processes.

☙ NONMODULAR ASPECTS OF CONCEPTUALIZATION.   Before illustrating the modular aspects, I argue in more detail that some aspects of conceptualization are nonmodular. Speaking is an *intentional* activity; that is, usually a speaker has a communicative intention he wants to convey, as Levelt (1989), among many others, points out. However, as the subtitle of his book (*From Intention to Articulation*) indicates: "Where intentions come from is not a concern of this book" (p. 59). What is more, he restricts his discussion to *communicative* intentions, intentions that underlie speech acts (Austin, 1962; Searle, 1969, 1979): "The mother of each speech act is a communicative intention" (Levelt, 1989, p. 108). He makes two further restrictions. First, he considers only *illocutionary intentions*: communicative intentions that are realized by no means of communication other than speech acts. Second, each communicative intention must be *recognizable* by the hearer as just that. Speech acts serving a different purpose, for example, to deceive the hearer, have no underlying communicative intention. This means that speakers follow Grice's (1975) *cooperative principle*.

It is no accident that Levelt restricts his account of speaking to a subset of communicative intentions. Although intentions are essential for characterizing our mental life, they are evasive. Even after some thousand years, there is no commonly accepted definition. A major reason is that intentions are the result of conscious, volitional processes, and *consciousness* is one of the most disputed terms in philosophy. For language production, this has the consequence that even if all processes of Levelt's architecture are fully understood one day and expressed in computational models, this will (most likely) not include the computation of the "initial spark," the spark that is the result of a volitional, conscious decision and sets everything into motion. One could say, the processes in Levelt's model take place after the spark came into being. Intentionality is a strong argument that language production cannot be modular in the strict sense, because it is accessible to conscious thought, that is, accessible to controlled processing. It also corroborates the view that conceptualization is the least modular component of language production. Although conscious thought can access all stages of language production, this becomes more difficult the farther away from the central system a component is located.

These prospects are discouraging, but all is not lost. Although the initial spark may well be beyond scientific discovery, one can focus on the situatedness of cognition, that is, the fact that humans are situated in an environment. This means that there is a strong *data-driven* aspect to conceptualization and language production. Although this, too, does not explain how initial sparks arise, it gives some answers to the question of how what I call *subintentions** arise in a data-driven scenario. If the communicative intention is *describe what happens* (while it happens), the subintentions are the communicative intentions that underlie speech acts realizing this goal. In AI terminology, communicative intentions are *verbalization goals*. Seen this way, speaking is a goal-directed activity, and subintentions are subgoals along the way to reach the overall goal.

Focusing on the data-driven aspects of conceptualization highlights the need for incremental processing, because it emphasizes the fact that the available resources are limited. First, *time* is limited, because an input increment must be processed before the next one enters the system. Otherwise, the system cannot keep up with the input stream like humans do. Second, the available *memory*, in particular working memory (Levelt, 1989), in which the input is processed is limited. So, a mode of processing is required that enables the system to cope with the available resources. Incrementality is just the way do this: Piecemeal processing that takes place on multiple stages in parallel means that the system is capable of reacting to new input all the time, even while already producing language.

Because working memory is also used by cognitive faculties other than language production, it is a particularly critical resource. In a natural (nonlaboratory) environment, a speaker is almost always occupied with additional tasks requiring working memory. Experiments reveal interferences between utterance planning and other cognitive tasks requiring working memory, whereas there are no interferences of such tasks and automatic articulation (Baddeley, 1986; Eysenck & Keane, 1995; E. E. Smith, 1999). In these experiments, the articulatory buffer is filled by letting participants articulate in a noncontrolled, automatic manner while other tasks have to be performed that require working memory. Because performance is not significantly affected, working memory is not needed for (automatic) articulation; that is, articulation employs different resources. However, planning tasks also require working memory, and the resource must be shared. Hence, working memory is only partly available for conceptualization.

---

* *Subintention* is perhaps not the best term for this, but I cannot think of a better one. With this I certainly do not want to propose a new kind of intention.

❧ MODULAR ASPECTS OF CONCEPTUALIZATION: LANGUAGE SPECIFICITY.
So, some aspects of conceptualization are nonmodular. Now I illustrate that conceptualization is a cognitive task in its own right. I do this by concentrating on its language specificity. Language specificity can mean two things:

1. How specific is conceptualization with respect to the production of language?
2. How specific is conceptualization with respect to the production of a particular language?

The first question is how specific conceptualization is with respect to the production of language in contrast to processing conceptual representations to perform other cognitive tasks, for example, navigating through an environment. The second question is whether conceptualization is different for, say, speaking Zulu than for speaking Latin. The overall question is *Is there only one conceptualizer performing one conceptualization task?* The answer is *perhaps* and *no*: There may be only one conceptualizer, but there is not only one conceptualization task.

To start with the question 2, von Stutterheim (1999) and Rieckmann (2000) show that conceptualizations differ even for speaking languages as closely related as German and English. Both investigated how participants describe events. They found that descriptions differ not only with respect to the linguistic means with which concepts are expressed (e.g., German knows no progressive forms), they also differ with respect to the use of the underlying conceptual representation: English native speakers tend to focus on the event itself, whereas German native speakers tend to focus on its result.* For example, when participants verbalize a scene in which they see a street with a bus stop on the opposite side and a woman who is pushing a pushchair while she crosses the street, then English participants tend to produce an utterance like (1) whereas German participants tend to produce one like (2).

(1) *A woman is crossing the street.*
(2) *Eine Frau geht zur Bushaltestelle.*
     'A woman walks to the bus stop.'

Similar evidence comes from Carroll (1997) and Levinson (1996, 1997), who present results from cross-cultural comparisons of spatial conceptions. Agreeing with Slobin (1996), they propose a *thinking for speaking* (see chap. 1): While humans are speaking,

---

* They might also have different underlying conceptual representations. However, the conceptual representations are built up by the conceptualization process as well (construction in INC), which does not affect the point I am making here.

they think in a particular way.

So, thinking for English must be different from thinking for German to some extent, because different parts of the conceptual representation are highlighted in the above utterances. Furthermore, the preverbal message must contain different information in different languages. For example, it does not need aspect information in German, but it does in English.*

But can one conceptualizer perform different conceptualization tasks? Bilinguals are a strong case in favor of this view, because they speak both languages as native speakers. So, at different points in time, their conceptualizer performs different conceptualization tasks. (If bilinguals also had two conceptualizers they should be able to produce output in both languages at the same time, say writing German and speaking English.)

Slobin's *thinking for speaking* offers a solution to the first question as well: Conceptualization (thinking) for speaking differs from conceptualization for other cognitive tasks. The alternative view is that native speakers of German and English differ not only in the way they verbally describe how to get from A to B but also in the way they plan their actions to get from A to B, which seems very far fetched. It cannot be fully rejected, because language is important for the way humans make sense of the world. Even though the extreme form of the Whorf hypothesis is accepted no longer (see, e.g., the not only instructive but also entertaining essay on "The Great Eskimo Vocabulary Hoax" by Pullum, 1991), language is the primary way for humans to gain knowledge and has, therefore, great influence on how we think of the world. For example, Wiese (2003a) argues that a speaker's language indeed has effects on conceptualization.

To sum up, conceptualization is language dependent to some extent. It is also a task in its own right. It is best seen as a quasi-module: It is a component between the central system and informationally encapsulated modules that is partly cognitively penetrable.

---

* The place in INC where conceptualization becomes language specific is PVM-generation. Here, some language-specific information, for example, temporal or aspect information, is included in the preverbal message.

$$\sim 3 \sim$$

CONCEPTUALIZATION

C ONCEPTUALISATION IS NOTORIOUSLY hard to investigate, because it is never directly observable. Using a data-driven (perception-driven) setting helps overcoming this difficulty (§12). Conceptualization is nonlinguistic, albeit particular for language production, as I argued in the previous chapter. However, although its endpoint is rather clear-cut (preverbal messages), it is hard to identify its starting point and internal workings. I, therefore, describe the starting point used by INC and characterize the tasks of which conceptualization consists (§13). The data-driven approach to conceptualization requires a working differentiation between perception and conceptualization (§14). At the end of this chapter, I give an outlook on how conceptualization is affected by incremental processing (§15).

§12   *Investigating conceptualization*

The previous chapter showed that conceptualization for language production is a nonlinguistic task but specific to language production. That is, it differs to some extent from conceptualization for other cognitive tasks, and its output is produced in order to be encoded linguistically. Thus, conceptualization is a bridge between the language production components proper—formulator and articulator—and other perceptual and cognitive faculties, for example, visual perception and long-term memory. Before I describe the subtasks of the overall task *conceptualization for language production* in more detail in §13, I first illustrate why it is difficult to investigate and provide more details on the method with which I investigate it.

The literature offers no generally accepted definition of *conceptualization for language production*. One of the major problems for the investigation of conceptualization results from this, because issues of conceptualization are often treated by theories of language. However, neither theories of grammar nor the cognitive components of grammar need to know that, for example, only animate entities can breathe. Instead, this information is part of the cognitive system that generates the input to the grammatical module, just as the conceptual system also decides which elements of the conceptual representation are verbalized, in which order, and in what way (Nuyts, 2001, p. 8).

There are three main reasons for this problem. First, there is no agreement among researchers about what they mean by *conceptualization*. Second, it is difficult to determine the degree to which conceptualization is specific to a task, such as language production or navigation through space (see chap. 2). Therefore, separating conceptualization from the task (e.g., speaking) is difficult. Third, and this may be the actual cause for all the confusion, conceptualization is not directly observable, because its output never surfaces directly but always serves as input to another system, the formulator in the case of language production. Whereas the first two issues are typical methodological problems of science, the last one makes studying conceptualization particularly difficult. One way to remedy this problem is to compare different behavioral patterns in different surface modalities in order to find commonalities, for example, between language and gestures. The commonalities then allow one to infer properties of conceptualization (Nuyts, 2001, p. 12).

I use a different method, namely focusing on the *data-driven* aspects of conceptualization. This is a means to strictly control its input. In this way, the output becomes comparable. Tomlin (1997), for example, uses this method to study how attention influences the order in which phrases are produced. He shows animated scenes on a computer screen of two fish swimming toward one another. A small arrow flashing over one of the fish shortly before they meet draws the participants' attention to one of them. Then, one fish opens its mouth, devours the other, and swims out of the visible area. The entity in the focus of attention—no matter whether it is the swallowing or the swallowed fish—is generally produced as the syntactic subject in the verbal descriptions of these scenes. He claims that this explains subject selection in English, without the need for intermediary pragmatic or textual levels; the element in the focus of attention is verbalized as subject. Although this conclusion may be correct in this particular case, it is also much too general, because it is not clear at all how it fits into a more general theory of selection and linearization of content to be verbalized. Additionally, this study has English-speaking participants only; a corresponding study for other languages may yield quite different results.

Tomlin's (1997) results point to a plausible mechanism for the incremental generation of preverbal messages: Starting from the element in the focus of attention, the preverbal message is generated increment by increment, where the element in the focus of attention is the first increment of a preverbal message. To emphasize the incremental way in which preverbal messages are generated, I call them *incremental preverbal messages*.* One should think of incremental preverbal messages as "sequences of well-formed propositional structures on a sub-propositional level" (Guhe et al., 2000, p. 88). This means that the proposition representing a preverbal

---

* The element in the focus of attention is the *focused element* introduced in chapter 5 and the *head of traverse buffer* of chapter 9. The decision of whether the element in the focus of attention is selected for verbalization is elaborated on in chapters 11 and 12. The idea of incremental preverbal messages was introduced in Guhe et al. (2000) and is described in detail in Guhe (2003) and in § 48.

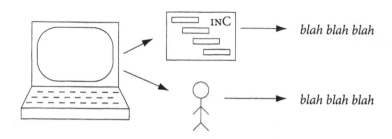

Figure 3.1: Overall setting of verbalization studies and simulating conceptualization

message is not produced as a whole but piecemeal, that is, in increments, and the increments themselves can be described by propositions.

Griffin uses an experimental setting "inverse" to Tomlin's in which the participant's attention is not guided but free (Griffin, 1998; Griffin & Bock, 2000; see also Bock, Irwin, Davidson, & Levelt, 2003; Bock, Erwin, & Davidson, 2004). Instead, an eyetracker monitors the participant's attention. (The underlying assumption in this line of research is that eye fixations reflect the focus of attention.) The participant's task is to verbalize pictures showing events. The events are transitive actions; that is, there are always two partakers A and B, and A is doing something to B (e.g., a dog is chasing a postman). It shows that there is a systematic temporal linkage between eye movements and the contents of spoken utterances. Eye movements and attention anticipate the order in which the partakers are mentioned in the corresponding verbalizations.

Such settings probe into conceptualization by correlating the input with the generated utterances. I use a similar setting for investigating the online description of events (figure 3.1. Scenes are presented on a computer screen, and the participant is instructed: "Describe what you see!" The verbalizations are recorded on tape and then transcribed for analysis. Two types of scenes are used in the studies: motion events and the drawing of sketch maps. In the studies with drawing of sketch maps, participants are asked in a first study to draw a sketch map of a known route, for example, the way from the campus of the computer science department to the main campus in Hamburg. This is recorded with a drawing tablet. In the following verbalization study, the recorded drawings—not the resulting sketch maps—are presented to a different group of participants. In the studies with motion events, synthetic movements are generated with a computer tool and shown to participants.*

---

* All studies were carried out with the help of tools we developed in the project ConcEv. The programs *Zeichnung* (Turhan & Erichsen, 1998) and *VirtualDraw* (Adiwidjaja & Gerhard, 2000) make it possible to record and replay sketch maps. *ConMotion* makes it possible to define movements of objects (e.g., taxiing planes) and play them to participants.

The advantage in both settings is that the data are not only used to present scenes to human participants but also as INC's input.* This allows a comparison of the output generated by INC with the analyzes of the human verbalization data in order to evaluate the quality of the model and the implemented system (see chapter 13). Note, however, that INC does not produce text or spoken output but preverbal messages, so that the comparison is not a one-to-one mapping.

§ 13   *Conceptualization tasks*

Conceptualization for language production can be briefly described as the cognitive process that builds up conceptual representations and produces preverbal messages from these representations, which can be encoded linguistically by the formulator. Thus, the conceptualizer is the mediator between the central system (and/or the systems working in other modalities) and preverbal messages. Put differently, conceptualization covers the stretch between linguistic encoding and higher level cognitive activities such as reasoning about the world, spatial cognition, social cognition, visual cognition, and so on. This means that conceptualization is particular for language production; it is *thinking for speaking*.

Understanding conceptualization this way draws on a close interdependence of conceptual representations and the conceptual tasks that operate on these representations. However, I will not stipulate the one and then develop the other from this, because it is hardly possible to distinguish them in representational or computational terms. Think, for example, of the standard method in functional programming languages or the predicate calculus to represent entities as functions with zero arguments (which are then part of the function/task, not part of a separate representation). Therefore, I will develop them in mutual dependence—using what is known about their cognitive basis.

I now describe the subtasks of conceptualization introduced in § 10: construction, selection, linearization, and the generation of preverbal messages.

❧ CONSTRUCTION.   Conceptualization starts with the construction of conceptual representations. For the task of online descriptions of events, this means that the conceptualizer reads in a stream of input increments and builds up a hierarchical representation of the external states of affairs from the input increments. The introductory example in § 2 already demonstrated the need for event hierarchies: A DOCKING event consists of subevents (cf. also Habel & Tappe, 1999). Although it is

---

* The only difference is that INC's input is processed by a perceptual preprocessing unit (PPU) first, which is necessary to get from spatio-temporal coordinates to perceived entities (§ 39).

possible to use a mode of presentation in which the DOCKING is perceived and conceptualized holistically, for example, by speeding up the movements, the normal case is that an observer sees the subevents and constructs the more complexDOCKING concept from them.

Because conceptualization is concerned with the processing of concepts, simple concepts have to be generated by a unit preceding the conceptualizer, a *preprocessing unit* (PPU). Both domains covered by INC (drawing of sketch maps and motion events) use a different PPU. A PPU reads in the same information that is used for the verbalization studies and generates output that is the input to INC. The interface between PPU and INC consists of *perceived entities* (PEs, §39). Having PEs as input to conceptualization just says that the entities are perceived but does not restrict their level of granularity. For example, a square in the drawing sketch maps domain may constitute a PE as well as succession of PEs that represent the lines the square consists of. For this reason, they are not called *perceptual* entities, which might imply that the perceptual system operates on a fixed level of granularity, for example, the level with the simplest concepts. The Levelt model neither addresses this important question where input comes from nor the fact that the structure of the conceptual knowledge depends on perceptual factors but simply states that the conceptualizer has access to different kinds of knowledge.

So, a major aspect of constructing a conceptual representation is matching PEs onto conceptual knowledge available in long-term memory. In most cases, the result of this matching is that construction inserts more complex elements into the conceptual representation that group simpler PEs. If a concept from long-term memory matches only partially and if it is possible that the missing parts will arrive as the next PEs, an *expectation* may be generated. An example of such an expectation in the DOCKING scene is that the WALKWAY will stop moving when it reaches the PLANE. Of course, it is an expectation only as long as the STOP event has not occurred. Afterward, the STOP event is a regular event of the conceptual representation. Note that humans will immediately and invariably say that the WALKWAY stops moving *in order* not to damage the PLANE. INC makes no such sophisticated inferences; the expectation is generated, simply because this STOP is part of the overall DOCKING event.

& SELECTION.   The next step toward generating preverbal messages is to select events from the hierarchical conceptual representation for verbalization. Because INC is specialized on the conceptualization and verbalization of events, the selection task only considers events for verbalization. (It could also generate verbalizations for other entities without changing the overall design and functionality; see §46.) It generates the subintentions discussed in §11, corresponding to Levelt's (1989) first part of macroplanning. For example, selection is the task that decides whether the subevents of the DOCKING event are verbalized, resulting in the four-utterance verbalization of the scene given on page 4, only one utterance like (1) below, or a mixture of both like (2).

(1)   *Ein Flugzeug dockt an.*
      'A plane is docking.'
(2)   a.   *Ein Flugzeug bewegt sich auf ein Gate zu.*
           'A plane is moving toward a gate.'
      b.   *Es stoppt beim Gate.*
           'It stops at the gate.'
      c.   *Es dockt an.*
           'It is docking.'

For the online description of events, the selection task can be reduced to looking at each change that the construction task makes in the conceptual representation. Selection decides whether the element that was changed by construction will be verbalized. This is possible because of the data-driven mode of operation. Deciding to utter a concept corresponds to generating a communicative subintention. In a full account of the selection task, many factors must be considered to determine the appropriateness of the selected content, including hearer model, discourse model, further communicative intentions that have already been decided on but are not yet realized, social appropriateness, estimation of reliability (information that is too speculative is not verbalized), and so forth. In the setting used for INC, two selection strategies proved particularly successful. The first can be phrased this way: *Always take the most complex concept that is currently not selected for verbalization.* In this selection strategy, only events that are not yet selected for verbalization are considered. If an event is already selected, then there is no need to select it a second time. For example, if the conceptualizer already decided on generating an utterance describing an event that would result in an utterance like (2a), then there is no need to produce a second utterance describing the same event. The other part of this selection strategy is that the most complex event available is selected. For example, if the event described by utterance (1) is selected for verbalization, then there is no need to select subevents like (2a). Conversely, if (2a) is selected but not yet verbalized when the overall DOCKING event is inserted into the conceptual representation, then this simpler event is replaced by the more complex one so that only an utterance like (1) is generated. (Note the importance of the fact whether a selected simpler event is still buffered when a more complex one becomes available for selection. The difference in the resulting verbalizations is a simple effect of the incremental mode of operation.) This strategy is based on empirical studies (Guhe & Habel, 2001, see also chap. 13). It conforms to the Gricean maxims *Be brief*, a submaxim of the maxim of manner, and *Do not make your contribution more informative than is required*, a submaxim of the maxim of quantity (Grice, 1975).

The second selection strategy used by INC can be phrased this way: *Retain the level of granularity if possible*. This strategy selects an event only if another event of the same level of granularity has already been selected (but not yet verbalized). Only if nothing else is currently selected for verbalization are events of another level of granularity selected. This strategy is motivated by the principles that (a) the ideal online description of events consists of utterances generated at a constant rate and (b) the utterances are on the same level of granularity. Reasons are that (a) the (imagined) hearer should be kept up-to-date about what is happening, or that gaps in verbalizations are undesirable, and (b) that permanent changes in the level of granularity make it difficult to follow the description. Because understanding this selection strategy requires more detailed knowledge about INC, I postpone its full explanation. With this strategy, sequences of utterances like the one given in the introduction on page 4 can be generated.

In the general case, one communicative intention does not necessarily lead to exactly one utterance. Instead, one communicative intention may lead to multiple utterances, or multiple communicative intentions may be aggregated to one utterance. However, for most purposes at hand, this is of no importance, for which reason I assume such a one-to-one correspondence as a working hypothesis. Analogously, utterances are different from sentences. However, the formulator must treat the problem of how utterances are matched onto sentences, because *sentence* is a grammatical notion. Thus, I use the term *utterance*, which is the linguistic correspondent to a communicative intention and which leaves open where exactly a sentence ends or where a new one begins.

❧ LINEARIZATION.   Linearization is the task of bringing the selected events into an order that is appropriate with respect to the goal of the discourse. Although linearization is perhaps the most investigated task of conceptualization (see, e.g., Levelt, 1983, 1989), it plays only a minor role in INC. First, linearization is the most dispensable task of the four: In contrast to linearization, verbalization cannot work without construction, selection, and the generation of preverbal messages. Second, in the online description of events, the input information is strictly chronological, so that adequate verbalizations can be generated without reordering the selected events. However, the difference of meaning in Levelt's (1989, 138–139) example:

(3)   She married and became pregnant.
(4)   She became pregnant and married.

makes clear the need for a linearization component. When these two events (marrying and becoming pregnant) are selected for verbalization it must be ascertained that they are generated in the chronological order in which they took place. Otherwise, the (implied) meaning differs from the one given in the conceptual representation of the speaker. If the order in which the events are verbalized differs from the chronological order, this must be marked overtly:

(5) She married after she became pregnant.

In the context of linearization, Levelt (1989) proposes the *principle of natural order*: *Arrange information for expression according to the natural ordering of its content* (p. 138). He develops this principle from a verbalization task in which participants linearize (and verbally describe) static constellations of colored dots linked by lines (Levelt, 1983, 1989). Although the principle of natural order quite plausibly captures the verbalizations recorded in this study, it is too simple to generally account for linearization phenomena (Habel & Tappe, 1999). First of all, it is usually difficult (or impossible) to determine the natural order of content. Although the chronological order is one natural order for motion events, it is often "more natural" to reorder events to generate a more coherent sequence in which the events are mentioned:

(6) a. *Das Flugzeug stoppt, nachdem es auf das Gate zugefahren ist.*
      'The plane stops, after it moved toward the gate.'
   b. *Es ist sehr schnell gefahren.*
      'It moved very fast.'

Linearization can be investigated in the online description of events by an extension of the task in which the participants have to verbalize *concurrent* events, that is, multiple events happening simultaneously. For example, more than one plane or different kinds of objects can move simultaneously. As language is purely sequential, the events must be brought into a linear order.

 GENERATION OF PREVERBAL MESSAGES. After the events to be verbalized have been selected and linearized, an appropriate utterance expressing the speech act is produced. Levelt (1989) lists four major aspects to the generation of preverbal messages: computing the accessibility status of the referents, topicalization, propositionalization, and acknowledging language-specific requirements.

The *accessibility status* determines whether a referent is known and by which expression it can be referred to. Accessibility strongly depends on the state of the system: which entity has been used last, or, for our data-driven setting, which entity has been perceived last. Hence, accessibility can be treated very elegantly by incremental processing. *Topicalization* is the assignment of the topic role to one of the referents of a preverbal message. *Propositionalization* is the task of generating a proposition for the event/speech act to be verbalized. This proposition is the preverbal message expressing the event. It is the latest point where information that is represented in another than propositional format must be translated. The ability of referential nets to represent multimodal knowledge facilitates the translation between formats (cf. appendix A). A major aspect of propositionalization is the assignment of perspective, or *perspectivization* (Levelt, 1989, pp. 152–157; see §15). Finally, the generated preverbal message must meet the *language-specific requirements* of the formulator in the sense that it must account for requirements of the particular language in which the preverbal message will be expressed. For example, if a language overtly marks tense, this information must be present in the preverbal message, whereas it may be left out in languages that do not mark tense. Language specificity is no major point in the following discussion, but see §11 on this issue.

Because the Levelt model contains no feedback from formulator to conceptualizer, it must be guaranteed that a preverbal message can indeed be linguistically encoded by the formulator. Otherwise, the verbalization is erroneous or fails completely. As humans do make mistakes, this is no absolute requirement; yes, a perfect model should even account for these mistakes. By and large, though, encodability must be given.* A possibility to ensure it is to check whether a preverbal message is encodable before it is handed on to the formulator. However, this contradicts the idea of incrementality, because it interrupts the flow of information from one stage to the next. In order to perform the check, the preverbal message must be available completely beforehand. Therefore, I consider encodability to be a requirement a conceptualizer must meet without explicit mechanism. That is, the normal functioning of the system must be such that preverbal messages are encodable.

Another problem at this stage of language production is the *verbalization problem* addressed, for example, by Bierwisch and Schreuder (1992). Just as there is no general, simple one-to-one mapping of communicative intentions onto preverbal messages, there is no one-to-one mapping of a preverbal message's parts onto lexical items. Whereas the first problem can be addressed as described above, the second problem is a problem of the formulator, not the conceptualizer, because preverbal messages are a special kind of conceptual representation and not linguistic representations.

---

* In the field of NLG, the encodability problem corresponds to the problem of the *generation gap* (Meteer, 1990, 1991). Although one can quite simply assure that only encodable prelinguistic representations are generated by restricting the possible representations, this is no real solution for a cognitive model, because it means that the system undergenerates; that is, the full richness and diversity of natural language are not used. This severely limits the quality of the system.

During the generation of preverbal messages, additional means of expressing the content to be communicated can be chosen. Especially prosodic information like loudness, rhythm, or intonational contour must be produced by the conceptualizer to some extent, for example, to realize a contrast between two parts of an utterance. Other means include gestures or facial expressions.

§ 14   *Conceptualization and perception*

Although perception and conceptualization are usually regarded as separate levels of cognitive processing, they are not independent of each other. Conceptualization and perception interact in both directions; that is, there is information streaming not only from perception to conceptualization but also in the opposite direction. For example, expectations—which can be seen as a preactivation of the corresponding concepts—can speed up processing of input if the expected concepts are indeed perceived (facilitation) or slow down processing if the expected concepts are not perceived (inhibition). The entire *priming* paradigm relies on this effect. Another well-known example of the influences of conceptualization on perception from the field of vision are ambiguous pictures like the duck–rabbit (e.g., as depicted in Pinker, 1999, p. 293), a picture that can be seen as showing either a duck or a rabbit. What one sees is strongly influenced by conceptual processing.

My data-driven setting makes necessary some perceptual preprocessing. However, I only provide a very coarse model of perception, because perception is not my main interest. I make only simple and widely used assumptions. My main assumption is that PEs constitute the interface between perception and conceptualization and that PEs are computed from sequences of spatio-temporal coordinates. I make no strong claims about the content of PEs and what they represent. The crucial point is that they can be used by the construction task to search long-term memory in order to build up a conceptual representation.

Additionally, because I focus on the conceptualization of events, I treat the perception and conceptualization of other entities only to the degree required for this purpose. In order to generate PEs, the PPU segments the input according to the empirically founded *cut-hypothesis* (Avrahami & Kareev, 1994, p. 239): *A subsequence of stimuli is cut out of a sequence to become a cognitive entity if it has been experienced many times in different contexts.* Because INC is capable of generating expectations, it is in principle also capable of generating feedback to the PPU in order to influence perception. For example, INC could send its expectations also to the PPU so that the PPU may more easily recognize the next input. If the next input does not match the expectation, this impedes recognition of the input. (As just mentioned, these facilitatory or inhibitory effects of expectations are the core idea of the priming paradigm.) Another example is that INC could send requests to the PPU to provide better or more information about a PE if the PE is not exact or detailed enough.

§ 15   *Incremental conceptualization: An outlook*

Incrementality is not just one possibility to perform conceptualization but is one of its essential properties. To elucidate this, I give an outlook on the effects of incrementality on conceptualization and describe how this challenges traditional notions of conceptualization. Incrementality is treated in detail in part B. Here, I elaborate three points:

1. The limitation of cognitive resources and how incrementality can explain that complex conceptual representations can be processed nevertheless,
2. The influence of the ordering of increments of incremental preverbal messages on the resulting utterances,
3. The temporal interleaving of the subtasks of conceptualization.

Incremental processing can reduce the complexity of computations. It can, therefore, operate with limited cognitive resources, in particular, limited memory and time. With respect to time, incrementality is similar to *anytime* processing, where the result of a computation can be requested at any time. More precisely, they yield a result for (almost) any amount of time that the algorithm is allotted. Often the run-time is specified when an anytime algorithm is called. This is one of the main differences between anytime and incremental processing, because in incremental processing there is no meta-computation of the time given to a particular algorithm or process; instead, the processing is triggered when input becomes available (§ 31). In anytime algorithms (and in the kind of incremental processing used in INC), the quality of the result improves over the course of time; that is, the later the result is requested, the better the quality of the result. Put differently, the depth of processing in anytime and incremental processing depends on the availability of the resource *time*. During the production of utterances, there is a time limit for the production of the next increment. If the limit is violated, audible gaps arise. A consequence in artificial systems is that the resulting speech sounds unnatural; a consequence for speakers is that another interlocutor may start speaking, although the speaker has not finished, because gaps are a means to signal the end of a turn. Such consequences for systems as well as for humans are undesirable.

Incremental processing helps coping with the limitations of memory by storing only parts of the currently produced utterance for a limited amount of time. This

Figure 3.2: A distractor set for the generation of referring expression

is necessary, because utterances can be infinitely long, whereas memory is limited. For conceptualization, this is mainly working memory. During utterance production, parts of utterances that are already handed on to the next stage of language production are deleted, and the freed space can be used to store the next increments.

Although incremental processing is a way to cope with limited resources, it has the consequence that the optimal result of a computation may not be found. A case in point is made by Dale and Reiter (1995). On the basis of work by Pechmann (1984), Dale and Reiter provide an incremental algorithm for the generation of referring expressions. The algorithm generates a uniquely identifying referring expression for an object that is chosen for verbalization from a set of objects. It does so by incrementally selecting properties of the object that distinguish it from the other objects in the set. The algorithm is not optimal in terms of the number of properties that are selected for describing the object. For example, if the set contains the three objects depicted in figure 3.2, the algorithm may generate *the small, black cup*, although *the black cup* would be the optimal (i.e., shortest) description. The algorithm is optimal, though, with respect to run-time (efficiency). Because it needs no backtracking it runs in linear time depending on the number of distractors, namely the objects that are not verbalized. Thus, incremental processing not only saves resources, it can also account for performance phenomena observed in empirical data, which non-incremental approaches can only explain with considerable difficulty. Dale and Reiter's algorithm is just one example of a large body of evidence that humans produce and process language incrementally (Altmann & Kamide, 1999; Amtrup, 1998; Chater, Pickering, & Milward, 1995; de Smedt, 1990a, 1990b; de Smedt & Kempen, 1987; Kempen, 1997; Kempen & Harbusch, 2003; Kempen & Hoenkamp, 1982, 1987).

Incremental processing can also be used to leave information implicit. For example, the sequence of the increments in a preverbal message can encode information for the formulator (§6). The output generated by formulators like the one of Kempen and Harbusch (2003) depends on the order of the input increments. A reordering or temporal suspension of operation is used only if the grammaticality would be violated otherwise. For example, topicalization and perspectivization do not need to be explicit transformational processes (like, e.g., in Ziesche, 1997) but are side-effects of incrementality. The incremental generation of a preverbal message commences with one concept; that is, this concept is handed on as first increment of a preverbal message to the formulator.* This is the referent the preverbal message is *about* (Levelt, 1989, p. 151) and, therefore, the concept that will be realized as topic (de Smedt, 1990a). The models by de Smedt (1990a) and Kempen and Harbusch (2003) show that this method allows to build generators without a separate perspectivization component.

Deciding on the first increment of a preverbal message is also the first step of perspectivization. For example, the decision, which of the two following utterances will be produced, is already made.

(7) David loves Sarah.
(8) Sarah is loved by David.

If the concept DAVID is generated as increment of the preverbal message before SARAH, utterance (7) is realized; if the order is inverse, it is (8). The two utterances describe the same state of affairs but from different perspectives. In the first, it is a statement about DAVID, whereas in the second one it is about SARAH (§6). (A second step in taking perspective, which is not related to the order of increments, is the decision how to refer to an entity. For instance, SARAH cannot only be referred to by her name, *Sarah*, but with many different descriptions: *Anna's daughter*, *the mother of Peter's children*, *Peter's wife*, etc.) INC's algorithm generating these expressions has a similar structure as Dale and Reiter's (1995). It consists of deciding on a designation associated with a refO and then recursively finding further designations for the refOs referred to by this designation in order to *ground* it (§49).

The temporal interleaving of the conceptualization tasks has important consequences for the way conceptualization proceeds. Consider the point in time when the generation of an incremental preverbal message commences. Obviously, the preverbal message that is generated can only contain information that is present in the conceptual representation. Thus, a preverbal message describing an event can differ from a preverbal message that is generated later even if it describes the same

---

* In INC, this depends on the interplay of selection and PVM-generation. As concepts are represented by refOs, the first refO that is sent to the formulator "sets the stage." All following refOs depend on this first one.

event. This is particularly true if the event was not completed before the generation started but can also be true afterward, for example, if additional inferences about the event were drawn in the meantime (e.g., connecting the event to other events). This issue is further elaborated in § 52.

CONCEPTUAL REPRESENTATIONS

C ONCEPTUAL REPRESENTATIONS GO hand in hand with the conceptualization process. First of all, it is paramount to have a sufficient understanding of the terms *concept* (the building blocks of conceptual representations) and *category* that serves the purpose at hand (§ 16). Based on these notions, the categorization task can be defined, namely the task that assigns categories to the perceived input (§ 17). A problem of concepts is the circularity of definitions of concepts, the symbol grounding problem, for which data-driven settings offer a solution (§ 18). The representations used by the conceptualization task are always internal representations of external states of affairs. This means the representations are particular to an individual human or system, and, therefore, they are subjective representations, not objective ones. Additionally, these internal representations change over time; that is, they are dynamic representations (§ 19). As INC is specialized on the conceptualization of events, I show how it represents events by elaborating how the conceptual representation for the docking example of § 2 is built up incrementally (§ 20). Finally, *thinking for speaking* requires *representations for speaking* (§ 21).

§ 16   *Concepts and categories*

Although the notion *concept* is central to several scientific disciplines, there is no clear-cut definition. I, therefore, use a working definition for INC. First, concepts are the "elements from which propositional thought is constructed" (Hampton, 1999, p. 176). Thus, they are the building blocks of conceptual representations. Second, concepts serve as a means of classification, for example, to identify different planes as being instances of the conceptPLANE and different walkways as instances of the conceptWALKWAY. Third, concepts are the means to relate new knowledge to prior or given knowledge, for example, to relate the plane instance that was just perceived to the conceptual knowledge about PLANES in order to retrieve additional information about this entity. Most researchers would agree that these are the central properties of concepts, and I will leave it at that and now concentrate on which concepts are used and how they are used in conceptual representations.

Among the plethora of ways to classify concepts in conceptual representations three are particularly important for the purpose at hand:

1. Part-of hierarchies
2. Subsumption hierarchies (ontology, sortal hierarchy, taxonomy)
3. Representations of entities (individuals) versus representations of categories

I already commented on the necessity of hierarchical conceptual representations in chapter 1 (e.g., figure 1.4, p. 10). Although part-of hierarchies are commonly accepted in the case of concepts representing concrete entities of the world, e.g., the fact that a PLANE consists of multiple parts, they are less common in the case of event representations. Nevertheless, having hierarchical representations is necessary as we already saw in the example in chapter 1, where two simpler events were taken together and constituted a more complex one. (Further reasons to treat event concepts similar to object concepts are given in §20.) Simple concepts are neither *basic* concepts nor *basic-level* concepts. Thus, they are not basic concepts, because I do not claim that the concepts I use here are in any way atomic or the most simple ones from which all other concepts are constructed. They also are not basic-level concepts (Rosch, Mervis, Gray, Johnson, & Boyes-Braem, 1976), which I do not consider as such. Simple concepts are really just this: simple. In particular, they are simple enough to be computed by the preprocessing unit (PPU). Thus, *perceived entities* (PEs; §13) are examples of simple concepts. Hence, simple concepts are not necessarily concepts that are at the bottom of the part-of-hierarchy. (Nevertheless, this is the case in the representations I discuss in this book.) The grouping and segmentation operations of the construction task create concepts on a neighboring level of the hierarchy—up or down, respectively. A consequence of this is that there are (theoretically) infinitely many levels of concepts.

Apart from distinguishing concepts by their position in the part-of-hierarchy, one can also discriminate them by their sort. The major distinction in the domain of motion events is the one between the sorts situation, spatial_entity, and object (see chap. 1). The sorts are hierarchically organized as well; they define the subsumption hierarchy. For example, the sort situation can be specified as state, process, or event, and these sorts can be refined further (see fig. 4.1, p. 57). This is usually phrased by saying that an *event is a* situation. Sorts allow the subdivision of a conceptual representation into multiple layers of representation, for example, the situation and the object layer (Tappe & Habel, 1998).

A third way to characterize concepts is to distinguish concepts of individual entities from concepts of sets of entities. Concepts of sets of entities are *categories*, and this is exactly the way the term concept is used most often: "Mental representations of categories are the entities psychologists mean by *concepts*. ... A category usually refers to a group of objects in the world, whereas a concept refers to a mental representation of such a group" (E. E. Smith, 1995, p. 3). (See Murphy, 2002, on concepts in general and a current exposition from a psychological point of view.) I extend this notion of concepts to include mental representations of individual entities, which will avoid unnecessary differentiations in the following—-unnecessary in the sense that INC would not profit from distinguishing knowledge about a set of entities from that of a single entity. It simplifies, for example, the definition of processes that retrieve or modify knowledge about what is perceived, that is, the same mechanisms retrieve knowledge about the categories and entities known to the system. Additionally, it allows the use of the same name for the items stored in INC's concept storage (cs) and its current conceptual representation (ccr). Using concepts in this way blurs issues that are important in other respects, in particular, the issue of abstracting over properties of different individual entities. However, in the current context this causes no problems. In short, I use categories and concepts as follows:

TERM 3: CATEGORY
A category is a set of abstract or concrete entities that share a set of common properties.

TERM 4: CONCEPT
A concept is the mental representation of a category or an entity. They are the symbolic elements from which a conceptual representation is constructed.

§ 17   *Categorization*

A central problem in the context of concepts and categories is how PEs that enter the system are connected to prior knowledge. Establishing these relations is the process of *categorization*—"the process by which distinct entities are treated as equivalent" (Medin & Aguilar, 1999, p. 104). More precisely, the categorization task is to compute which PEs are to be treated as equivalent, that is, as belonging to one category. It is "a rule for classifying objects" (Gärdenfors, 2000, p. 60); that is, it is a cognitive task, not an abstract relation between entities and categories. Note that categorization processes of a different kind are required to build up (learn) concepts representing categories, but I do not consider this problem.

Categorization in INC is a two-stage process. The first stage takes place in the PPU, where the perceptual input is classified and simple concepts are generated that represent PEs. The second stage follows in INC, which summarizes sets of PEs to more complex concepts or analyzes a concept into simpler concepts. This is done recursively for all concepts generated in this fashion, that is, also for the ones computed by INC. Each newly perceived entity (and each self-generated concept) is compared to the available knowledge about concepts. For example, INC can relate the PE representing the PLANE of the introductory example to knowledge about

PLANES in general, which it retrieves from the CS, for example, the fact that a PLANE
has an OWNER. If the OWNER is not known, an empty concept can be introduced
into the conceptual representation. This concept stands for the OWNER and also
represents that nothing more about the OWNER is known than the fact that he/she/it
owns the PLANE. However, the more important function of category knowledge
serves to group simpler concepts into more complex concepts (or to segment them
into even simpler concepts). For example, the simpler events in the introductory
example can be grouped to the DOCKING event.

The main problem of categorization is that entities can be categorized in infinitely
many ways. Categorization is mainly accomplished by measuring similarity. Two
ways to do this are the *feature-based* and *metric-based* measurement of similarity
(E. E. Smith, 1995). In the former, the similarity between two concepts is measured
by counting their shared features. In the latter, similarity is measured as metric
distance in a multidimensional vector space or a metric space. A third approach to
categorization is *theory based*. The theories provide coherence between the concepts,
which extends (and does not contradict) the feature- and property-bases approaches.
The advantage of the theory-based approach is that the underlying theory specifies
"which features are relevant and how they might be interrelated" (Medin & Aguilar,
1999, p. 104).

INC employs a categorization method that first uses theories to determine
concepts, which are then compared by measuring their similarity. In the case of the
grouping and segmentation of concepts, the similarity of two concepts is the ratio
of the parts they share to the parts they do not share (§ 45). Thus, it is a combination
of theory- and feature-based categorization.

Alas, the measurement of similarity faces the same ubiquitous problem as categorization in general: All entities are similar in infinitely many dimensions. Hence,
one has to decide with respect to which features/metrics similarity is computed.
Because this is a general modeling problem, I do not pursue it as problem in its own
right but only insofar as concepts used by INC are concerned.

§ 18   *A remark on the symbol grounding problem*

A pervasive problem for symbolic approaches to cognition is the *symbol grounding
problem* (Harnad, 1990). It is the problem that symbols, in particular concepts, cannot be defined by other concepts alone, because this results in circular explanations.
In order to avoid this circularity, concepts must be expressed in nonconceptual
terms (Hampton, 1999, p. 177). In data-driven approaches, the problem still exists
but is less grave, because the used concepts are connected to and defined by extra-
conceptual properties. At least this solves the problem for cases in which the simple

concepts of a representation are tied to perception. A solution along these lines is also suggested by Harnad (1990).

Because IN C does not require a full solution of the symbol grounding problem, I do not propose an elaborated solution. Nevertheless, the approach by Gärdenfors (2000) is similar to the one used in IN C. (Dörner, 1999 handles the symbol grounding problem in a similar fashion.) I will therefore outline it in order to show how symbols (concepts) can be grounded.*

Gärdenfors's (2000) account is based on the notion of *dimensions*. Examples of dimensions are temperature, pitch, or brightness, which are all tied tightly to the sensory systems. But there are abstract, nonsensory dimensions as well. He then defines a *domain* as "a set of integral dimensions that are separable from all other dimensions" (p. 26). The color domain, for example, can be described by the dimensions hue, chromaticness, and brightness. Yet, there can be no temperature–color domain or the like, because such dimensions would not be *integral*. Integral dimensions depend on each other to a certain degree.

Based on dimensions, Gärdenfors (2000) defines *conceptual spaces*. A *conceptual space* is a collection of one or more domains (p. 26). Thus, all in all, there are three levels. Connecting the symbolic (conceptual) and the subconceptual level is the level of conceptual spaces. (See Deacon, 1997, for a similar tripartite distinction.) Conceptual spaces (more precisely: *regions* within conceptual spaces) are then defined as *natural properties*† and *natural concepts*. Gärdenfors characterizes these in the following way: "A *natural property* is a convex region of a domain in a conceptual space" (p. 71). "A *natural concept* is represented as a set of regions in a number of domains together with an assignment of salience weights to the domains and information about how the regions in different domains are correlated" (p. 105). Thus, properties and concepts differ in that a property is defined with respect to one domain. For example, in the color domain, *red* is a property, and a concept is defined with respect to multiple domains. APPLE in table 4.1 shows the region for the domains in which the value for a particular apple can be located.

The definition of natural concepts contains the additional notion of *salience weight*. Domains are *weighed* with regard to their respective *salience*. The salience weight depends on the context in which a concept is used: For eating an apple, its taste is more dominant than for throwing it (p. 103). Giving some domain particular attention corresponds to taking perspective when using the concept. Salience weights are also influenced by the knowledge and interest of the user.

---

* My approach is also close to the one by Gärdenfors (2000) in that he describes it as "instrumentalist cognitive epistemology" (p. 106). This means that he is not interested in ontological and epistemic questions of concepts but only how they can be used.

† (Gärdenfors, 2000) regards properties as a special, simple kind of concept (p. 60). *Natural* means that properties "are, in a sense, *natural* to our way of thinking" (p. 66).

DOMAIN	REGION
colour	red–yellow–green
shape	roundish (cycloid)
texture	smooth
taste	regions of sweet and sour dimensions
fruit	specification of seed structure, flesh and peel type, etc according to principles of pomology
nutrition	values of sugar content, vitamins, fibres, etc

Table 4.1: Domains and regions for APPLE (Gärdenfors, 2000, p. 103)

§ 19   *Dynamic representations of the external world*

Conceptual representations are internal representations; that is, they are particular to an individual. From this follows that the conceptualization process always operates on a subjective representation of the state of affairs, not an objective one. To assume the existence of objective representations, one would need to know the situation-independent factors that define such representations. (And humans could only obtain such representations on the basis of their experiences and subjective knowledge, which means there is nowhere to start.) Because humans are shaped by their experience, conceptualization means that newly perceived information is interpreted with respect to the available information. This is one of the key properties of incrementality.

Apart from experience, conceptualization depends on a multitude of factors, such as available knowledge, context, attitudes, current state of the cognitive system, and available resources. These factors influence how conceptual representations are constructed and used. Consequently, the ensuing representations possess only limited generalizability, and rules like the cut-hypothesis (Avrahami & Kareev, 1994, p. 239) are no way to find events "in the world." Instead, it is a way to explain why humans experience a succession of perceived states as a coherent whole.

This is only part of the problem, though, because it is difficult to decide whether a representation is correct. Representing always means abstracting away from some details. It makes little sense to represent the world in full detail (think of the absurd notion of a street map in scale 1:1), because a representation always serves a purpose. For the language production system the purpose is to produce language, in the case of a whole organism, major purposes are survival and reproduction. This means that *correct* can only mean 'correct' with respect to a purpose. Glenberg (1997) emphasizes that memory always *is for* something, especially representations of the current state of affairs. Because memory supplies an organism with an internal representation of the perceived world, memory must be seen as *embodied*. According to Glenberg this means that memory contains representations of the organism's experiences and that it contains the next possible actions in the environment. So, an individual's memory contains representations that are, although dependent on the environment, representations for the individual, because they are stored experiences and possible actions for the particular individual.

Despite the internal character of conceptual representations, it is nevertheless possible to identify errors in them. For example, it is acceptable to represent a PLANE as an unidentified OBJECT but not as HANGAR, for example, due to an erroneous categorization, because this will lead to errors when the representation is used, say when the represented scene is described verbally. (Systematically occurring errors in human behavior can, therefore, provide important insights into cognition.) In the online description of events the correctness of a conceptual representation can be evaluated by comparing the descriptions produced by the system—the implementation of INC—with descriptions recorded in the verbalization studies. If there are significant deviations, it is likely that the representation is erroneous.

A key factor for understanding conceptual representations is the dynamic character of representations. Formulated more strongly: Representations must be dynamic if they are to account for cognition. The traditional view on representations, however, is static, disembodied, and context independent (Prinz & Barsalou, 2000, p. 52). Dietrich and Markman (2000) suggest that proposals to completely do away with representations are a reaction to the shortcomings of traditional approaches to representation. Yet, such use of representations must fail, because representations in cognitive systems are constantly changing. Sources for these changes are external stimuli as well as internal causes, such as integrating results from computations. So, representations must be dynamic, embodied, and context dependent (Bickhard, 2000, p. 47), and approaches that do not account for this are doomed to fail.

From this follows that "time constraints have implications for what kind of representations situated agents can deploy" (Prinz & Barsalou, 2000, p. 70). I will mention just two consequences that arise from this insight. First, due to the complexities and the sheer amount of knowledge contained in conceptual representations, the cognitive processing time does not suffice for the system to ascertain truth-maintenance and absence of contradictions. Second, a representation is never used in the same context twice. Even if the same external stimulus is present, the internal state of the system is different, yielding a different context.

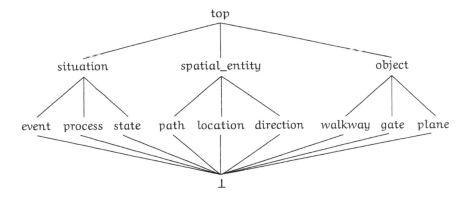

Figure 4.1: The part of the sort hierarchy (lattice) used in the motion event domain

§ 20   *Event representations*

The bulk of the scientific literature on concepts deals with object concepts. A reason
for this is that events are less accessible to experimentation than are objects. Event
concepts, just like object concepts, serve as building blocks of conceptual representations; they have the same function and are learned and used similarly. The main
difference is that events are immaterial. In addition to events (situations) and objects,
conceptualizing motion events requires spatial entities (§ 2). The rationale for assuming spatial entities is twofold. First, spatial entities (e.g., locations or directions)
are neither objects nor events. Nevertheless, they can be identified (e.g., a location
close to an object or the directionNORTH). Second, they have the same function as
the other kinds of concepts; see Landau and Jackendoff (1993) for an argument that
where something is in space (the spatial entity) is differently represented than *what*
is located there (the object).

INC represents concepts as referential objects (refOs). Different kinds of refOs
are distinguished by their sort (§ 6; appendix A). Sorts partition referential nets, and
INC's conceptual representation is partitioned by the three sorts object, situation,
and spatial_entity. The sorts themselves are organized in a subsumption hierarchy.
Figure 4.1 shows the sort hierarchy of the motion event domain.

Temporal relations play an important role in connecting situations. The temporal
relations used in INC's conceptual representations are listed in table 4.2. These
relations are based on Allen (1983, 1991; see also van Benthem, 1990). However,
Allen's relations define only relations between time intervals. INC also uses time
points, which means that the temporal relations must be defined for time points
as well. This approach follows the proposal of Vilain (1982). I will write a relation

RELATION	INVERSE	EXAMPLE
X before Y	Y after X	XXX YYY
X equal Y	Y equal X	XXX YYY
X meets Y	Y met_by X	XXXYYY
X overlaps Y	Y overlapped_by X	XXXX YYYY
X during Y	Y contains X	XXX YYYYYYY
X starts Y	Y started_by X	XXX YYYYYYY
X finishes Y	Y finished_by X	XXX YYYYYYY

Table 4.2: Temporal relations

r between two intervals as r, between an interval and a time point as ·r or r·, and between two time points as ·r· so that, for example, the *after* relation becomes ·after for the relation between a time point and a time interval, after· for the one between a time interval and a time point, and ·after· when two time points are related.* For a detailed discussion of this problem see Guhe, Habel, and Tschander (2004).

In the remainder of this section, I show how the conceptual representation for the docking example is built up incrementally and point out particulars of the representation. The final state of the conceptual representation is shown in figure 4.2. Because the refNet is rather large, I use a special numbering of refOs. It groups refOs belonging to one movement and refOs that have the same sort. $r6_P$ is the path of the plane movement, $r6_W$ the path of the walkway movement, $r7_S$ is the location of the start of the walkway movement, $r7_F$ the location of the final point of both movements. The subscripts of the situation refOs indicate the order in which the segments of the respective overall situation occur. However, this is only a naming convention; using different names would not change the referential net.

To take up the motivation from §2 again, when you look out of the window

---

* Keeping the different kinds of temporal relations apart is important as can be seen from the following example. If a punctual event occurs between two time intervals, these time intervals could not be in the meets relation, because if the time point were between the two intervals, there would be a gap between them. However, if the time point is part of one interval, it must also be part of the other interval, which means that the intervals are in the overlap relation. Using different sets of temporal relations means that such interferences do not occur, and the temporal relations involving punctual events allow temporal reasoning in an Allen-like style (Vilain, 1982).

while waiting to board, you will first see a configuration of objects. Consequently, the initial state of the conceptual representation contains two refOs that stand for the GATE and the WALKWAY.*

(1)

$$
\text{gate} \longrightarrow r1 \Longleftarrow
\begin{array}{l}
\eta x\, \text{gate}(x) \\
\text{'B21'}
\end{array}
$$
$$
\text{parts}([r2])
$$

$$
\text{walkway} \longrightarrow r2 \longrightarrow \eta x\, \text{walkway}(x)
$$
$$
\text{part\_of}([r1])
$$

The fact that the WALKWAY is part of the GATE is represented by the attributes parts and part_of that establish the part-of hierarchy between refOs. (The parts attribute can be read as *has parts*.) Both are list attributes, which means they have a list as argument.† The designations represent that r1 can be described as *a gate*, as *B21*, or as *gate B21* and r2 as *a walkway*. When the PLANE enters the scene in phase 1 (see fig. 1.1, p. 4) three refOs are simultaneously added to the conceptual representation.

(2)

$$
\text{plane} \longrightarrow r3 \Longleftarrow
\begin{array}{l}
\eta x\, \text{plane}(x) \\
\eta x\, \text{chpos}(r4_1, x, r6_P)
\end{array}
$$

$$
\text{situation} \longrightarrow r4_1 \longrightarrow \eta x\, \text{chpos}(x, r3, r6_P)
$$
$$
\text{—complete}
$$

$$
\text{path} \longrightarrow r6_P \Longleftarrow
\begin{array}{l}
\eta x\, \text{straight}(x) \\
\eta x\, \text{chpos}(r4_1, r3, x) \\
\eta x\, \text{to}(x, r1)
\end{array}
$$

The situation refO ($r4_1$) and the three chpos descriptions that come with it connect the triple. The chpos descriptions represent the fact that in the situation ($r4_1$),

---

* Actually, the conceptual representation should contain an additional refO for the situation. I left it out, because it has no bearings on what follows. Note that it would be necessary if INC were to generate an utterance at this point like *There is a gate*, because INC requires a situation refO to be able to start producing an incremental preverbal message.

† From a formal perspective one attribute would suffice. For example, if part_of were left out, the information stored with parts could be used to compute the part_of information. The whole refNet is searched for parts attributes referring to a refO. This refO would otherwise have the part_of attribute. In this mini-refNet, this is only r2. r2 is then a part_of all the refOs having such a parts attribute (r1 in this case). Thus, one of the attributes is redundant and could be left out. Although it is a fairly short computation in this mini-example, in bigger refNets these searches require much time, because the whole net must be searched. Because incremental processing is mainly about efficiency with respect to run-time and not storage use, INC, therefore, uses both attributes.

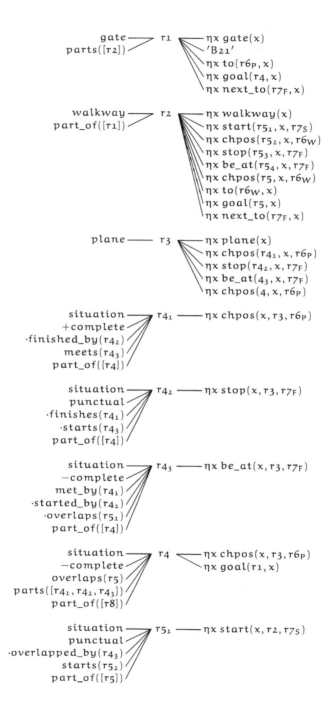

gate ———→ r1 ◄——— ηx gate(x)
parts([r2])   'B21'
                              ηx to(r6$_P$, x)
                              ηx goal(r4, x)
                              ηx next_to(r7$_F$, x)

walkway ———→ r2 ◄——— ηx walkway(x)
part_of([r1])   ηx start(r5$_1$, x, r7$_S$)
                               ηx chpos(r5$_2$, x, r6$_W$)
                               ηx stop(r5$_3$, x, r7$_F$)
                               ηx be_at(r5$_4$, x, r7$_F$)
                               ηx chpos(r5, x, r6$_W$)
                               ηx to(r6$_W$, x)
                               ηx goal(r5, x)
                               ηx next_to(r7$_F$, x)

plane ——— r3 ◄——— ηx plane(x)
                   ηx chpos(r4$_1$, x, r6$_P$)
                   ηx stop(r4$_2$, x, r7$_F$)
                   ηx be_at(4$_3$, x, r7$_F$)
                   ηx chpos(4, x, r6$_P$)

situation ———→ r4$_1$ ——— ηx chpos(x, r3, r6$_P$)
+complete
·finished_by(r4$_2$)
meets(r4$_3$)
part_of([r4])

situation ———→ r4$_2$ ——— ηx stop(x, r3, r7$_F$)
punctual
·finishes(r4$_1$)
·starts(r4$_3$)
part_of([r4])

situation ———→ r4$_3$ ——— ηx be_at(x, r3, r7$_F$)
−complete
met_by(r4$_1$)
·started_by(r4$_2$)
·overlaps(r5$_1$)
part_of([r4])

situation ———→ r4 ◄——— ηx chpos(x, r3, r6$_P$)
−complete   ηx goal(r1, x)
overlaps(r5)
parts([r4$_1$, r4$_2$, r4$_3$])
part_of([r8])

situation ———→ r5$_1$ ——— ηx start(x, r2, r7$_S$)
punctual
·overlapped_by(r4$_3$)
starts(r5$_2$)
part_of([r5])

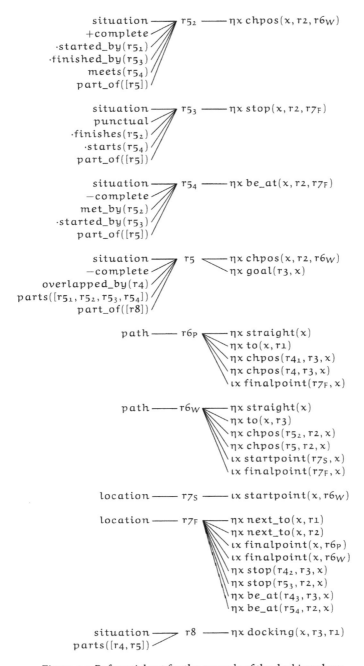

$$
\begin{aligned}
&\text{situation} \longrightarrow \mathrm{r5_2} \longrightarrow \eta x\, \mathrm{chpos}(x, r2, r6_W)\\
&+\text{complete}\\
&\cdot\text{started\_by}(r5_1)\\
&\cdot\text{finished\_by}(r5_3)\\
&\text{meets}(r5_4)\\
&\text{part\_of}([r5])
\end{aligned}
$$

$$
\begin{aligned}
&\text{situation} \longrightarrow \mathrm{r5_3} \longrightarrow \eta x\, \mathrm{stop}(x, r2, r7_F)\\
&\text{punctual}\\
&\cdot\text{finishes}(r5_2)\\
&\cdot\text{starts}(r5_4)\\
&\text{part\_of}([r5])
\end{aligned}
$$

$$
\begin{aligned}
&\text{situation} \longrightarrow \mathrm{r5_4} \longrightarrow \eta x\, \mathrm{be\_at}(x, r2, r7_F)\\
&-\text{complete}\\
&\text{met\_by}(r5_2)\\
&\cdot\text{started\_by}(r5_3)\\
&\text{part\_of}([r5])
\end{aligned}
$$

$$
\begin{aligned}
&\text{situation} \longrightarrow \mathrm{r5}
\begin{cases}
\eta x\, \mathrm{chpos}(x, r2, r6_W)\\
\eta x\, \mathrm{goal}(r3, x)
\end{cases}\\
&-\text{complete}\\
&\text{overlapped\_by}(r4)\\
&\text{parts}([r5_1, r5_2, r5_3, r5_4])\\
&\text{part\_of}([r8])
\end{aligned}
$$

$$
\text{path} \longrightarrow \mathrm{r6_P}
\begin{cases}
\eta x\, \mathrm{straight}(x)\\
\eta x\, \mathrm{to}(x, r1)\\
\eta x\, \mathrm{chpos}(r4_1, r3, x)\\
\eta x\, \mathrm{chpos}(r4, r3, x)\\
\iota x\, \mathrm{finalpoint}(r7_F, x)
\end{cases}
$$

$$
\text{path} \longrightarrow \mathrm{r6_W}
\begin{cases}
\eta x\, \mathrm{straight}(x)\\
\eta x\, \mathrm{to}(x, r3)\\
\eta x\, \mathrm{chpos}(r5_2, r2, x)\\
\eta x\, \mathrm{chpos}(r5, r2, x)\\
\iota x\, \mathrm{startpoint}(r7_S, x)\\
\iota x\, \mathrm{finalpoint}(r7_F, x)
\end{cases}
$$

$$
\text{location} \longrightarrow \mathrm{r7_S} \longrightarrow \iota x\, \mathrm{startpoint}(x, r6_W)
$$

$$
\text{location} \longrightarrow \mathrm{r7_F}
\begin{cases}
\eta x\, \mathrm{next\_to}(x, r1)\\
\eta x\, \mathrm{next\_to}(x, r2)\\
\iota x\, \mathrm{finalpoint}(x, r6_P)\\
\iota x\, \mathrm{finalpoint}(x, r6_W)\\
\eta x\, \mathrm{stop}(r4_2, r3, x)\\
\eta x\, \mathrm{stop}(r5_3, r2, x)\\
\eta x\, \mathrm{be\_at}(r4_3, r3, x)\\
\eta x\, \mathrm{be\_at}(r5_4, r2, x)
\end{cases}
$$

$$
\begin{aligned}
&\text{situation} \longrightarrow \mathrm{r8} \longrightarrow \eta x\, \mathrm{docking}(x, r3, r1)\\
&\text{parts}([r4, r5])
\end{aligned}
$$

Figure 4.2: Referential net for the example of the docking plane

an object (r_3) moves along a path (r_{6P}). For this reason, the *sort frame* of chpos is (situation, object, location). The sort frame defines of which sort the arguments of an expression must be in order for the expression to be *sort-correct* (see appendix A for details). Because r_{4_1} represents the first SITUATION of the scene, it has no temporal relations yet. The −complete attribute says that the SITUATION is not yet completed, which implies that it is extended, this is, takes place in a time interval. The situations that have the −complete attribute are the *ongoing* situations in a scene. The set of ongoing situations is important, because for these situations, the temporal relations are established that are added to the conceptual representation. Temporal relations between other situations must be computed when they are required. (The set of ongoing situations is also important if the temporal relation between two situations cannot be uniquely determined, which is particularly relevant in the case of concurrent events (Guhe et al., 2004).) The description ηx straight(x) of r_{6P} represents the shape of the PATH of the movement. Note that PATHs are no real-world tracks but abstract (invisible) spatial entities (Eschenbach, Habel, & Kulik, 1999; Eschenbach, Tschander, Habel, & Kulik, 2000). The description ηx to(x, r_1) (sort frame (path, object)) says that the PATH is leading toward the GATE (r_1).

This representation already gives rise to some inferences. First of all, the description ηx to(x, r_1) says that the PATH is leading toward the GATE. Together with the fact that in the SITUATION a change of position is occurring (because of the chpos descriptions), this leads to the inference that there is an overall SITUATION (r_4) in which the goal of the movement is the GATE. The sort frame of goal is (situation, object).

(3)   situation ———→ r_4 ⟵——— ηx chpos(x, r_3, r_{6P})
                         −complete ———↗   ⟍——— ηx goal(r_1, x)
           parts$([r_{4_1}, r_{4_2}, r_{4_3}])$ ↗

The next inference is already indicated in r_4 by the parts attribute: The complex SITUATION brings with it additional simple ones. Although the PLANE reaches the GATE only in phase 2 of the scene, this can already be anticipated (expected) in phase 1 by adding two refOs to the representation.

(4)

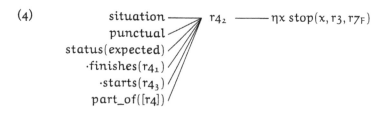

                         situation ———→ r_{4_2} ——— ηx stop(x, r_3, r_{7F})
                          punctual ↗
           status(expected) ↗
             ·finishes(r_{4_1}) ↗
               ·starts(r_{4_3}) ↗
             part_of$([r_4])$ ↗

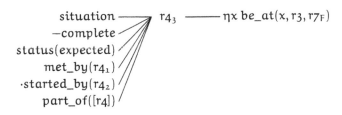

The fact that these two refOs were not actually perceived but are only anticipated is represented by the status attribute, which can have the values expected, regular, or discarded. Perceived or inferred refOs of which all parts are regular have status(regular). Expectations that were not fulfilled are discarded. The refOs are not deleted from the conceptual representation, however. From a cognitive viewpoint, this would mean that INC contained a "forgetting mechanism," which it does not. Deleting these discarded refOs would make it impossible to generate utterances like *At first I thought the plane would crash into the gate, but then ...* Currently, however, INC verbalizes no discarded refOs, and no descriptions referring to discarded refOs are used. For reasons of brevity, I only specify the status attribute when it is relevant. The refOs in figure 4.2 all have status(regular). (Expectations in INC are discussed in chap. 10.) At this stage, the first temporal relations are inserted ($r4_1$ is updated accordingly). $r4_2$ finishes the movement (the PLANE stops) and starts the SITUATION where the PLANE stands still ($r4_3$). Because $r4_2$ represents a punctual situation—that is, it has no temporal extension—$r4_1$ and $r4_3$ are in a meets relation.

Adding these refOs to the conceptual representation causes the insertion of yet another refO, $r7_F$, which represents the LOCATION where the STOP event takes place and subsequently the PLANE is standing. This location is next_to the GATE and the WALKWAY. Furthermore, it is the final point of the PATH $r6_P$. Again, $r1$, $r2$, and $r6_P$ are updated with the according descriptions.

(5)   location ──── $r7_F$ ⎰── $\eta x\ next\_to(x, r1)$
                                      ⎰── $\eta x\ next\_to(x, r2)$
                                      ── $\iota x\ finalpoint(x, r6_P)$
                                      ── $\eta x\ stop(r4_2, r3, x)$
                                      ⎱── $\eta x\ be\_at(r4_3, r3, x)$

In phase 2 of the scene, the PLANE stops next to the GATE at the location introduced as $r7_F$. This has the effect that the two status(expected) of $r4_2$ and $r4_3$ change to status(regular). So, during this phase, no new refOs are inserted into the conceptual representation; the representation is only modified. Note that I simply assumed without further comment that the INC introduces these expectations. What is more, I assumed that the overall situation, represented by r8, is not expected. The reason for this is that I chose a "medium willingness" of the speaker to generate expectations that was high enough for the first one but too low for the second. This willingness varies across verbalizations (see part C). In INC, it is modeled by the parameter DOAT (degree of agreement threshold, §38). A low value of this parameter means that no expectations are generated; with a high value, INC would also create r8.

Conceptualizing the movement of the WALKWAY in phases 3 and 4 changes the conceptual representation analogously. During these phases, the DOCKING refO (r8) is created as well. Note that a full representation would include a refO $r5_0$ for the SITUATION when the WALKWAY is at LOCATION r7s.

I want to conclude the discussion of event representations with two short remarks. First, there are many other event sequences that can constitute the docking of a plane. Hence, I do not claim to have presented a full account of all possible conceptual representations for docking events. Second, the way I represent entities takes into account that they are the conceptual representations from which language is produced; that is, they are representations *for speaking*. I will turn to this aspect now.

§ 21   *Representations for speaking*

Conceptual representations can serve many purposes. Therefore, it should be emphasized that INC's conceptual representations, which I described in the previous section, are particularly tailored for language production. To paraphrase Slobin's (1996) formulation, it means that *thinking for speaking* requires *representations for speaking*. This is not to mean that representations for other purposes must be completely different. For example, the representation a pilot uses to maneuver the plane toward the gate will have elements in common with the conceptual representation in figure 4.2.

For producing incremental preverbal messages, though, a speaker needs additional knowledge apart from a representation of the observed state of affairs (Levelt, 1989), most notably:

- The common ground
- The speaker's own contributions
- The interlocutors' contributions
- The information the speaker still wants to convey

INC does not need all of these representations. Because only one person (system) is speaking, no provision needs to be made for the *contributions of the interlocutors*. Similarly, the *common ground* (the interlocutors' shared knowledge) can be left implicit. That is, it is not necessary to represent the knowledge that the speaker believes to share with the hearer (H. H. Clark, 1996); a default hearer can be assumed instead.

The *information the speaker still wants to convey* must always be represented; otherwise, no utterance planning is possible. In order to produce a coherent discourse (and not only isolated utterances), a memory for the *speaker's own contributions* is needed. This is the only information contained in INC's *discourse memory*, because there are no other interlocutors whose contributions could be part of the discourse memory. Thus, INC's *discourse model* consists of the information the speaker still wants to convey and the speaker's own contributions.

The discourse memory is represented as path through the conceptual representation that is represented as a referential net. This path is simply called the *traverse*, because it is built up by traversing the referential net. It consists of the refOs that have been used in a preverbal message.* For instance, in the generation of an incremental preverbal message for an utterance like (6a), the refOs r4, r3, r6p, and r1 are taken (in this sequence) and added to the traverse.

(6) a. *Ein Flugzeug bewegt sich auf ein Gate zu.*
'A plane is moving toward a gate.'

b.

$$\text{situation} \longrightarrow \text{r4} \longleftarrow \begin{matrix} \eta x \, \text{chpos}(x, r3, r6p) \\ \eta x \, \text{goal}(r1, x) \end{matrix}$$

$$\text{plane} \longrightarrow \text{r3} \longrightarrow \eta x \, \text{plane}(x)$$

$$\text{path} \longrightarrow \text{r6p} \longrightarrow \eta x \, \text{to}(x, r1)$$

$$\text{gate} \longrightarrow \text{r1} \longrightarrow \eta x \, \text{gate}(x)$$

The information stored in the traverse after this preverbal message was generated is, for example, that the GATE was described as *a gate*, not as B21 or *gate B21*. The mechanism that generates an incremental preverbal message consists basically in attempting to *ground* chosen designations. (This use of the term *grounding* is different

---

* This is not quite correct but accurate enough for the moment. The actual mechanism creates a new refO each time a refO is used in a preverbal message. The new refO stores the current state of the verbalized refO at that point of time and the information used in this verbalization. Otherwise, the discourse memory could contain each refO only once and only in its current state, that is, not in the state in which it is verbalized. See chapter 12 for the full explanation.

from H. H. Clark's 1996 use.) In this example, the designations ηx chpos(x, r3, r6ₚ) and ηx goal(r1, x) of r4, for example, refer to other refOs (r3, r6ₚ, and r1), for which designations must be chosen, because the refOs are already "announced" by sending r4 to the formulator as first increment of the incremental preverbal message. This is a consequence of INC's early-commitment strategy (cf. Extended Wundt's Principle, term 6, p. 70).

The information to be conveyed is stored in the *traverse buffer*. The traverse buffer contains pointers to situation refOs that were selected by the selection process but for which no preverbal messages were generated yet. Until refOs in the traverse buffer are verbalized, they can be deselected. That is, the decision to verbalize a refO can be reverted by the selection process. Therefore, they are stored in a buffer. However, since the function of the traverse buffer depends strongly on the incrementality used by INC, I defer its detailed description to part C. I now turn to the issue of incrementality.

~ 5 ~

INCREMENTALITY

I NCREMENTALITY WAS DEVISED within the field of computer science in the 1960s. It originated in compiler theory, as a mode of processing that applies modifications to a compiled program without compiling the whole program again. Instead, only the modified parts are recompiled and integrated into the existing program. This makes the compilers more interactive and efficient. The general idea to process only changed information is widely used, for example, in spell-checker algorithms of word processors, where only modified words are checked by the algorithm but not the whole text.

The notions of incremental processing discussed in the literature focus on the externally observable behavior of computing devices (usually systems). The characteristic behavior of incremental systems is that they produce output before all input that may have effects on the correct and complete computation of the corresponding output is available. This chapter focuses on two different aspects. First, I emphasize the fact that each new input increment is interpreted with respect to the current state of the system. Second, a corresponding output increment is computed with respect to the input increment and the currently available knowledge.

In this chapter, I first introduce the relevant properties of incremental processing (§ 22) and report on distinctions between different kinds of incrementality put forward in the literature (§ 23). Based on this discussion I develop a blueprint for incremental models (§ 24) and discuss the dimensions along which these incremental models can vary (§ 25).

§ 22 *Approaching the phenomenon*

Incremental processing has been known in computer science for quite a long time considering the youth of the discipline, namely since the 1960s (Finkler, 1997; Wirén, 1992). It originated in the area of compiler construction where it describes techniques to change only those parts of a compiled program that changed in the source code; recompiling the whole program is not necessary (Lock, 1965; Ryan, Crandall, & Medwedeff, 1966). Thus, the main advantage of incremental processing is that it reduces the complexity of computations by reusing results of previous computations. Put more generally, incremental algorithms consider only the information that changed since the last execution of the algorithm and relate it to the current state of the knowledge, which is result of the last executions of the algorithm. This makes them especially suited for models like INC that are situated in a dynamic environment.

The notion of incrementality that I put forward here additionally reduces the complexity of computations in that not all available knowledge is considered when a new piece of information is acquired. Instead, that part of the available knowledge used for the previous computation is the starting point for evaluating the new information. The advantage is that, in most cases, this enables the system to correctly incorporate the new information into its knowledge. Accordingly, only in a minority of cases does all knowledge need to be considered.

The notion of incremental processing prevalent in language production is more specific. It was first put forward by Kempen and Huijbers (1983; see also de Smedt & Kempen, 1987; Kempen & Hoenkamp, 1987; Levelt, 1989). It has two major properties: it is a *piecemeal* processing mode and it uses a *cascade* of subsequent processes (cf. chap. 1). Piecemeal—sometimes also called *chunking*—means that computations take place before all information that may be relevant for the complete and correct computation of an output is available. Thus, not all input is available when the generation of output commences. Piecemeal processing means that not a continuous flow of information is processed but rather discrete increments (fragments/pieces/chunks). This property of piecemeal processing restricts incrementality to systems based on discrete, symbolic representations.

Different architectures can be used for incremental processing. The most prominent of these are *cascaded architectures*, a symbolic representation of which is shown in figure 5.1. The cascade metaphor represents the idea that, just like a water stream in a water cascade, a stream of increments exists on different computational stages at the same time; and on each stage, a different increment of the stream is processed. After a process finishes its computations for an increment, it "splashes" down to the next process. Thus, a cascaded architecture performs a parallel processing of a sequential information stream. In figure 5.1, the information stream is represented by arrows. It is processed by processes p_1, p_2, and p_3. The three increments i_1, i_2, and i_3 can be understood in two ways. Under the first perspective, the figure shows a snapshot of the system where they stand for three *different* increments belonging to the same information stream at a particular point of time. Under the second perspective, the x-axis represents the flow of time and the dots stand for the *same*

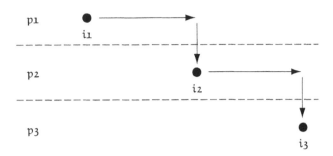

Figure 5.1: A piece of information running through a cascade of processes

increment at three subsequent points of time. Apart from being resource-efficient, such cascaded systems have the advantage that they can keep up with the pace in which input arrives and produce output at a constant rate. Moreover, they can simultaneously read input and produce output. They are therefore suited for the data-driven online setting in which INC operates.

There are also substantially different notions of incrementality proposed in the literature. To give just one example, Liu (2000) presents a program analysis and transformation technique she calls *incrementalization* with which she derives an "incremental" function from a nonincremental one. She shows that these functions are more efficient than their nonincremental counterparts. So, the main advantage of this approach is also to save resources (run-time). However, the main principle underlying this technique is to store (intermediate) results so that they need not be re-computed when the function is called the next time with the same arguments.

In contrast to this, the notion of incremental processing I am presenting also improves run-time if a result has not been computed before, because an increment is always processed in relation to the current state of the available knowledge. This increment is the *focused element*. Furthermore, because the knowledge is not unstructured, the knowledge that is relevant for processing the focused element surrounds it. For referential nets, this means that the relevant knowledge is either directly connected to the focused element or is only a few links apart. This relevant knowledge is the *local context* with respect to which the focused element is interpreted.

This method, however, may also *increase* run-time if an inappropriate or no local context is found, because in this case a new local context must be determined, and the incremental algorithm is executed again. This may result in a complete search of all knowledge. Thus, performance may even be worse than if all of the available knowledge were taken into account right from the start. Yet, this property is a strong argument in favor of the cognitive adequacy of this incremental processing mechanism, because it models a cognitive attention mechanism: The focused element is the item in the focus of attention. What is more, the increase in run-time can model *priming* phenomena, where the elements in the local context are the preactivated knowledge. This facilitates the response to new input, because less information is processed, which means that the run-time for the computation is reduced. If the computation fails, however, the response time increases, because then different local contexts have to be tried, and in the end, all available knowledge is used (or the system has to give up). Because these extreme cases can only be detected after processing commences, the overall beneficial function of incrementality comes at a certain cost.

My notion of incrementality is grounded on a general processing principle proposed by Levelt (1989, p. 26). Levelt names it *Wundt's Principle* after Wilhelm Wundt, who first proposed such a mode of processing. It states a general cognitive processing principle, namely that cognitive processes are *hungry* or *eager*; that is, processing starts as soon as possible.

TERM 5: WUNDT'S PRINCIPLE
Each processing component will be triggered into activity by a minimal amount of its characteristic input.

There are two important points about this principle. First, the characteristic input (cf. p. 31) must be defined individually for each processing component. Second, it must be identified what a minimal amount of input is for a processing component. It can be said, however, that a minimal amount is an increment—which in turn raises the question of the size of increments, but more on that later. Saying that a minimal amount of input is an increment does not mean that all increments constitute a minimal amount; increments for one processing component can be of different sizes.

In the following, I use a stronger, extended version of Wundt's Principle. The extension consists in that components not only start processing as soon as possible but also produce output as quickly as possible.

TERM 6: EXTENDED WUNDT'S PRINCIPLE
Each processing component will be triggered into activity by a minimal amount of its characteristic input and produces characteristic output as soon as a minimal amount of output is available.

Extended Wundt's Principle implies that processes do not evaluate their output; that is, they make no decision whether the overall output would benefit if it were not immediately sent to the subsequent process but if the process waited longer until, say, the quality of the output can be judged more reliably. There is various support for this view, for example, by Bock et al. (2003), and de Smedt (1990a)—citing work by Hoenkamp—states that "what can be uttered must be uttered immediately" (p. 27). It is also nourished by results of studies on language processing (e.g., Altmann & Kamide, 1999; Crocker & Brants, 2000), although it is not clear whether language production and language comprehension work according to the same principles. Extended Wundt's Principle stands in opposition to the principle proposed by Kilger and Finkler (1995) which says to "output as soon as *necessary* ..., not as soon as *possible* for subsequent output increments" (p. 9; i.e., after the initial output increment) so as to optimize quality and reliability of the output.

§ 23   *Kinds of incrementality*

This section describes kinds of incrementality that are put forward in the literature, before the next section presents my account of incrementality. I adopt formulations to my use of terminology as necessary. Because I am concerned with language production, I mainly discuss this literature. The following dichotomies serve to characterize possible variants of incrementality and to distinguish the kind of incrementality used by INC from other proposals—which may be adequate for other purposes.

LEFT-TO-RIGHT (LR) VERSUS FULL.   Wirén (1992) distinguishes *full* incrementality from *left-to-right* (LR) incrementality. In full incrementality, an input increment can cause changes at any place in the knowledge representation, whereas in left-to-right incrementality, this can only happen to the part of the knowledge representation that is "right" of what was processed before. (*Left-to-right* metaphorically refers to the direction of texts in Western culture. Hebrew or Arabic notions would probably appeal to a *right-to-left* incrementality.) Wirén uses incremental processing for NLP, and he considers LR incrementality to be the important variant for parsing. Full incrementality has mainly applications in information systems, for example, in text editors.

Full incrementality describes the original notion referred to in § 22 (Finkler, 1997; Wirén, 1992): An incremental compiler must allow changes anywhere in the program. Fully incremental systems have to discern the parts of the program that need to be altered from those that remain unchanged. In AI, replacing *program* by *knowledge representation*, this is tantamount to the *frame problem* (§ 32). LR incrementality is a special case of full incrementality that is particularly useful for NLP (including generation), because language is a sequential "left-to-right" medium.

Neither of the two forms of incrementality can account for conceptualization alone. The restriction of LR incrementality to allow changes only to a defined point in the knowledge representation is too limited for conceptualization. For example, in the taxiing scenario, a second plane may appear at any time, which cannot be interpreted with respect to the most recent movements of the first plane. That is, it cannot be interpreted by attaching the new information to the "right" of the current knowledge representation. Full incrementality, on the other hand, is costly in terms of resources, because changes can occur anywhere, affecting any element of the representation. INC, therefore, employs a combination of both: Although the conceptual representation can change anywhere, it does not allow random access. Instead, INC assumes that the most recent change is related to the last change, which means it starts at the focused element and considers a local context first. Because additional local contexts may have to be constructed, this method can be more costly than full incrementality in case of repeated failures (§ 22).

❧ MASSIVE VERSUS MODERATE.   Hildebrandt, Eikmeyer, Rickheit, and Weiß (1999) make a distinction between *massive* and *moderate* incrementality. In massive incrementality, each increment is processed as quickly as possible, which means it is similar to Extended Wundt's Principle. In moderate incrementality, output is not always immediately generated, but the process may wait some time, store the intermediate result, and wait for the next input increment. Thus, buffering is necessary for moderate incrementality, except if the system design ascertains that there is no danger of losing increments (or that this does not matter).

An example of massive incrementality in INC is the use of selection strategies. The decision whether to verbalize a newly perceived event is made immediately. For example, as soon as a plane movement is perceived, INC decides whether to describe it. (The decision can be reverted afterward, until a corresponding verbalization is generated.) Altmann and Kamide (1999), Crocker and Brants (2000), and Hildebrandt et al. provide empirical evidence that massive incrementality (Extended Wundt's Principle) is an adequate processing principle for cognitive models. In contrast, a conceptualizer using moderate incrementality would evaluate whether the decision should already be made or whether waiting might pay off, for example, waiting until information about where the plane is heading becomes available.

This dichotomy stems from the area of language comprehension, where it poses eminent problems, because some expressions cannot be parsed unequivocally while information that is still to follow is still missing. However, all incremental models are subject to the overall problem. There are three ways to handle this problem:

1. Delay the decision until all information is available.
2. Commit to one solution.
3. Generate all solutions in parallel.

The first possibility seems to be the most attractive one: The system generates no errors, and no corrections or recoveries are required. This is the route taken in most NLG and NLP systems. However, it is the opposite of incremental processing, because it contradicts the idea of a pace-keeping way of processing: If the system waits until all information is available, no output can be produced before then. For systems (and humans) situated in an environment to which they must react, this is no viable solution, because input is infinite, and there is no reliable way to ascertain that the following input does not invalidate output generated earlier on. Furthermore, assuming that all information *can* be available is a strong idealization in the first place, because this takes into account neither the limitations of time and knowledge that humans must cope with nor the fact that they use cues from the available information to make decisions instead of global optimizations (cf. the discussion of *bounded rationality* in § 30).

The second possibility seems to be less attractive at first sight, because reverting a decision is costly in terms of resources. It is the best solution, though, if

· Reverting a decision is comparably cheap,
· The goal is to model characteristic human errors (e.g., talking oneself "into the corner"),
· The decision procedure is so accurate that only seldom do decisions have to be reverted.

The third possibility may seem equally unattractive, because there usually are many solutions to consider, sometimes even infinitely many, and to pursue them all is impossible. However, there are also cases in which the number of solutions is small so that it is reasonable (advantageous in terms of resources) to generate them all (cf. the discussion on the number of increments that are processed in parallel, pp. 92–93).

§ WORD-BASED VERSUS CONSTITUENT-BASED.   Apart from the massive/moderate dichotomy Hildebrandt et al. (1999) also distinguish *word-based* from *constituent-based* incrementality. This is a case of the general problem of identifying increments. In word-based incrementality, the increments are mainly words; in constituent-based incrementality, they are mainly constituents of sentences. I say "mainly," because incremental processes should be flexible to some degree in what increments they can handle.

Although words and constituents are not processed by the conceptualizer, two things can be learned from this dichotomy. First, Hildebrandt et al. find that a massive, constituent-based incrementality is supported by linguistic and psycholinguistic evidence. Although they only appeal to the linguistic notion of constitu-

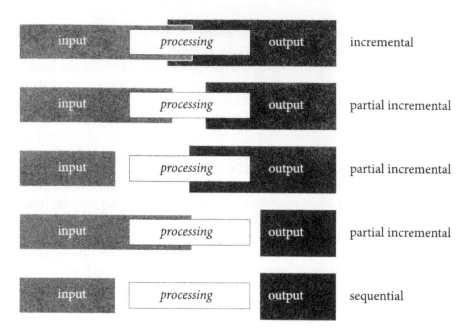

Figure 5.2: Kinds of incrementality according to Finkler (1997)

ents in general and provide no definition, constituents are larger increments than words. That is, the characteristic input and characteristic output of incremental processes need not consist of the smallest increments possible. INC's selection process, which decides on subintentions (§13), uses rather large increments as well. Because subintentions are about whether a situation is described or not, one could call this *situation-based incrementality*. Second, the output generated by INC is rather close to constituent-based incrementality, because a refO that is an increment of an incremental preverbal message corresponds roughly to a constituent in its informational content. This could be called *refO-based incrementality*.

✿ PARTIAL INCREMENTALITY.   Finkler (1997) defines incrementality in terms of the behavior exhibited by incremental systems. In contrast to my notion of incrementality, which uses multiple processes, Finkler bases his definitions on a single system. He distinguishes three kinds of processing modes: *incremental, partial incremental,* and *sequential,* cf. figure 5.2. The defining property of the incremental processing mode is that the generation of output starts before the input is complete, which corresponds to what I call *incremental behavior* (term 20, p. 88). Partial incrementality has temporal overlap of input and processing, or processing and output, or both, but no temporal overlap of input and output. (That would be incremental, not partial incremental.) The sequential processing mode has no temporal overlap of input, processing, and output. Thus, all relevant input for computing the corresponding output is completely available when processing starts, and the processing is finished before any output is generated.

Partial incrementality is, therefore, simply a special case of incrementality. However, since the main property that distinguishes incrementality from sequential processing is the interleaving of reading input and producing output, identifying systems as being partially incremental is problematic. For example, can an incremental system also behave partially incremental? Are there cases in which a partially incremental system may also behave incrementally? How can the different kinds of partial incrementality be distinguished by means of the externally observable behavior? In other words, it is unclear how this distinction can be used to classify systems, in particular how systems are classified that behave differently for different inputs.

Additionally, this distinction makes only very weak claims about cognitive processes, because it is only concerned with the externally observable behavior but not with the internal mechanisms that bring it about. See also Lewis (1999) on this problem and the discussion of different levels of architecture by Newell (1990).

❧ QUALITATIVE VERSUS QUANTITATIVE.   Finkler (1997) also distinguishes *qualitative* and *quantitative* incrementality. A system works in a qualitative incremental fashion if it always obtains a complete input. When the input data change the system not only receives the new information but all information, including all old information. The assumption is that the quality of the input information increases over the course of time. A quantitative incremental system receives only new or changed information. This means there are two different kinds of increments: those that contain new information and those that are updates (corrections/enhancements) for previous increments. In qualitative incrementality, there is only one kind of increment: a complete representation of differing qualities.

For INC, qualitative incrementality would mean, for example, that the construction process always receives a complete representation of the scene from the PPU. Thus, it would receive not only the information about the current position of the plane—as in a quantitative incremental system—but also the fact that there is a gate and a walkway, that the color of the plane is black, and so on. (If this idea were taken seriously, INC would need to receive even information about all past events each time.) Because this is no cognitively adequate way to model conceptualization, INC uses quantitative incrementality.

But this is just part of the problem with this dichotomy. Whereas quantitative incrementality is just another name for piecemeal processing, qualitative incrementality can hardly count as incrementality at all, because input and output do not consist of pieces (increments, chunks, new information) but of all information. Indeed, qualitative incremental systems have more in common with *anytime* algorithms. The most notable difference is that anytime algorithms gradually improve the quality of their output over time, whereas incremental algorithms simply process an input increment for which they may produce one or more output increments. Another difference is that the time anytime algorithms have available is determined by an external entity (the process calling the algorithm), whereas incremental processes determine their processing time themselves. So, it is much easier and much more accurate to use the well-established notion of anytime computation instead of qualitative incrementality. (This does does not mean that there are no similarities between incrementality and anytime algorithms; see §31.)

§ BOUNDED VERSUS UNBOUNDED.   Ramalingam and Reps (1993) make a distinctions between *bounded* and *unbounded* incremental algorithms (p. 503). An incremental algorithm is bounded if its processing time depends only on the size of the input increments. If the processing time also depends on factors other than increment size, an incremental algorithm is unbounded.

INC's incrementality is unbounded. The time that its processes need to process an input increment not only depends on the size of the input increment but even more on the reasoning processes that are carried out for the input increment. First of all this means that the time required by the categorization task (§16) and the other tasks of the concept matcher, for example, finding a more complex concept for the input, depend on the content of the input, not its size. However, because there is not much variation in the size of the input increments, the processing time is rather constant. Note that bounded incrementality not the same as bounded rationality (cf. §30). Although INC uses unbounded incrementality, it is a boundedly rational model.

§ LINEAR VERSUS HIERARCHICAL.   Bock et al. (2003) differentiate *linear* and *hierarchical* incrementality. In linear incrementality, an incremental process generates one increment after another without making any plans concerning future increments. In hierarchical incrementality, the preparation of an increment may involve making such plans; that is, following increments can partially (or completely) be prepared, but they are not yet generated. In other words, the hierarchical structure is generated before it is filled with increments.

INC uses mostly linear incrementality. For example, the selection process only considers one increment at a time and does not generate structures for futures ones. Hierarchical incrementality is used at an important point, though: The initial increment (ref0) of an incremental preverbal message induces a framework for the following increments in that it specifies what other refOs have to be verbalized. Moreover, each refO that is an increment of an incremental preverbal message may induce additional frames, that is, announce further refOs.

♠ FREE-FORMAT VERSUS PREFORMATED.   The last dichotomy I report here is similar to the previous one. It was put forward by Kempen: *free-format* versus *preformated* incrementality.* In free-format incrementality, the order of increments is established while they are generated; that is, increments are generated as they become available. In preformated incrementality, a sequence of output increments is generated by editing a previous sequence of output increments. The hierarchical structure and linear order of a previous sequence are simultaneously available. Some increments from the old structure are replaced by other ones; the remaining increments and their linear order are reused in the new increment sequence.

Although the hierarchical structure and the linear order of an increment sequence are simultaneously available, the editing and generation of output takes place piecemeal, because an incremental system does not have the ability to process a structure as a whole. In the case of the human language production system, this means that even if a whole utterance is available it cannot be generated as a whole.

Kempen is mainly concerned with syntactic priming, where he finds empirical evidence for preformated encoding. As preformated encoding also occurs in self-corrections and in coordinations, both modes of operation are relevant for conceptualization as well (§ 28). The most relevant point for INC is that, according to Kempen, a speaker prefers to reuse existing structures for pointing out meaning contrasts between the current utterance and an earlier one; that is, he prefers preformated incrementality. This has consequences for the processes selection and PVM-generation (preverbal message generation). In the following utterances, the structure of the first is reused in the second, which points out the meaning contrast:

(1)   a.   *Ein Flugzeug fährt auf Gate B21 zu.*
           'A plane moves toward gate B21.'
      b.   *Ein anderes Flugzeug fährt auf Gate B23 zu.*
           'Another plane moves toward gate B23.'

---

* This idea was presented at a meeting of the DFG priority programme *Language Production* on September 9, 2002, in Frankfurt.

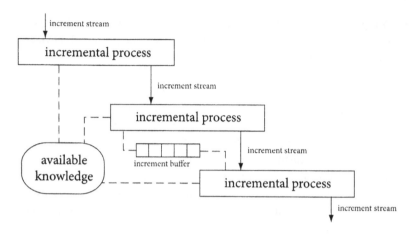

increment stream

incremental process

increment stream

incremental process

increment stream

available
knowledge

increment buffer

incremental process

increment stream

Figure 5.3: A blueprint for incrementality

§ 24   *A blueprint for incrementality*

These kinds of incrementality and the characterization of incrementality given in §22 are the basis for the terms I define in this section. These terms provide a basis for talking about incremental models. Their main purpose is to explain the incremental mode of processing, not to describe externally observable behavior of incremental models. Furthermore, they are formulated so that they are useful in building incremental models. In this sense, I now present a blueprint for incremental models.

In a nutshell, the blueprint is this. A number of processes arranged in a fixed sequence (pipeline, cascade) operate on an information stream that is read in by the first process of the sequence and output by the last process (cf. figure 5.3). Each process has exactly one predecessor and one successor—except the first and the last process. They all operate on a shared memory containing the model's available knowledge on which they all have different views. The pieces of information sent from one process to the next are increments.

Incrementality is a property of computational devices: models, systems, agents, processes, algorithms, functions, procedures, and so on. Thus, any device that is capable of computing and behaving in some way, that is, is capable of producing output for input, can be incremental. The central notions in the following are *incremental algorithm*, *incremental process*, and *cascade*, which is the combination of incremental processes in a model, system, agent, or any means of encapsulating multiple incremental processes.

TERM 7: INCREMENTALITY
Incrementality is the property of a model, system, algorithm, or process to compute information in a piecemeal manner and the ability to produce output before all input is available.

Because incrementality can be adequately be described as piecemeal processing, the question now is what the pieces are. First of all, they are called *increments*.

TERM 8: INCREMENT
An increment is a piece of information that is the input of an incremental process (input increment), *the output of one* (output increment), *or both.*

Formally, increments are defined as words of a formal language. For INC, this formal language is defined within referential nets (see chap. 4). The words of this formal language serve as input and/or output of incremental processes. According to their function, they are called input and/or output increment. Thus, an increment is defined with respect to the processes of which it is the input and/or or output. An increment for visual processing, for instance, must be different from an increment for phonological processes. An example for increments in INC are the input increments to the selection process, which are the refOs that the construction process inserts into the current conceptual representation (CCR, § 46).

Because increments are just pieces of information and the information can change if the system is nonmonotonic (§ 25), there must be a mechanism to cope with these changes. In particular, later computations can reveal that already generated output increments must be changed, for instance, when a later computation on new input shows that a previously generated increment is false, faulty, or can be improved. For these cases, *update increments* are needed.

TERM 9: UPDATE INCREMENT
An update increment is an increment that updates an increment previously read or sent by an incremental process.

Update increments are just special increments. There are two major cases for update increments: modifying a previous increment and informing a subsequent process to ignore a previous increment. If the reading process has already made computations based on this increment, it must perform a recovery. If the reading process has not used the increment up to then, it can simply be ignored. Because there is usually no direct feedback in incremental models, the sending process cannot know whether the update was successful. If this information is necessary, increment buffers (term 17) can be used to give *indirect* feedback (term 21).

TERM 10: INCREMENT STREAM
An increment stream is an ordered sequence of increments that changes over time. Increments can be appended to and popped from the increment stream.

(Popping means that the head of the stream is read and simultaneously removed from the stream.) An increment stream is a FIFO (first-in-first-out) buffer of unlimited size containing increments. (But see also the discussion of increment buffers, term 17.) In particular, an increment stream serves to connect two incremental processes in order to form a cascade (term 18). Increment streams connect the four conceptualization tasks identified in part A, which are realized in INC as incremental processes.

TERM 11: INCREMENTAL PROCESS
An incremental process is a process that behaves incrementally. It reads input from an increment stream, writes its output to another increment stream, and recursively executes the following two steps: (1) It determines a local context and (2) calls an incremental algorithm with respect to the available knowledge. The recursion ends if (a) a new input increment is available or (b) the result(s) cannot be improved. In the second case, the process suspends itself until a new input increment is available. An incremental process runs in an infinite loop until it is explicitly terminated from the outside.

This notion of incremental processes emphasizes the proximity to anytime processing. Other variants are conceivable, especially processes that do not execute an incremental algorithm in a infinite loop, for example, processes that execute the algorithm repeatedly until a termination condition is met. Such processes are not terminated from the outside but terminate themselves. Another variant is an incremental process that executes its incremental algorithm only once for each input increment. If the algorithm is reliable, this saves a lot of processing time. Such a method is similar to the *one reason decision making* of Gigerenzer, Todd, and ABC Research Group (1999).

Explicit termination from the outside is necessary, because the incremental algorithm is executed recursively until a new input increment is available or the results cannot be improved. In these cases, an incremental process suspends itself. From this follows that the process has no means to determine that it processed the last input increment, and the process runs until it is terminated by an external signal. The signal will usually indicate that no further input increment will follow but can also be sent in other cases. Especially the property of external termination makes this notion of incremental processing similar to anytime processing.

The interplay between the next four terms—*model knowledge, available know-*

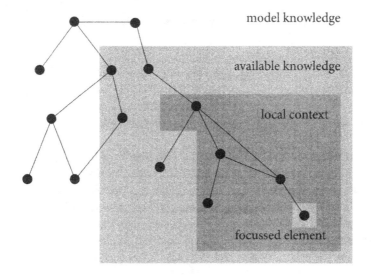

Figure 5.4: Model knowledge, available knowledge, local context, and focused element

ledge, *local context*, and *focused element*—which describe the processed knowledge, is depicted in figure 5.4. This figure implicitly assumes a representation using referential nets; yet, the following notions can equally be used with other representational formalisms.

TERM 12: MODEL KNOWLEDGE
The model knowledge is the declarative knowledge of an incremental model.

In INC, the model knowledge consists of the conceptual representation in the CCR and of the concept formation rules in the concept storage (CS). The part of the model knowledge that is accessible by an incremental process and its incremental algorithm(s) is its *available knowledge*.

TERM 13: AVAILABLE KNOWLEDGE
The available knowledge is the model knowledge that is accessible by an incremental process and its incremental algorithm(s).

An incremental process usually does not have access to all knowledge of the incremental model but only to a part. So, the knowledge that is available to the process is not the complete knowledge of the incremental model. The view of an incremental process on the model knowledge is managed by the model, that is, the model determines what knowledge is seen by an incremental process.

TERM 14: FOCUSED ELEMENT

A focused element is an element of the available knowledge. Each incremental process has one focused element. It is the entry point to the available knowledge of an incremental algorithm executed by the incremental process. An incremental algorithm starts evaluating the available knowledge from this element.

The focused element is the "hot spot" of the available knowledge of an incremental process. It either results from the last recursion of the incremental algorithm, or it is the most recent input increment. Each incremental process has only one focused element. (Although an incremental process may have the choice between different incremental algorithms, it can only execute one algorithm at a given time.) For example, after INC's construction process inserted an element into the CCR, this element is the increment sent to selection, and it becomes the focused element of the next call of selection's incremental algorithm.

Focused elements in referential nets are usually refOs, but there are other possibilities. For example, after PVM-generation chooses the description of a refO for verbalization, this description is repeatedly the focused element, once for each refO referred to in this description as these refOs are verbalized one after the other.

TERM 15: LOCAL CONTEXT

The local context is that part (subset) of the available knowledge that is used by an incremental algorithm in its computation. It is a connected subpart of elements in the available knowledge around the focused element. In each recursion of the algorithm, the local context is different. It is determined by a heuristic that is specific to the incremental algorithm.

The basic idea of local contexts is that only the part of the available knowledge surrounding the process's focused element is used by an incremental algorithm. Thus, it is defined as interconnected subpart of the available knowledge around the focused element. Local contexts reduce the complexity of the algorithm's computations, because less knowledge is considered. So, there are two reductions of the knowledge considered: the reduction of model knowledge to available knowledge and of available knowledge to local contexts. Local contexts are similar to the notion of *locality* by Ghidini and Giunchiglia (2001), who propose two principles:

> *Principle 1 (of Locality).* Reasoning uses only part of what is potentially available (e.g., what is known, the available inference procedures). The part being used while reasoning is what we call context (of reasoning);

> *Principle 2 (of Compatibility).* There is compatibility among the kinds of
> reasoning performed in different contexts. (p. 222)

The locality principle captures what I call local context. Problems of compatibility are hard to solve, for example, the problem that after a process modified a shared representation, the other processes operating on this (part of) the representation must still be able to process it. Problems of compatibility are beyond the scope of this book. Hence, I assume that the builder of the incremental model ascertains compatibility.*

Because the local context is determined by a heuristic, it is not ascertained that globally optimal local contexts are determined. Globally optimal means that, first, the local context captures all knowledge that is relevant for the computations of the incremental algorithm and, second, that the next execution of the incremental algorithm leads to results consistent with the available knowledge. Thus, the resulting representations can be inconsistent. Here is an example of how an inconsistency can arise. Assume that INC gets the information from the PPU that a plane is standing at a gate. As long as this information is not changed by new information, this is held to be true. Consider further that INC may not be informed that the plane is leaving its position and moves out of the observed area. A reason for this may be that the PPU is occupied with other movements, and there is not enough time. If now another plane is moving to the position at the gate where the first plane was standing, INC may not notice that according to its conceptual representation, this position is already occupied by another plane. This can happen, because the local contexts are established starting from the moving object and without checking locations. Now two planes occupy the same location.

Not all incremental systems can work on inconsistent representations, for example, compilers or text editors. However, inconsistencies contribute to the cognitive adequacy, because humans cannot take into consideration all facts known to them due to resource limitations (§ 30). As a consequence, humans do not have consistent representations, that is, representations without contradictions or representations that cannot lead to contradicting inferences or deductions. Thus, mechanisms must be provided for either resolving inconsistencies or for allowing to continue processing in spite of them.

The above definition leaves open the possibility that local context and available knowledge may be identical. This view is taken by approaches that formalize dynamic systems (see, e.g., R. Reiter, 2001).

---

* The frame problem—determining the knowledge needed for a computation and the knowledge that is changed by the computation—that overshadows such reductions is solved by assuming that it does not need to be solved due to the goal of cognitive adequacy (§ 32).

The notions of focused element and local context correspond to Levelt's *focal center* and *focus*, respectively (Levelt, 1989, p. 119f–120). My definition is more general; in particular they are not defined not specific to a task. Nevertheless, the notions are very similar, which is a good indication that they are important for cognitively adequate models.

TERM 16: INCREMENTAL ALGORITHM
An incremental algorithm is an algorithm that has the following properties: (a) It obtains a triple of focused element, local context, and available knowledge as input. (b) It only considers the local context for its computations starting from the focused element. (c) The output consists of modifications in the available knowledge, a new focused element, and an output increment.

There are some important points about this definition. First, remember that the representations used by an incremental algorithm—focused element, local context, available knowledge, and output increment—are managed by the incremental process calling the incremental algorithm. This includes storing the newly determined focused element until the incremental algorithm is called again and sending the computed output increment to the subsequent process.

Second, an output increment can be an update increment that modifies a previously generated output increment. In this case, the incremental algorithm must have information about its previous output increments. There are three ways to realize this:

1. The incremental algorithm uses the available knowledge together with time stamps that indicate the point of time at which the relevant elements last changed.
2. The output increments are sent to an increment buffer (term 17), not an increment stream. As long as they are in the buffer, they are still accessible and can be updated.
3. The incremental algorithm stores its output increments internally.

Because in incremental models subsequent components cannot give feedback to previous ones, a subsequent process cannot send an acknowledgment when an update is successful. Hence, only the first two methods provide a means to establish the success of an update via indirect feedback (term 21). In the third method, the algorithm can only guess whether the subsequent process already processed the output increment that is to be updated and whether an update can still be successful.

Third, an incremental algorithm operates on incomplete knowledge, not only because it uses a local context but also because the available knowledge changes over time. In particular, new information is integrated into the available knowledge. As future changes cannot be known to an incremental algorithm, it produces its output with respect to the knowledge that is available when it is executed. In other words, not all information necessary for the complete and correct computation of an output may be available. In this respect, incremental algorithms are like *online algorithms* (Albers, 1996; Borodin & El-Yaniv, 1998).

Fourth, incremental algorithms are a class of algorithms. Thus, they do not refer to a particular algorithm as, for example, the Reiter and Dale algorithm for generating referring expressions (Dale & Reiter, 1995; E. Reiter & Dale, 1992, 2000).

Finally, the computations take place with regard to the current state of the available knowledge. The important point is that the representation containing the available knowledge must exist longer than a call of the incremental algorithm. This is a key property of incremental processing and, therefore, a crucial condition for an algorithm to be an incremental algorithm.

TERM 17: INCREMENT BUFFER
An increment buffer is a buffer between two or more incremental processes. It can store a limited number of increments that either cannot be processed further at the moment, because the reading process is not yet ready to take an increment from the buffer as input increment.

Most incremental models require a limited buffering mechanism between incremental processes, because it usually cannot be assumed that an incremental process is ready to process an input increment when it becomes available. This is the function of increment buffers but also by increment streams. Whether to use increment streams or increment buffers between two incremental processes is a design decision for each model. Often the simpler increment streams are adequate, especially if the processes it connects are comparably fast, that is, most of the time the stream is empty. The slight buffering mechanism of increment streams only serves to smooth the information flow; it has no storage function. Hence, if the unlimited size of the stream distorts the model by storing substantial numbers of increments, then the limitations of storage capacity must be addressed explicitly by the model.

Further important differences between increment buffers and streams are that the access to increment streams is very restricted and that more than one process can access an increment buffer. Whereas increment streams are FIFO-buffers (i.e., the can only be accessed at their ends), increment buffers can allow random access. (Yet, each incremental process should only have a defined set of operations it can carry out on a buffer.) This random access can be allowed for multiple processes.

According to Extended Wundt's Principle, incremental processes generate output rapidly. This often has the consequence that immediately after an output increment is generated, an update increment follows in order to improve the output increment. For these cases, it is much more efficient if the reading process does not process the increment for a latency. This latency can be seen as a time span in which the certainty increases that the increment has an adequate quality. Another advantage is that the output increments may not be ordered in a way in which they should be read by the subsequent process. The reordering can take place in an increment buffer, or the reading process can pick the next increment best suited to its current state. In INC, the traverse buffer has this function. It is located between the processes selection, linearization, and PVM-generation. The refOs selected for verbalization by the selection process are inserted into the traverse buffer, linearization can reorder them, and after a latency PVM-generation takes them out in order to generate incremental preverbal messages.

Although increment buffers are limited in size, which allows cognitive models to simulate memory limitations, the available knowledge has no such limitation. This corresponds to the distinction between general memories, where elements can be stored for an unlimited time and which is unlimited in size, whereas more specialized buffers store elements only temporally and are limited in size. Levelt (1989) lists three such buffers relevant for language production: working memory, the syntactic buffer, and the articulatory buffer (p. 26).

TERM 18: CASCADE
A cascade consists of incremental processes that work in parallel and that are arranged in a fixed, sequential order in such a way that each process has one preceding and one succeeding process. The incremental processes of a cascade are connected by increment streams and/or increment buffers. A process reads input increments from its preceding process and sends output increments to its succeeding process. The first process of a cascade has no preceding process but reads input from the environment, and the last process has no succeeding process but sends its output to the environment.

The idea of a cascade lies at the heart of incremental processing, because it captures the special combination of sequentiality and parallelism that is so characteristic for incrementality. A cascade is close to E. Reiter's (1994) *pipeline*, which is the idea of subsequent processes that perform their computations one after the other. The difference is that E. Reiter restricts his definition to sequences where the processes do not work in parallel. Instead, they perform their computations in the order in which they are arranged.

The definition of cascades explicitly allows that incremental processes are connected by increment streams *and* increment buffers. This is useful when incremental processes exchange their increments via an increment buffer. In this case, it is more efficient that an incremental process sends a notification about a change in the increment buffer via an increment stream to its successor instead of letting the subsequent process poll the buffer. In INC, the traverse buffer connecting and coordinating the processes selection, linearization, and pvm-generation is a case of a combined use of increment buffers and increment streams.

TERM 19: INCREMENTAL MODEL

An incremental model is a model that contains a cascade of incremental processes and a representation of the model knowledge. The incremental model manages (a) the views of the incremental processes on the model knowledge and (b) the access of the incremental processes to the model knowledge so that only one process has access to the representation at a given point in time.

Whereas it is quite common to use a cascade in an incremental model, the idea of encapsulating it in a model and using only one shared representation (shared memory) is a bit unusual. (In inC, this shared memory is the ccr.) There are three main reasons for using a shared memory. First, it saves storage capacity. If each process represented its own knowledge, much of the knowledge would be represented more than once. The shared memory avoids such redundancies. Second, it conforms to psychological memory models, which consider human memory as one integrated structure. Third, a shared memory allows indirect feedback. Usually, incremental models are strictly unidirectional, allowing no feedback. Although this is desirable, because it makes them simple, efficient, and fast, it has the disadvantage that decisions cannot be changed. This means that errors can only be detected by a monitoring component. Therefore, it can pay off if a process depends on changes in the shared memory made by a later process. However, this can only be a very limited dependency. Most importantly, the operations of the dependent (preceding) process must not relie on feedback being available; that is, indirect feedback must be optional. The discussion in chapter 2 showed that the components of the language production system are not strictly informationally encapsulated, which supports the notion of indirect feedback in cognitively adequate models. More on indirect feedback on pages 91–92.

The view of an incremental process on the model knowledge that constitutes the available knowledge of this process is generated and managed by the incremental model. Additionally, it must be ascertained that only one process has writing access to the shared memory at a given point of time. Otherwise, typical synchronization problems of parallel processing like racing ("last writer wins") arise. Although this is a critical issue in building artificial machines like computers, it plays only a minor role in cognitive models. The main reason for this is that computers must be deterministic devices in order to function properly. For example, computers are usually not equipped with mechanisms for handling inconsistent representations, which are a typical result of racing. In the following, I assume that only one writing process has access to the shared memory at any given point of time. This makes building and implementing the model easier without losing anything essentially required for cognitively adequate models.

This is all that is required to build an incremental model, and these notions can be transferred easily to incrementally operating systems and agents. The resulting behavior of a model with the described architecture is the following.

TERM 20: INCREMENTAL BEHAVIOR
The minimal *condition for calling the behavior of a model incremental is that it is capable of producing output before it receives all input possibly relevant for the correct and complete computation of the corresponding output. The* strong *condition for incremental behavior is that additionally input and output are read and written in parallel.*

The minimal condition captures the processing of incomplete knowledge. This behavior can be found in systems like compilers and text editors that interact with humans and process a user's input (cf. the discussion of partial incrementality on pp. 74–75). The strong condition is a requirement for cognitive systems like agents navigating through space or for INC. A navigating agent (e.g., a robot) cannot be called cognitively adequate if it scans its environments and then does not move while it evaluates this input before initiating a movement. If INC did not meet the strong condition, it could not generate online descriptions of events. Thus, in order to be cognitively adequate, incremental models interacting with an environment must fulfil the strong condition.

All models that have a cascade of more than one process are, in principle, capable of behaving incrementally in the strong sense. Having such a cascade does not automatically mean, however, that the model exhibits this behavior. For example, the processes may not run in parallel; that is, the cascade is in fact a pipeline. Whereas architectures other than cascades can behave incrementally (e.g., an incremental process alone can behave incrementally in the minimal sense) strong incremental behavior requires a cascade of at least two incremental processes. A one-process model could only achieve incremental behavior if it were internally structured in a way that it has subcomponents for reading input and generating output simultaneously. But that would just be using different names for the same underlying idea.

The definition above does not explicitly require that in order to have incremental behavior proper, an incremental model must indeed behave incrementally if it has the ability to do so. It may behave differently in certain situations, for example, not producing output when it considers the output as not reliable enough or when the output is not yet needed. However, this contradicts Extended Wundt's Principle. So, if an incremental model always behaves nonincrementally, it would hardly be

justified to say that it exhibits incremental behavior—unless one considers such
behavior as the degenerate case of incremental behavior.

§ 25   *Dimensions of incrementality*

In § 23, I demonstrated that incrementality is a complex notion that encompasses different phenomena. In the previous section, I presented a blueprint for constructing
an incremental model, which also constitutes the skeleton of the INC architecture.
However, this skeleton not only describes the particular architecture of one model
but describes a class of models. In this section, I describe the dimensions along
which these models can vary. I do this with special consideration of the issues relevant for conceptualization. Hence, while describing the dimensions along which
incrementality can vary, I discuss the variants that are suitable for conceptualization
and that are, accordingly, used in INC.

❦ MEANS OF STRUCTURING.   Processes are only one way to structure incremental models, and agents are an interesting alternative (§ 24). However, agents can
hardly be arranged in a cascade, because they are used for building flexible models
in which the agents depend on each other to a much lesser degree than processes
do. Furthermore, agents typically model independent, autonomous (sub)systems
acting on their own behalf and interacting with each other and with the environment. Consequently, the fixed, unidirectional flow of information used in cascaded
models makes little sense, so that using agents as means of structuring would mean
giving up the use of a cascade.

   A more interesting possibility for using incremental agents is to take multiple
incremental models, each one being an agent, and let them interact with each other.
Then, the input to an incremental agent is generated by other agents and/or the
environment, on which the agents can also act. For a conceptualizer model, however,
agents offer no advantages compared with the approach taken here.

   Instead of incremental models, one could also use incremental programs or
systems as means of structuring. Functions, procedures, or tasks could then be used
instead of incremental processes. This would shift the focus of the proposed notions
less than using incremental agents.

❦ MONOTONICITY.   Incremental processing can be monotonic and nonmonotonic. In the nonmonotonic case, an incremental process can generate update
increments if a previously computed result was wrong or inaccurate. Monotonic
incrementality is, therefore, only useful in cases where no internal recomputations
take place, that is, in cases where the processes produce results that will not be

changed afterwards (e.g., spell-checkers). Generating update increments enhances the robustness of incremental models (pp. pp. 93–94). Increment buffers can be used to reduce the amount of updates in the nonmonotonic case, because the incremental processes can change output increments that they stored in an increment buffer. INC's incremental processes are nonmonotonic, and reducing the number of changes is a main function of the traverse buffer.

Humans can change (parts of) a planned utterance. If a self-correction is possible before articulation takes place, it is called a *covert correction*; otherwise it is called an *overt correction*. Because the three main components of Levelt's (1989) language production model do not give feedback (§10), a covert correction can only be performed in two cases:

1. if the output increment is still available in an increment buffer, or
2. if one of the subsequent processes receives the update increment early enough to perform the change before this process produces the corresponding output.

Due to the lack of feedback, the preceding process cannot know whether the update increment reaches the subsequent process in time in the second case (p. 84). An overt correction can be initiated if a covert correction did not succeed or if the error was detected by the monitor component, not by the process itself.

The increments used in self-corrections are no update increments but regular output increments, because the previously generated increments are not changed. Instead, the utterance is extended, usually by a correction term like *uh no*, or *er* followed by the correct content, for example:

(2) *Flug CK-314 bewegt sich auf Gate B21 zu … äh nein … auf Gate B23.*
     'Flight CK-314 moves toward gate B21 … uh no … gate B23.'

INC generates corrections like these as covert corrections (§27). It can generate overt corrections with its rudimentary monitor component (chap. 14).

❧ BUFFERING.   Incremental models can use increment buffers to improve their robustness and efficiency. Buffering means that an incremental process stores its output increments in an increment buffer. This is advantageous when the writing process needs to update previously generated output increments. If the wrong increment is still in the buffer, the writing process can apply the changes of the update increment directly. This reduces run-time and increases robustness, because the reading process makes no computations with the old version of the increment. However, if the reading process already removed the increment from the increment buffer, the update increment must be stored in the buffer in order to be processed by the reading process. This is one case of indirect feedback (term 21, p. 92). Incremental models that use no buffering must either take special precautions that no increments get lost between incremental processes, or they must be able to function properly despite the (occasional) loss of increments. In such models, the processes are typically fast, and only a few increments are transmitted between the processes.

Buffering is crucial for handling phenomena like word order scrambling as a consequence of incremental sentence production (Kempen & Harbusch, 2003). Their model of an incremental formulator obtains the parts of an utterance increment by increment, which need not arrive in the order in which they appear in the generated sentence. Their model generates all increments that are in agreement with the syntactic restrictions of the language, and it temporarily stores the increments that would lead to a syntactically erroneous utterance. (They do not call it increment buffer, but the idea is the same.) For example, if in producing a German or English declarative sentence, the information that will become the verb arrives before the information that will become the subject, the formulator will delay generating the verb until the subject has been generated. In the meantime, the delayed information can be processed to some degree; for example, the lexical access for the verb can take place. INC's traverse buffer fulfills a similar function.

☙ LOOKAHEAD.

Lookahead means that a few subsequent input increments, which are likely to be relevant for processing the current input increment, are available. This makes incremental processing easier and more reliable. Because more input increments are known, it is less likely that an update increment must be generated directly afterward. Generating fewer updates, however, increases the efficiency and robustness of an incremental model. Increment buffers, in which a few increments can be collected, are one way to realize lookahead. Certain problems of language production require some lookahead (Levelt, 1989, pp. 24–25).

For incremental processing, the lookahead can only be minimal. If an incremental process waited until more than just a few input increments are available, the rapid (and sometimes uncertain) production of output, which lies at the heart of incremental processing, would no longer be given. Thus, the advantages and disadvantages of lookahead must be weighed against each other for each incremental model.

☙ FEEDBACK.

A crucial question for each incremental model is whether feedback between components is allowed, and if so, between which ones. Incremental models complying to the blueprint proposed in the previous section contain no feedback. If this restriction is dropped, feedback in a cascade of incremental processes means that a (subsequent) incremental process p_s can send information back to a preceding process p_p in order to influence its operation, for example, to request missing information or to report that an increment has been processed. Although this sounds like another possibility to enhance the reliability and robustness of incremental models, it comes at a high cost, namely that an incremental process using feedback gets more complex, because it needs some knowledge about the functioning of the process(es) it sends feedback to (p_p) and/or receives feedback from (p_s). This is true for p_p as well as for p_s, because p_s has to generate the feedback information and p_p must be able to interpret it.

INC uses as simple a cascade as possible. This includes that it uses no feedback and that its incremental processes are as simple as possible. However, INC uses *indirect feedback*, which means that an incremental process p_s can influence p_p by either modifying the contents of an increment buffer or by changing a part of the model knowledge that is part of the available knowledge of both incremental processes. p_p can change output increments in an increment buffer accessible by p_p and p_s as long as it is actually in the buffer. After p_s has taken it out, it is no longer accessible to p_p, which means that p_s influenced the functioning of p_p by making it impossible for p_s to modify the increment. In INC, the only increment buffer by which indirect feedback is given is the traverse buffer (§ 41). More generally:

TERM 21: INDIRECT FEEDBACK
Indirect feedback is feedback that is not realized as direct transmission of information. Instead, the component giving feedback alters a representation that the component receiving feedback is using as well. If the modification of the representation by the one component affects the operations of the other component, an indirect feedback has been given.

This *minimal feedback principle* cannot be used for incremental agents because of the independent and interactive character of agents, which means that the flow of information is not as fixed as in a cascade. Hence, there are multiple information flows between the single agents, and some of the information is feedback, for example, cases where an agent a_1 generates output to which agent a_2 reacts by generating output to which, then, a_1 reacts. In dialogues, such feedback consists of signals from the hearer to the speaker, for example, by nodding or facial expressions.

❧ NUMBER OF INCREMENTS.   Incrementally working models like IPF (de Smedt, 1990b, 1990a) or Performance Grammar (Kempen, 1997; Kempen & Harbusch, 2002, 2003) process multiple increments in parallel—input increments as well as candidates for output increments. Thus, they possess an additional dimension of parallelism and additional mechanisms apart from the standard cycle of reading, processing, and generating increments. These mechanisms coordinate and evaluate the increments existing in parallel.

The blueprint for incrementality supports the parallel processing of increments, for example, by providing increment buffers in which these increments can be stored. Because increment buffers can only store a limited number of increments, they can model the limits in the number of increments that can be processed in parallel. Models not concerned with limitations of resources may, of course, compute all possibilities.

❦ DISCRETENESS.   Computational models can be discrete or continuous. Symbolic models are always discrete, and connectionist models are continuous. (One of the main tenets of connectionism is the refusal of discrete symbols.) However, connectionist models can, in a certain sense, be regarded as being incremental. The change of activation occurring in one place and "rippling" through the network resembles the characteristic parallel processing of a sequential information flow. What is more, the distinction between discrete and continuous models is not always as clear-cut as this. Sometimes it is just a question of the perspective taken and of the properties of the model that are taken into account. For instance, hybrid models that use nodes to represent symbols as well as the spreading of activation to perform computations are continuous models on the one hand (because of the spreading of activation) and discrete models on the other hand (because of the use of symbols). ACT-R (Anderson & Lebiere, 1998) and Word Grammar (Hudson, 2003a, 2003b) are two such approaches.

As INC is based on symbols, it is discrete. Yet, it also uses a (very limited) kind of activation to represent the degree to which the elements of representations are focused, which influences the likelihood of them being used by processes. So, there are some continuous aspects as well (§ 49).

❦ ROBUSTNESS.   Incremental models are more error-prone than other models, because they produce incomplete output on incomplete input. Nevertheless, they should be as robust as possible. Thus, they should contain error correction mechanisms to improve their overall robustness and reliability, which leads to a better overall performance of the entire model. As I already argued, buffering, lookahead, and feedback are means to enhance the robustness of an incremental model; that is, they are methods to reduce the number of errors (see also Foth, Menzel, Pop, and Schröder (2000), who explore this issue from a parsing perspective).

There are four possibilities when an error arises in an incremental model:

1. The error is detected but not corrected.
2. The error is detected, and correction is tried but fails.
3. The error is detected, and correction succeeds.
4. The error is not detected.

Each time an incremental process detects an error, it must evaluate whether the error is so severe that it requires a correction. The decision not to correct an error may only make things worse. However, (small) errors should not affect the overall performance of the system, because incremental models should be able to cope with errors up to a certain degree. If an error is not detected, some even more cumbersome corrections may follow. This may well lead to a situation in which a correction is not possible and the system has to start anew. There are two possibilities for corrections: update increments and further output increments. Which one to use depends, first, on whether it is possible to make a modification and, second, on whether the flawed output increments can be updated before they leave the system.

There are three main sources for errors: structural errors in the system, malfunctions of the system (performance errors), or errors due to changes arising from information that is read in after the output was generated. Although errors of the first kind should not occur in a well-designed system, they can be compensated to a certain extent if multiple systems perform the same computations and compare their results, a technique common in safety critical systems like airplanes or spaceships. Incremental models should be able to cope with the other two error sources cf. the discussion on monitoring in chap. 14). For conceptualization, *conceptual changes* are a particularly interesting example of the third error source. In conceptual changes, the conceptual representation changes while an incremental preverbal message is generated for the changing content. (The term *conceptual change* is also used to describe changes in the meaning of a concept. I never use it in this meaning in this book.)

The human language faculty obviously is quite robust; that is, it continues processing as long as the errors are not too grave. Typical examples are minor mispronunciations or using a suboptimal concept, for example, using the concept OBJECT instead of PLANE in the example of chapter 1. Although self-monitoring is the most important means for detecting errors (Levelt, 1989), errors should be detected and corrected internally as far as possible before the erroneous (part of an) utterance leaves the system, because it saves the effort of an overt correction (Levelt, 1983).

🍂 PARALLELISM.   Although incremental models with only a single incremental process can exhibit minimal incremental behavior, they usually contain a cascade of multiple incremental processes that work in parallel. Therefore, incremental models face the standard problems of parallelism, the most important of which are cooperation, competition (for resources), scheduling,* communication, synchronization,

---

* Scheduling is part of the competition for resources, especially if the parallelism is only simulated (concurrency) and the processor is one of the resources that has to be shared by the processes.

indeterminism,* independence versus interdependence, indivisible instructions, critical sections, and interleaving. Generally, all these issues must be addressed by incremental models, but as there is a huge amount of literature on these topics (e.g., Bic & Shaw, 1988; Herrtwich & Hommel, 1994; Tannenbaum, 1987), I only comment on some issues that are relevant for INC.

Parallelism is usually distinguished from *concurrency* and *sequentiality*. In sequential models, the sequence of all operations is fixed and cannot be changed. Concurrent or *quasi-parallel* systems simulate parallelism, for example, the operating systems on most current computers, which have only one physical processor on which all (virtual) processes are executed. That is, the operating system assigns and interleaves time slices in which the processes run on the processor. INC is a parallel model that is implemented as a concurrent system. Because scheduling is not part of its implementation, it is a close enough approximation to real parallelism.

There is another kind of parallelism that could be used in incremental models: multiple cascades that work in parallel. In models containing multiple cascades (e.g., one for language comprehension, one for language production, one for visual cognition, etc.), the coordination problems multiply, because there are now two interdependent kinds of parallelism: the parallelism of the incremental processes and the parallelism between the cascades. The more these systems are seen as (part of) the central executive, the more such interacting cascades exist.

🔊 DETERMINISM.   Computational models are either deterministic or indeterministic. In a deterministic model, the next step of the computation (or its next state) is unequivocally determined at each point of time; that is, each computation—given the same input and the same state of the model—always yields the same result. In indeterministic models, this condition does not hold. (This means that determinism is a special case of indeterminism.) Hence, the mapping of input to output is a function in the deterministic case and a relation in the indeterministic case.

Marcus (1980) introduces the additional notion of *strict determinism* and demonstrates its usefulness for parsing. Strict determinism means that the computations are not indeterministic in a hidden way; that is, there is no *backtracking*. Backtracking itself is in fact deterministic. However, after a step was taken back, the computation is back at a point in the solution tree where it was already before. Thus, it has the same choice again but chooses a different option this time (Marcus, 1980, p. 12). This could also be called a *temporally discontinuous indeterministic decision*. In the context of incrementality, there is a fourth useful notion: *quasi-indeterminism*.

---

* Deterministic parallel systems are conceivable if the processes are coordinated accordingly; but because this is contrary to the fundamental ideas of parallelism, they are not really an option. Nevertheless, a sequential system can be regarded as the degenerate case of a parallel system.

These are indeterministic computations carried out by a deterministic device, for example, a computer processor. Quasi-indeterminism is equivalent to concurrency.

Incremental processing usually means that the model is indeterministic because of the parallelism in the cascade. INC is an indeterministic model, which is simulated by the programming system in which it is implemented.

CONSISTENCY. Performing computations only with respect to a local context can mean the loss of consistency (§24). The reason for this is that only part of the model knowledge is considered for the computation of new results, which then become part of that knowledge. Only if it can be ascertained that all relevant knowledge for a computation is part of the local context can the representation stay consistent. For example, the spell-checker of a word processor has to check only modified words. Say if a *p* is inserted in the middle of *aple*, the spell-checker will detect that *apple* is now a correctly spelled word, and it can be certain that this local change does not affect the correctness or incorrectness of the other words in the text. Thus, the representation (which words are spelled correctly) stays consistent. However, in order to do so the frame problem must be solved (§32). Because this is a very hard problem (apart from simple cases like the one just laid out), consistency can often only be achieved if local context and available knowledge (or even model knowledge) are identical. Yet, in some cases, inconsistencies can be avoided without considering all available knowledge: first, if all operations carried out on the representation are conclusions in the formal sense or, second, if there are no changes in the environment that are not caused by the system (agent) itself.

Because I use local contexts for processing incremental representations, it is hardly possible to demand consistent representations, especially from the perspective of cognitive adequacy, because realistic cognitive representations are inconsistent. For cognitively adequate models, the inconsistencies in the model should be as close to empirically observable inconsistencies as possible. Nevertheless, I will not consider inconsistencies in the following, because the scenes INC can process are not yet complex enough. Hence, the conceptual representations used here are consistent.

MODULARITY. I already dealt extensively with the issue of modularity in chapter 2. Therefore, I want to make just one point here: nonmodular models can also work incrementality, although the blueprint in §24 implicitly assumes a modular approach and would have to be adapted accordingly.

Modular approaches stand mainly in opposition to those using network representations in which computations are carried out by the spreading of activation. The most prominent examples are connectionist networks, but there are also models that use a combination of symbols and spreading activation (e.g., Hudson (2003b) claims that all of cognition really is just one giant network) and, therefore, there are no boundaries that could be identified as interfaces between modules. As already mentioned in the discussion of discreteness, such activation-based networks can be seen as performing their computations in an incremental fashion in that a change of activation of one place "ripples" through the net. Additionally, when comparing modular and nonmodular models, one can observe that in modular models the modularisation is done by the creator of the model, whereas nonmodular models very often are based on the assumption that the model possesses self-organizing capabilities. Thus, self-organization would have to be incorporated into a notion of nonmodular incrementality.

6

INCREMENTAL REPRESENTATIONS

*I*NCREMENTAL REPRESENTATIONS ARE representations that can be used by incremental processes, that is, processes as I described them in the previous chapter. The main requirement, as I repeatedly pointed out previously, is that incremental representations are dynamic representations, that is, representations that can change over time. IN C uses two kinds of incremental representations: the CCR and incremental preverbal messages. Whereas the first one is a constantly expanding representation from which no elements are deleted, incremental preverbal messages exist only temporarily and "disappear" as soon as they are sent to the formulator (apart from the fact that the refOs are also copied into the CCR).

In this chapter, I describe requirements for incremental representations (§ 26). The main part of this chapter, however, consists of describing how semantic underspecification formalisms can be used as incremental representations (§ 27)—in particular, how the Constraint Language for Lambda Structures (CLLS) can be used for generating incremental preverbal messages (§ 28).

§ 26 *Requirements for incremental representations*

A representational formalism must have two main properties in order to be used for incremental processing: It must be changeable over time, and it must make possible to define increments. To be used with the blueprint for incrementality, it must, furthermore, represent knowledge in a localized fashion, which is required for the computation of local contexts, and it must support different views on the representation for each incremental process.

To be used for conceptualization, a representational formalism must have additional properties. It must be able to represent (hierarchical) conceptual knowledge. It also must provide means for linking the conceptual knowledge to nonconceptual knowledge, that is, perceptual and linguistic knowledge (cf. the remark on the symbol grounding problem in § 18). In addition, it must represent knowledge in a cognitively adequate manner; for example, it must allow the representation of inconsistencies.

I already showed that referential nets have these properties. In comparison, the Constraint Language for Lambda Structures (CLLS, Egg, Koller, & Niehren,

2001) only has the first two properties (changeability, definition of increments). Localization and different views require additional definitions, and although it certainly possesses some cognitive adequacy, it is not suited to represent conceptual knowledge and to link conceptual to nonconceptual knowledge.

INC requires two kinds of knowledge representations: conceptual representations and incremental preverbal messages. Both are built up by assembling the representation piecemeal; referential nets can be used for both. The changes in the representation can be subdivided into adding or deleting refOs and designations and adding, deleting, and modifying the attributes associated with a refO or a designation. The pieces of knowledge that are used by these operations are the increments.

I extend referential nets by a rudimentary activation concept, which is not part of the standard version (Eschenbach, 1988; Habel, 1986). Each element of a representation has an activation value, which determines its prominence (salience) in comparison to the other elements. However, the current version of INC only uses the activation of designations (cf. part C for details). Additionally, the activation is static: An activation value is assigned once and then never changed. In order to enhance its cognitive adequacy, mechanisms for the decay and reactivation of items must be integrated (Anderson & Lebiere, 1998).

§ 27   *Underspecification and incrementality*

Semantic underspecification formalisms have been proving their usefulness over the last years.* There are two main reasons for this. The first reason is that underspecification makes it possible to represent ambiguous utterances by only one structure for *all* readings instead of one structure for *each* reading, in particular in the case of scope ambiguities. At the same time, it is an elegant representational method for the semantic description of anaphora, reinterpretation in lexical semantics, and the meaning of elliptical expressions (Egg et al., 2001; Schilder & Guhe, 2002). Although the idea of semantic underspecification is not particular to one direction of language processing, it has—with few exceptions—only been used in comprehension up to now. This probably is so, because the mentioned problems are typical problems in parsing sentences and discourses, whereas they can be more or less avoided in generation. The problem that particularly sets aside comprehension from generation is that during parsing, ambiguities arise that usually can only be resolved by considering the corresponding context. Most parsers, though, work without a context,

---

* The ideas presented up to the end of this section were developed in cooperation with Frank Schilder and were previously published in Guhe and Schilder (2002a, 2002b) and Schilder and Guhe (2002).

because their goal is to build up a *semantic* representation, which is—by and large—independent of context. As one of the main advantages of underspecification is to represent ambiguous utterances in one structure, only one underspecified semantic structure has to be built up during parsing which can then be disambiguated in a further step—if there is need at all (cf. Knight and Langkilde (2000), who describe a system that preserves ambiguities during translation).

However, these parsing problems have no real counterparts in NLG and language production (§ 8). The main reason is that the knowledge representation from which language is generated usually is completely available. For example, when I use the name *Tom*, I always know which Tom I am talking about even if I know more than one person with this name. Yet, a person or a system hearing me say *Tom* will have to infer which of the, say, seven Toms known to us both is meant. In the case of anaphora, the generator always knows what the anaphora is referring to; for an ellipsis, the implicit content is known, and because it is known what is meant when the lexical semantics is generated, there is no need for reinterpretations. Most builders of NLG systems even explicitly try to avoid these problems if they arise while specifying a system. However, the generated output sounds much more natural if certain information is left implicit, in particular if the goal is to build a cognitively adequate system. This can also be done in referential nets, where it is called *underdetermination* ("Unterbestimmtheit"; Habel, 1986), which has additional, different connotations. For example, the cardinality of a refO representing a group of entities can be underdetermined by stating that the number of entities the group consists of is between, say, three and twelve; the exact number is not specified.

The second, and in this context the important reason for using underspecification is that it allows representations to change over time. Because underspecified representations are usually specified in some parts, it is possible to distinguish those parts of the representation that cannot be modified (without creating an error or reanalysis) from those parts that can, that is, where elements can be added or inserted. It is this extendability property of underspecification that can be exploited for the incremental generation of preverbal messages.

Underspecified structures have been used in NLG before. For example, Pianta and Tovena (1999) present a hybrid generation system that combines template-based and "proper" NLG methods. In the resulting system, the information to be verbalized can be specified on different levels. That is, the underlying data structure can contain a completed string that is output as is, and, at the same time, it can contain other knowledge representations for which output must still be generated by other NLG techniques. However, this is more of a hybrid system instead of one that systematically uses underspecified representations. The Verbmobil system, a machine translation system (Wahlster, 2000) that uses a semantic transfer approach, comes closest to the idea put forward here. It uses underspecification in the semantic representations and components for parsing and generation that work incrementally. However, it translates entire dialogue acts, which means that each dialogue act is completely parsed into an underspecified semantic representation and then completely translated before generation commences. In this way, the mentioned advantages of underspecification—plus preservation of lexical ambiguities—can be used but not the fact that an utterance can be generated incrementally while planning is not finished. Finally, Gardent and Thater (2001) propose to use underspecification on the level of the formulator. A modified output of INC could in fact be used as input to this system. However, none of these approaches exploits the extendability property of underspecification formalisms.

Incrementality is a way to cope with dynamically changing states of affairs, for example, for models working in a dynamic setting (part A). The dynamics of the environment and incremental processing necessitate changes in the representation of the states of affairs. The main advantage of underspecification is that these representations need not be restructured or constructed from scratch after each change. Quite the contrary: Like in the referential nets approach, new information can be added to the already existing underspecified representation at the allowed places. One can imagine these places as holes in the representation where new information can be filled in. However, this is not obligatory; the representation is already complete as it is. This method facilitates models that need not plan a whole utterance in advance to generate a valid structure but that can plan an utterance piecemeal while it is already leaving the system.

Summing up, underspecification can be employed for incremental language generation, because an underspecified representation can be extended without reverting earlier made planning decisions. Subsequently planned increments can be inserted where the underspecified representation left room. Because underspecification is not mainly motivated by cognitive considerations, an additional aim of this section is to show that NLG techniques can be enhanced by transferring work from cognitively oriented language production to NLG in the sense of E. Reiter (1994).

§ 28 *Generating incremental preverbal messages with the Constraint Language for Lambda Structures (CLLS)*

CLLS (Egg et al., 2001) is a formalism for the partial (underspecified) description of lambda structures. Lambda structures are represented as ordinary trees amended by the two partial functions lam for binding variables of the λ-term and $ante$ for modeling anaphoric expressions. The lambda term $Mary(\lambda x.sleep(x))$, for

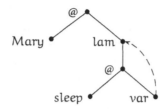

Figure 6.1: The CLLS representation for *Mary sleeps*

instance, can be represented as the tree structure shown in figure 6.1.* The label
@ indicates application, a dashed line between two nodes labeled by lam and var
ensure the correct binding between variables and the λ-abstractor. Additionally,
variables denoting tree nodes (e.g., $X_0, X_1, X_2, ...$) are added to the lambda tree
structure in order to allow for underspecification, the specification of anaphoric
references, and so on. Formally, a CLLS formula is described as a conjunction of
atomic literals. In order to satisfy such a formula, a lambda tree structure, such as
the one in figure 6.1, and variable assignments have to be found such that every
literal is satisfied.

Several constraints are defined in CLLS. Crucial for the definition of underspecification is the dominance relation holding between tree nodes: $X \lhd^* Y$ is satisfied if
and only if X denotes an ancestor of Y in the lambda tree structure. The constraint
graph indicates this relation via the dotted lines, for example, the relation between
the nodes labeled by Y_1 and Y_2 in figure 6.2. The dominance relation is reflexive and
transitive; thus, the nodes connected via a dotted line can be identical, or there can
be an infinite number of further tree structures inserted between the nodes. Another
constraint ensures that the binding between variables and lambda operators is given:
$λ(X) = Y$ is satisfied if and only if the denotation of X maps to the denotation of Y.
Within the constraint graph, the mapping is indicated by the dashed line pointing
from the variable to the lambda operator (lam).

For the representation of coordination-structures, the *parallelism constraint*
is particularly interesting. It defines a parallel structure between tree segments.
Segments in a lambda structure are defined as X/Y where X denotes the *root* of
the segment and Y a *hole* such that $X \lhd^* Y$. The segment covers all nodes that are
dominated by the root X with the exception of the node Y and the nodes dominated
by Y. In other words, a segment is a subtree starting with the node X with the
exception of a further subtree, which has Y as root node. For instance, in figure 6.2,

---

* NPS including PNS are type-raised. Hence, the term Mary in $Mary(λx.sleep(x))$ is actually a
function from sets of entities to truth values.

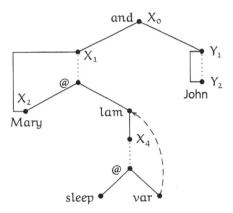

Figure 6.2: The parallelism constraint for the elliptical sentence (1)

the segment X_1/X_2 has the root node X_1 including all nodes dominated by it apart from node X_2 and the subtree of which X_2 is the root. The actual parallelism constraint $X_1/X_2 \sim Y_1/Y_2$ is satisfied if and only if the segment X_1/X_2 of the lambda structure is parallel to a segment Y_1/Y_2. The segments are described by brackets in the constraint graphs (see figure 6.2). Formally, the parallelism between two segments is captured via a correspondence function, which is defined as a bijective mapping between the two segments (see Erk (2000) for further details).

The parallelism constraint proves to be especially useful for the description of VP ellipses and for self-corrections, like in the following examples:

(1) Mary sleeps and John does, too.
(2) Mary sleeps ...uh no ...is awake.

The corresponding CLLS representation for (1) is given in figure 6.2 and the one for (2) in figure 6.3.

The advantage of CLLS and underspecification formalisms in general is that semantic representations for utterances like these need not be generated at once. In the first stage of generating the above examples, the representation in figure 6.1 is produced; or, to be more precise, this structure is generated in its underspecified version shown in the left side of the tree in figure 6.2. This is done in two steps. First, the tree containing the underspecification for $\lambda x.sleep(x))$ is produced; second, the node for Mary and the application (@) of the lam tree to the Mary node are produced. This tree can now be extended at two points, above the upper @ node and between X_4 and the lower @. The latter can be used for utterances like the following:

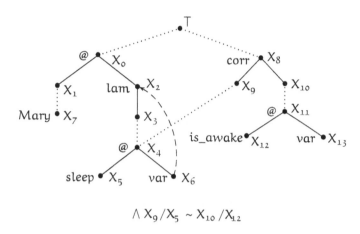

$$\wedge\, X_9/X_5 \sim X_{10}/X_{12}$$

Figure 6.3: The underspecified preverbal message of the self-correction in (2); the parallelism constraint is not written in the bracket notation but as constraint below the tree.

(3)   Mary sleeps and snores.

The former possibility is used in the examples presented here: VP ellipses and self-corrections. After the generation of the initial tree, the conceptualizer may detect that not only is Mary sleeping but John as well, or it may detect that Mary in fact is *not* sleeping in contrast to its former belief. In the first case, a VP ellipsis can elegantly extend the utterance generated so far; in the second case, the erroneous part of the utterance can be corrected. Note that in the case of a change of belief, it would be misleading to simply generate an utterance that reflects the new current state.

(4)   Mary sleeps. Mary is awake.

This utterance must be regarded as a faulty description of the state of affairs, because it will confuse the hearer with respect to which of the two utterances is actually true. It cannot be expected that the hearer simply overwrites former beliefs. Instead, it must be made explicit that part of the previous utterance is wrong.

The parallelism constraint $X_1/X_2 \sim Y_1/Y_2$, occurring in figure 6.2, is reflected in the graph via two brackets denoting the two parallel segments (X_1/X_2 and Y_1/Y_2). The brackets precisely determine the part of the source sentence (*Mary sleeps*) that has to be copied into the target sentence (*John does, too*) as well as the part that has to be kept separate (*Mary* and *John*). One of the lambda tree structures satisfying this constraint graph is given in figure 6.4. This specification step is tantamount to

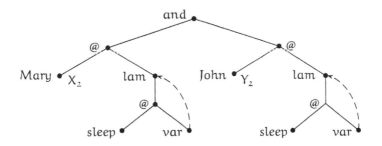

Figure 6.4: A lambda structure that satisfies the constraint graph in figure 6.2

deciding on one reading of the sentence. A few more details are necessary in order to use this approach with INC, for example, a function translating designations and refOs to CLLS terms (cf. Guhe & Schilder, 2002b), which are of no interest here.

Underspecification is a very powerful idea, as can be seen by the fact that it can be taken even one step further: Not only the structure but also the constraints themselves can be underspecified. In particular, the parallelism constraint can be underspecified in order to capture all three readings of the gapping example (5), given in (6) (see Schilder & Guhe, 2002).

(5) Peter gave Mary a book and John, too.
(6) a. Peter gave Mary a book and Peter gave John a book.
    b. Peter gave Mary a book and John gave Mary a book.
    c. Peter gave Mary a book and Peter gave Mary John.

Distinguishing the first two readings is a standard problem of semantics and is, therefore, not further commented on. The third reading is usually ruled out by standard pragmatic assumptions but may be the correct reading if, for instance, John is Mary's favorite doll. The basic idea of underspecifying the parallelism constraint is that the reading that actually fits the state of affairs is not specified, that is, the attachment point of the gapping expression is not specified. In other words, it is left open which of the three argument positions of the VP formed by *give* the gapping construction is attached to. The discussion of the technical details required for this are given in Schilder and Guhe (2002) and are of no interest here, because underspecifying the parallelism constraint is mainly interesting for language comprehension as the attachment point is known to the generation system. However, it demonstrates that underspecification in this dimension (i.e., underspecifying a constraint) reduces the amount of information that has to be transmitted from speaker to hearer and, thus, is another means to save resources.

Concluding, one can say that CLLs allows the specification of very flexible and concise structures that can be modified in the course of time. For this reason, they are suited for incremental processing.

7

RESOURCES, RATIONALITY, ANYTIME, AND THE FRAME PROBLEM

ESOURCES ARE ONE of the main reasons for using incremental processing—apart from the simultaneous processing of input and production of output. In this chapter, I provide characterizations of resources and related terms (§29). The most important point about resources in the context of cognitive processing is that the behavior of a cognitively adequate model is influenced by how much of each required resource is available. Because most resources are limited, cognitive systems cannot be perfectly, unboundedly rational, but they are rational within bounds (§30). Another well-known approach for saving resources are anytime algorithms, and although they have similarities to incremental processing, there are also significant differences (§31). The problem of limited resources in a dynamic system is not only a relevant problem in a cognitive context but also a general problem of computability. A standard AI problem in this respect is the frame problem, especially in the form of the persistence problem (§32).

§29   *Resources*

Resources are a very broad notion (Jameson, 1997; Jameson & Buchholz, 1998):

TERM 22: RESOURCE
A resource is a—material or immaterial—auxiliary means required by a task in order to perform a function in achieving a goal. The performance or even the overall success of the task depends on allocation of the required resources, or how much of the required resources are allocated to the task.

Resources are always defined with respect to a specific task. Typical resources are physical objects, human abilities, information, energy, and time (Jameson & Buchholz, 1998, p. 96). Some resources are consumed when they are used (e.g., energy or time), whereas others are not (e.g., information). Some resources can be divided (e.g., time), whereas others can only be used as a whole (e.g., a telephone number).

For incremental processing, the limitations of two resources are especially of interest: time and storage capacity (memory). In particular, increment buffers are suited to model these limitations: storage capacity by restricting the number of items

107

that can be stored in the buffer, time by the length of time an increment can remain in the buffer. In INC, these limitations are varied by parameters that determine the length of the traverse buffer and the time that it stores an increment (§38).

TERM 23: ALLOCATION
The allocation of a resource is the assignment of (part of) the resource to a task in order for the task to be carried out.

With respect to allocation, the notion of resources is too general for the following purposes, because information is not exhausted when it is used. Hence, it would be misleading to call this allocation (Jameson & Buchholz, 1998, p. 97). For the present purpose, I therefore narrow down this term to resources that are exhausted when they are used. This excludes, in particular, knowledge.

Allocation of resources is usually carried out with the goal to maximize (optimize) their usefulness; that is, the available resources should be used in a way that maximal gain is achieved with them. The means to measure this usefulness are *metrics*.

TERM 24: METRIC
A metric determines the degree of usefulness of a resource for performing a task.

The use of metrics is one important difference between incremental and anytime processing. Whereas anytime algorithms typically perform explicit estimations of the optimal use of the available resources, incremental algorithms typically only change their behavior if a resource is in danger of becoming too scarce. For example, if working memory or a specialized buffer is close to being completely filled, the system may decide to switch to another level of granularity in order to cope with the available resources. This is called *adaptation*.

TERM 25: ADAPTATION
Adaptation is the adjustment of the behavior of a computing device in a way that its available (allocated) resources suffice to accomplish a task.

Agents that adapt to the available resources are usually divided into two main components (cf., e.g., the agents by Larson & Sandholm, 2001). The first component does the computation proper, that is, the computation the agent was designed for. This is often done with anytime algorithms (§31). The other component determines how much of a resource the agent spends on each computation. Incremental models, in contrast, do not reason about resources and, consequently, have no such components. Therefore, adaptation plays only a minor role. In particular, INC cannot regulate the allocation of its resources, and the amount of available resources is fixed when the system is started and does not change afterward. However, there are possible extensions, for example, by monitoring the fill-rate of the traverse buffer (§ 58 and § 59).

§ 30   Bounded rationality

For cognitive models, it is particularly important to cope with the limitations of the available resources. A particularly important idea was put forward by Herbert Simon (1955, 1982): When an agent makes decisions, it does not behave globally optimal; that is, he/she/it* does not make the optimal decision with respect to the current state of the world. This is due to the limited resources it has available, most of all, deliberation time and knowledge about the world. Thus, it has to make the best of the resources it has available. As a consequence, its decision is not perfectly rational but the rationality is *bounded* (Simon, 1982, vol. 1, p. 409).

Simon's idea is mainly directed against the notion of a perfect, unbounded rationality, which was the prevalent theory in the 1940s and 1950s when he first proposed the idea. And despite the fact that Simon's theories were and still are widely acknowledged, this situation did not change. For example, the highly praised AI book by Russell and Norvig still dismisses the notion of bounded rationality, because they want to build agents that are "actually useful in the real world, whereas … satisficing agents might or might not be, depending on their own whims" (Russell & Norvig, 2003, p. 973). (See p. 17, this vol., for a critique of this argument.)

Simon showed that unbounded rationality is unsuited to explain the behavior of natural agents, because the computational and predictive ability of natural agents are too restricted. The key factors are the agent's limited knowledge and the complexity of the environment, which would require too much time to be fully taken into consideration (Simon, 1982, vol. 2, p. 241). Hence, models based on unbounded rationality produce unrealistic and, therefore, unreliable predictions of human behavior. In order to investigate and model people's behavior Simon proposed not to make ideal world assumptions but rather to study the exhibited human behavior directly.

Based on this analysis, Simon considered humans as what he called *satisficing* rather than optimizing beings. *Satisficing* means that humans often do not consider all available possibilities; rather they consider them one at a time and stop the

---

* I will use *it* in the following, because, first, it solves the unsolvable *he/she* or *he or she* or *he and she* or even *s/he* problem and, second, because it emphasises the fact that my goal is to build a model of an artificial agent. However, *it* can be understood as encompassing natural (*he* or *she*) agents.

search "once they discover the one that they regard as satisfactory" (Simon, 1982, vol. 2, p. 413). However, there is another kind of bounded rationality that fits even better to incremental processing, namely the *fast and frugal heuristics* by Gigerenzer (Gigerenzer et al., 1999; Todd & Gigerenzer, 2000). In this approach, making a decision consists of three major components:

1. Heuristic principles guiding search
2. Heuristic principles for stopping search
3. Heuristic principles for decision making

Although Gigerenzer et al. have classical decision making problems in mind (e.g., deciding which of two cities has more inhabitants), the overall approach is similar to incremental processing. There are two heuristic principles guiding search: (a) the overall principle that each input increment is taken and processed in relation to the available knowledge, and (b) the heuristics that establish the local contexts on which the incremental algorithms operate. The heuristic principles for stopping search correspondingly are that a new input increment is available or that the results of the incremental algorithm are not improved any more. The heuristic principles for decision making are integrated in the way the incremental algorithms work, for example, the selection strategy that decides which event is verbalized.

Without going into too much detail here, it should be noted that the fast and frugal heuristics by Gigerenzer et al. do not impair the quality of the results. On the contrary, the quality is comparable to that of techniques using unbounded rationality, such as multiple linear regression. Yet, their approach is also much more robust with respect to new input data, which underlines its cognitive adequacy: Although suboptimal performance can be tolerated to a certain degree, an agent must be able to make decisions of constant quality in different settings and environments.

Hence, incrementality enables humans to act, despite their limited resources, in a bounded rational way, which is not only cognitively adequate but also robust.

§ 31   *Anytime processing*

Bounded rationality greatly enhances a model's cognitive adequacy, because it behaves in a rational way without the unrealistic assumptions of unlimited resources. Anytime algorithms were developed for very similar reasons. In particular they enable agents acting in an environment of a realistic (natural) complexity to reach decisions in a limited amount of time. The term *anytime algorithm* was coined by Dean and Boddy (Boddy & Dean, 1994; Dean & Boddy, 1988). Anytime algorithms are algorithms that improve the quality of their results over time; that is, the more time they have available, the better the result is. They are used, for instance, for constraint satisfaction problems, the interpretation of sensory data, and path planning like in the traveling salesman problem.

> The defining property of an anytime algorithm is that it can be stopped at any time to provide a solution, and the quality of the solution increases with computation time. This property allows a trade-off between computation time and solution quality, making it possible to compute approximate solutions to complex problems under time constraints. (Hansen & Zilberstein, 2001, p. 14)

Anytime algorithms extend the usual notion of computation by being able to return not only one result but a range of results, the quality of which can be determined by different metrics. Three metrics have been proving particularly useful (Zilberstein, 1996, p. 74): (a) *Certainty* is the metric that measures the degree of certainty that a result is correct. (b) *Accuracy* measures how close the result is to the global optimum. (c) *Specificity* determines the level of detail of the result. The last metric presupposes that the algorithm only produces correct results, and only the level of detail increases for each result.

The point in time when an anytime algorithm stops can either be determined beforehand, for example, by stochastic evaluations of previous executions, or by monitoring its progress (Hansen & Zilberstein, 2001). Accordingly, there are two kinds of anytime algorithms: *interruptible* and *contract* algorithms. The former can be interrupted at any time (e.g., by a signal from the outside) and present the best result they computed so far. The latter know the amount of time in advance; thus, the optimization of result quality and run-time is performed beforehand. Anytime processing faces a problem unknown to incremental processing, the *meta-level control problem*: "the problem of determining the stopping time for an anytime algorithm that optimizes the expected value of computation" (Hansen & Zilberstein, 2001, p. 14).

According to Zilberstein (1996, p. 74) an anytime algorithm should have the following properties:

1. *Measurable quality*: the quality of the result can be determined precisely
2. *Recognizable quality*: the quality of the result can be determined at run-time
3. *Monotonicity*: the quality of the result increases with time and input quality
4. *Consistency*: the quality of the result is correlated with time and input quality
5. *Diminishing returns*: the improvement in quality diminishes over time
6. *Interruptibility*: the algorithm can be stopped at any time and provide an answer
7. *Preemptability*: suspending and resuming the algorithm requires minimal overhead

As this list shows, the main concern of anytime processing is the quality of the result. Most properties are desirable for incremental algorithms as well, which is one of the reasons why incrementality and anytime are kindred processing mechanisms. In particular both are similar in the following respects:

· They need less resources for producing their results than algorithms that search for the global optimum.*
· They can produce output before the computation has yielded the optimal result.
· They do not ascertain to produce the globally optimal result; that is, they are methods of bounded rationality.

Yet, incremental and anytime algorithms also differ in important respects:

· Incrementality does not know the meta-level control problem.
· Anytime "is about" the quality of a result, incrementality about producing output at a constant rate.
· Anytime processes are used for tasks in which the result can be improved gradually; incremental processes produce output of (more or less) constant quality—although corrections are possible.
· In anytime, the resources that are spent on a computation are the object of computation itself; that is, the model reasons about the amount of time it allocates for performing a task. In incrementality, resources are "just used" (but adaptations may be performed).
· Anytime processes usually work on demand; that is, they are called in order to return a result. Incremental processes are more autonomous in that they just work at a steady rate and produce output as soon as it is available.
· Anytime processes return the best result they have got up to that point, whereas incremental processes just produce output as quickly as possible.†
· Anytime algorithms usually do not deal with dynamic input in a way where the difference of new and present knowledge is considered; this is what incremental processing is all about.

Despite the substantial differences between anytime algorithms and incremental processing, both can be combined in order to build more reliable systems. Menzel (1994), for example, describes a constraint-based approach to natural language pars-

---

* However, there are cases in which incremental processing needs more resources than a corresponding nonincremental mode of processing (cf. the remark on priming in §22).
† If Extended Wundt's Principle is not used and if, in particular, incremental processes generate some candidate results before deciding on one of them, anytime and incremental processing operate identical in this respect.

ing that combines both techniques. For this purpose, he introduces *weak* anytime algorithms, which are anytime algorithms for which it is not possible to establish the optimal trade-off between output quality and required run-time before the algorithm starts computing. Their progress is measured by determining the remaining ambiguity of the parsed language. The goal is to generate a representation without ambiguities. This parsing technique proves to be more robust and fault-tolerant than incremental systems without anytime mechanisms. Parsing of ungrammatical language is performed by these algorithms without extra effort.

§ 32   *A remark on the frame problem*

The *frame problem* was first observed by McCarthy and Hayes (1969). Originally it termed a quite narrow problem in the *situation calculus*. The situation calculus is a first-order logic for reasoning about time and a changing world; see McCarthy and Hayes (1969) for the original description and R. Reiter (2001) for a recent version. Within this calculus, *actions* define changes of states of the world. For example, in a model of the well-known blocks-world, it is possible to describe how the representation of the world changes if a block is moved on top of another one. Because this action does not change size or color of the blocks, such nonchanges must be specified by so-called frame axioms; for example, *the size of a block is not changed by movements*. Each time an action is carried out, the changes as well as the non-changes must be computed. Because there usually are many more facts that do not change than facts that do change, the number of frame axioms is huge. The frame problem leads to an explosion of complexity, which means it causes problems in systems that have to cope with limited resources.

The original frame problem has led to much discussion about this particular problem of the situation calculus and about related problems in this and other calculi (cf. Morgenstern, 1996, for a concise overview and Shanahan, 1997, for a history of proposed solutions to the frame problem including a further proposal). The reason is that all calculi dealing with changeable representations eventually face this or a similar problem. I do not want to discuss the frame problem as such here, but there is one point in incremental processing that is subject to it, namely the point where a heuristic determines the local context for an incremental algorithm.*
The assumption up to now is that all relevant information that is required for the

---

* A. Clark (2002) discusses a similar version of the frame problem and proposes to use an intriguing technique by Kleinberg (1999) to solve it. The upshot is that in a densely interlinked knowledge representation like the World Wide Web much can be gained by not evaluating the information but the *structure* of the information. Put informally, in order to find an entity, one has to look at the links, not the linked entities. A similar solution can be used for referential nets.

incremental algorithm to make its computation is available in the local context, which leads to a reduction of the required resources. Thus, this method could already be considered a solution of the frame problem, because only few frame axioms have to be applied. This is even more true, because it is supported by the most obvious solution to the frame problem, which was already suggested by McCarthy and Hayes (1969). This solution consists in proposing the general axiom that no facts are changed by an action, except those that are explicitly modified.

Morgenstern (1996) argues that although this is the original frame problem, it is not the real problem, and the solution suggested by McCarthy and Hayes is no real solution. Instead, the real frame problem is the *persistence problem*, the problem of deciding which facts are changed by an action and which persist. To my knowledge, no general solution of the persistence problem has been found yet. The solution I use here is, therefore, not to solve it at all. Instead, the goal for a cognitively adequate model must be to build a model that is "good enough for government work" as Dennett (1996, p. 6) puts it. In continuation of the discussion on bounded rationality, the frame problem seems to be an artificial AI problem from a cognitive standpoint. The problem is artificial (ill-posed), because to solve it means to build agents that perform better than those found in nature. Given that natural organisms are particularly adapted to their environment, it remains to be seen whether that is possible.

My goal, therefore, is to build a model that works "according to the ubiquitous biological design principle: oversimplify and self-monitor" (Dennett, 1996, p. 4). This design principle can be read in two ways. First, the first version of a model design need not be perfect. Cases in which the model does not behave the way it should are examined, and a better version is built. In nature, this is done by the learning of an organism and by evolution in a population. Second, a model needs mechanisms that enable it to correct errors, because it should be robust. In the conceptualizer, this is done by the monitor (cf. chap. 14).

~ c ~

INC—THE INCREMENTAL CONCEPTUALIZER

~ 8 ~

ARCHITECTURE

*A*FTER DISCUSSING CONCEPTUALIZATION and incrementality as separate issues in the previous two parts, this—rather technical—part describes INC (the incremental conceptualizer) in detail. INC integrates the issues of the discussion so far by providing a working model that is implemented as a system. INC is not a complete conceptualizer model but more like a framework that has been elaborated in some parts. This is the consequence of modeling a large stretch of cognition. Thus, INC contains gaps and hooks, places for further enhancements that will lead toward a more complete model of the conceptualizer.

This chapter gives an overview of INC as a whole, and the following chapters deal with its components in more detail. Before describing INC's architecture, I compare INC to unified cognitive architectures and explain why they are too restrictive for my purposes (§33). I then describe the architectural principles underlying INC's design (§34). The ensuing sections have the following topics: INC's processes (§35), its representations (§36), the increments between the processes (§37), its parameters (§38), and, finally, INC's preprocessing unit (PPU) and the corresponding increments (§39).

§ 33 *Unified cognitive architectures*

Apart from cognitive models that perform only one specific task, there is a long tradition of unified theories of cognition (Newell, 1990), which I refer to as *unified cognitive architectures* because I am more concerned with the architectural side of cognition. The first of these architectures was the General Problem Solver (GPS) developed by Newell and Simon (1963). More recent architectures are Soar (Laird, Newell, & Rosenbloom, 1987; Newell, 1990); ACT-R (Anderson & Lebiere, 1998), which contains an additional subsymbolic level, and EPIC (Kieras & Meyer, 1997; Meyer & Kieras, 1997), which emphasizes perception and action. Finally, PSI

115

(Dörner, 1999) is based on artificial neural nets and takes a wider approach in that it models not only cognition but "the soul," which means that it includes, among other things, models of emotion and motivation.

Models like INC (sometimes called *one-shot models*) are subject to a major criticism initially brought forward by Newell and being a main inspiration for proposing a unified cognitive architecture in the first place. The criticism is that such models capture only one aspect of cognition and that it is easy to build a model that fits a set of data. There are three main problems (Lewis, 2001). First, the problem of irrelevant specification: Computer programs, especially complex ones, contain many details, and it is often difficult to distinguish those aspects with theoretical merit from those that are merely technical assumptions, that is, those required to get the system running but that have no bearing on the theory. Second, the problem of too many degrees of freedom: The more degrees of freedom there are, the easier it is to fit a computer program to a data set. Third, the problem of identifiability: The more general a program or representation is, the easier it is to use it to match any kind of input to any kind of output.

Unified cognitive architectures address these problems by restricting the possible computations to computations that are cognitively plausible and supported by empirical data. And, to cut a long discussion short, because INC has no such restrictions, it has all these problems. (However, see Cooper & Shallice, 1995 for arguments that unified cognitive architectures, especially Soar, actually face similar problems.) Given this situation, would it be better to develop INC within one of these frameworks? These are really two questions:

1. Is it possible to implement INC in a unified cognitive architecture?
2. What are the advantages of (not) doing this?

Is it possible to implement INC in a unified cognitive architecture? Put differently: Are the assumptions of INC compliant with the assumptions of unified architectures? Yes and no. On the one hand, there are important similarities between the approaches, and there is no obvious reason why INC could not be implemented in a unified cognitive architecture. There are two major similarities. First, INC distinguishes between working memory and long-term memory: working memory for the conceptual representation of the current state of affairs and other temporary knowledge, long-term memory for the rules on how to construct complex concepts from simple ones. Second, the recognize–decide–act cycle of unified cognitive architectures has a counterpart in the incremental processes: Identify the focused element, determine the local context, execute the incremental algorithm.

On the other hand, there are also significant differences. Considering the second question, one has to bear in mind that INC has a different purpose than unified cognitive architectures. Apart from modeling conceptualization for language production, the incremental processing mechanism itself is an equally major issue. In unified cognitive architectures, the processing mechanisms are not the research focus. For example, it is rarely questioned whether production rules are an adequate way to model cognition. I want to mention four major differences here.

First, incrementality in a cascaded architecture includes a kind of parallelism different from the one in the mentioned architectures. Instead of considering all productions of the model in parallel, defined processes work simultaneously on one information stream on different stages.

Second, the Soar control structure, to take just one example, uses a least-commitment strategy (Lewis, 2001). Changing this strategy to comply to the early-commitment strategy of Extended Wundt's Principle would substantially change the Soar architecture. However, there is no guarantee that the resulting architecture still fulfills the original constraints.

Third, although ACT-R, for example, contains distinct modules, they differ from INC's quasi-modular processes (cf. chap. 2). Modules in unified cognitive architectures are not about the generation of preverbal messages or the construction of a conceptual representation but, for example, contain the current goal of the system. Put differently, the processes (modules) of unified cognitive architectures are general processes of cognition, not processes specialized on a particular task. (EPIC can be seen as an exception, because its perceptual processors function comparably to INC's processes.) A Soar model that comes close to being modular in the INC sense is NL-Soar by Lewis (1996), a Soar model for natural language processing. Generally, this model, as all other Soar models, uses Soar's nonmodular processing mechanisms (Lewis, 1996). Thus, NL-Soar is a *horizontal* architecture in the sense of Fodor (1983), that is, an architecture that shares mechanisms and resources across domains. Yet, the model also exhibits modular properties: informational encapsulation, domain specificity, mandatoriness, and speed (operators need on the order of 100 ms; cf § 11). However, it must be doubted whether the claimed informational encapsulation stands the test: Because of the learning mechanism, each rule can be taken to be combined with other rules, or the function of a rule can change.

In continuation of the discussion of modularity (chap. 2), this raises the following question: What does a process like selection in INC model? A general selection faculty or a specialized one? (In Fodor's (1983, pp. 10–23) terms, are the processes horizontal or vertical faculties?) Remember that the conceptualizer is a mediator between the central executive and language-specific modules (§ 9). Comparing INC to a model like NL-Soar places INC somewhere between the domain-general, central processes and the specialized, informationally encapsulated, peripheral modules like the manual motor module of EPIC or ACT-R. This supports what I stated already in chapter 2: The components of the conceptualizer are quasi-modules that are cognitively impenetrable but informationally encapsulated (p. 31).

The fourth difference between unified cognitive architectures and INC is that in INC, the degree of informational encapsulation of a component is an important aspect of modeling. In particular, an incremental process does not have access to all knowledge of the model. Furthermore, allowing indirect feedback has the consequence that informational encapsulation is not strict. This does not mean that in a unified cognitive architecture, all knowledge can be used to solve a problem. However, as Lewis (2001) states, there are no architectural barriers to the knowledge that can be used for a computation. The consequence is that unified cognitive architectures rely heavily on the self-organization of the (given and learned) knowledge, whereas in models like INC, the builder of the model defines the informational encapsulation of the components during the model's development.

In addition to these differences, it is telling that (with the notable exception of NL-Soar) unified cognitive architectures are rarely used to model language phenomena—despite the fact that language plays a key role in understanding human cognition. It is likely that unified cognitive architectures would have to be extended and adapted to account for language. (See, for example, Guhe, 2006, on problems to capture refNet-like representations in ACT-R.) From a practical perspective, this implies that it is currently easier to write new models for language-related issues.

Summing up, there are certain problems with building a specialized model and not using a unified cognitive architecture. Furthermore, it is likely that at least a similarly working model of a conceptualizer can be constructed within a unified cognitive architecture. Nevertheless, investigating incremental processing in the way I do it here can hardly be achieved within a unified cognitive architecture.

§34   Principles used in building INC

In the first two parts, I laid out the general framework that I used in designing INC. However, because this framework is scattered over many chapters, I now lay out in a concise form the architectural principles that guided its design.

The most important principle is Extended Wundt's Principle, which can also be referred to as *massive incrementality* or *early-commitment strategy*. It is the main mechanism by which the bounded rationality of INC is realized. Extended Wundt's Principle means, in particular, that there is no explicit reasoning about the *when-to-say* (p. 71). From this follows the use of simple, small, "dumb" processes, which are very fast. The complex behavior of the model is a result of their interaction.

Neither left-to-right nor full incrementality is desirable in its pure form for a cognitive model. For this reason, INC uses the strategy to evaluate local contexts within the available knowledge around the focused element that step by step take different and/or more knowledge into account. Although the issue of word-based versus constituent-based incrementality is not applicable here as such, the underlying question of defining the increments of the single processes will be answered in detail in this part. Although the notions of *partial* and *qualitative* versus *quantitative* incrementality are not particularly useful, in those terms INC is a quantitative, incremental model. INC is an unboundedly incremental model; that is, the amount of time that is required for processing input not only depends on the size of the input (p. 76). Most of the incremental processes of INC use linear incrementality most of the time. Hierarchical incrementality is only used by PVM-generation when it decides to verbalize a description that refers to other refOs (chap. 12). Although preformated incrementality is a very attractive possibility to generate subsequent preverbal messages that stress a contrast, it is not yet used by INC. Thus, INC only uses free-format incrementality.

INC's means of structuring are processes, and because it uses update increments to keep track of the changes in the external state of affairs, it is nonmonotonic. Due to the lack of lookahead and the use of Extended Wundt's Principle, buffering and indirect feedback are the means to reduce the number of updates and to enhance the robustness of the model—apart from an experimental monitoring component. The processes in INC generate no parallel increments, so that the number of increments is always 1. The parallelism of the incremental processes in a cascaded architecture means that the model is indeterministic, and the use of local contexts means that consistency is not ascertained. (However, the representations in the current version of INC are consistent, which means that INC has no mechanisms for resolving inconsistencies.) Finally, INC is a discrete, modular model.

§ 35   *Processes*

INC's overall architecture is shown in figure 8.1. It consists of four main processes that form the cascade of this incremental model (terms 18 and 19 in §24), one auxiliary process (the concept matcher), and two storages (memories) for representations. The four main processes that constitute the cascade are construction, selection, linearization, and PVM-generation (§13). In short, construction reads the output of the perceptual PPU, called *perceived entities*, and builds up the current conceptual representation (CCR) from them with the help of the concept matcher. (Concept matcher and *concept storage* [CS] could also be seen as part of construction; cf. §36.) Each time construction modifies the CCR, it informs selection of the change, which decides whether the changed element will be verbalized. If it changed the plans for verbalization it notifies linearization, which checks whether the sequence of the events selected for verbalization needs to be reordered. PVM-generation, finally,

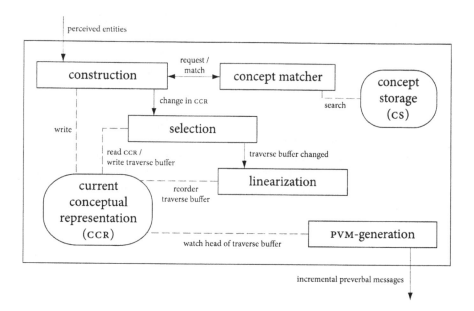

Figure 8.1: The architecture of INC

takes one of the events and generates an incremental preverbal message for it. There is no increment stream between linearization and PVM-generation, because these processes coordinate their operations via the traverse buffer, which contains the events that were chosen for verbalization by selection but for which PVM-generation did not generate an incremental preverbal message yet (§ 41).

The discussion on the number of increments (pp. 92–93) showed that there is an alternative to an architecture with a fixed cascade of processes, namely to use multiple instances of a process that run in parallel (de Smedt, 1990a, p. 142). For an incremental formulator, de Smedt (1990a) argues as follows:

> Clearly, a parallel formulator has an advantage compared to one which operates in a sequential mode. Newly incoming fragments which take little processing time can be uttered before older but more difficult fragments are ready. This suggests that the time when a fragment can be uttered depends not only on the moment when it has entered the formulator, but also on how much processing time the formulator spends on it. Extraposition of long and complicated phrases at the end of the sentence, which is often found in spontaneous speech, is indeed predicted by this model. (p. 82)

Spawning multiple processes raises new problems. First, either the results of the processes must be integrated when the processes terminate, or the result of one process must be determined as the overall result. Second, processes spawned simultaneously will terminate at different times; that is, there is a new coordination problem. Thus, spawning processes increases overhead for managing the instances. However, it can reduce the overall run-time. The processes in INC that could profit from this are the concept matcher and PVM-generation and, to a lesser degree, also construction.* Whether using this method would actually improve INC will have to be evaluated in future versions.

In the implementation of INC, there are maximally two instances of a process and only for a very short period. This happens when a process has finished one iteration of its loop and just waits for an acknowledgment that a change in the CCR has been completed before it starts the next iteration. For example, when construction inserted a new refO into the CCR, the CCR acknowledges the modification. (More precisely: the acknowledgement is sent by the process in which the CCR is encapsulated; see chap. 9.) Before construction can operate on the CCR again, it has to wait for this acknowledgment, so that it does not operate on an old state of the CCR. Nevertheless, it can already read the next input increment from the PPU and prepare it for processing. Thus, these operations can be carried out in parallel. However, cases like these are the exception in the implementation of INC, and the mentioned coordination problems do not arise.

§ 36   *Representations*

INC does not possess a detailed memory model; it contains no learning or forgetting mechanisms. Furthermore, INC makes no claims about access and storing of information. The memories are linearly searched without accounting for an organization of memory, say, with regard to the domain. INC has two memories, the CCR and the CS, which is analogous to the well-known distinction between working memory (CCR) and long-term memory (CS). Put differently, the CS contains encyclopedic knowledge and the CCR contains situation and discourse knowledge. Thus, INC's model knowledge (term 12) consists of the CCR and the CS. This is a more differentiated memory structure than Levelt's (1989).

The CCR could be split up in multiple representations so that each incremental process of the cascade contains its own memory. There are three arguments against this. First, multiple memories cause unnecessary redundancies. Second, no indirect

---

* The concept matcher could match the candidate list handed over by construction against multiple concepts in parallel. PVM-generation could chose designations for multiple refOs in parallel. Construction could generate multiple candidate lists that could be sent to multiple instances of the concept matcher. (Candidate lists are introduced in § 43.)

feedback could be given via the shared memory. Third, all models of memory assume an integrated structure (e.g., Newell (1990, p. 164)).

The CCR is not subdivided further into articulatory buffer, visuo-spatial sketch-pad, and central executive (Eysenck & Keane, 1995, pp. 129–134). It can be said, however, that the latter two are relevant for conceptualization, whereas the articulatory buffer need not be considered because it is located further down in the language production system. Hence, I consider no interferences between the articulatory buffer and other parts of working memory, if there are any. Furthermore, I will say nothing about the division of labor between the visuo-spatial sketchpad and the central executive. However, the processes operating on spatial knowledge—which object is located where and which object is moving how—mainly use the visuo-spatial sketchpad, and the processes that reason about verbalizations mainly use the central executive. As both are located in the working memory, it is likely that there are interferences. Yet, nothing of this is considered in INC.

The CS can only be accessed by the concept matcher, and the concept matcher is connected only to construction. Thus, CS and concept matcher could be integrated into construction. They are modeled separately in INC, because (a) they have well-defined, self-contained functions, (b) the concept matcher executes an incremental algorithm different from construction's, and (c) this algorithm is only indirectly involved in building up the CCR. The concept matcher can be seen as interface to long-term memory that can be replaced by a different process without affecting the way construction works.

It is arguable whether it is the best way to call the distinction between CS and CCR the one between working memory and long-term memory, even if it is analogous to the way this is done in unified cognitive architectures. The more important distinction in INC is the one between the previously available knowledge that is used for constructing a conceptual representation (CS) and the conceptual representation that contains the knowledge constructed while INC is running (CCR).

§ 37   Increments

The following list gives an overview over the increments used by INC. They are described in more detail in the following sections and chapters in the context of the corresponding processes and representations:

- Perceived entities (INC's input),
- The increments of incremental preverbal messages (INC's output),
- Candidate list and best match (the latter consisting of match list and DOA; § 38)—this is information exchanged between construction and concept matcher,

- Notification of changes in the CCR sent from construction to selection and from selection to linearization,
- The pointers to refOs in the CCR that are stored in the traverse buffer, including update increments for modifying the traverse buffer.

§38 Parameters

INC is a parameterized model, a property not depicted in figure 8.1. When INC is started, values are assigned to these parameters and influence INC's behavior. Note that they only influence INC's behavior and do not determine it, because INC is an indeterministic model (§34).* Thus, despite identical parameter values and identical input, the behavior and the generated output can differ. INC has four parameters (§59 describes ideas for additional ones).

❧ DEGREE OF AGREEMENT THRESHOLD (DOAT).   The concept matcher determines the degree of agreement (DOA) between a list of refOs that it obtains from construction, the candidate list, and the concepts stored in the CS. It gives back the entry with the highest DOA to construction, which is the best match. Construction then decides whether the DOA of best match and candidate list is high enough to insert the best match into the CCR. This is the case if DOA ⩾ DOAT. DOA and DOAT are values between 0 and 1. This decision is relevant in cases in which the candidate list does not contain all elements that the best match comprises. (Otherwise DOA = 1, and DOA ⩾ DOAT.) If DOA ⩾ DOAT and DOAT < 1, the missing elements of the best match are also inserted into the CCR by construction. As they were not actually perceived, they are marked *expected*. For a detailed account of these computations, see chapter 10.

❧ LENGTH OF TRAVERSE BUFFER (LOTB).   The parameter LOTB determines the length of the traverse buffer, that is, the maximum number of elements that can be stored in the traverse buffer. The traverse buffer is an increment buffer that contains pointers to the events that were selected for verbalization but for which PVM-generation did not yet generate a preverbal message. While the elements are in the traverse buffer, linearization can reorder them. The minimum value of LOTB is 1 (LOTB ⩾ 1), because PVM-generation needs to access an element of the traverse buffer to start generating an incremental preverbal message, and a buffer of

---

* The indeterminism is caused INC's parallel processes. The Mozart/Oz system in which INC is implemented simulates this parallelism; that is, it uses concurrency. The important point here is that INC cannot influence the scheduling of the processes, which makes it an indeterministic system.

length o cannot store anything. If LOTB = 1, no linearization can take place, because it requires at least two elements. If selection appends an element to the traverse buffer while it is filled, the first element (the head of traverse buffer) is removed ("forgotten").

☙ LATENCY (LT).   The latency is the time that an element is kept in the traverse buffer until it is taken out by PVM-generation. LT is realized in the following way: When selection inserts an element into the traverse buffer, a time stamp (t_s) of the current system time (t_c) is saved with it. PVM-generation monitors the head of traverse buffer. When $t_s + LT \geqslant t_c$ (i.e., when the latency expired), the element is removed by PVM-generation, and a preverbal message is generated for it.

☙ ACTIVATION THRESHOLD (AT).   The activation threshold is used in PVM-generation. After PVM-generation decided to verbalize a refO, designations from the refO are chosen that constitute an adequate verbalization. Because a refO can have a large number of designations, constraints are used for deciding which designations are used in the preverbal message. One of these constraints checks the activation* of designations a_d, and if $a_d \geqslant AT$, this constraint is not violated. However, the designation may still be chosen if it is required for completing a preverbal message.

§ 39   *Preprocessing unit (PPU) and perceived entities (PES)*

Although there is no sharp boundary between perceptual and conceptual processing (see, e.g., Barsalou, 1999, p. 588), INC is a model of conceptual processing only. The perceptual preprocessing is carried out by a separate component, the PPU. The output increments of the PPU are INC's input increments (more precisely construction's). These increments are *perceived entities* (PES). This section gives a rough sketch of how the PPU computes PES. The exact way this is done is beyond the scope of this book; a detailed description for the sketch maps domain, for which INC was first developed (§53), is given in Guhe and Huber (1999).

   PES are computed from spatio-temporal coordinates, which are generated by the environment playing the scenes on the screen. For motion events, the input to the PPU consists of sequences of 5-tuples of the following form:

(1)   (frameID, objectID, x-coordinate, y-coordinate, direction)

   For example, a sequence of

---

* INC uses static activations for designations; that is, the activation is assigned when a designation is created and does not change afterward. This should be extended by a decay and reactivation mechanism (§58).

(2) $\langle (1, 1, 50, 100, 90), (2, 1, 54, 112, 89), (3, 1, 52, 127, 91) \rangle$

of positions of an object, say, a plane, with the identifier 1 is translated into a PE that represents a straight movement in the time interval [1, 3] from coordinates (50, 100) to (52, 127). The direction of the object is the most recent one—91 in this example. As can be seen in this made-up example, the PPU must be able cope with noise: The object is not moving along a completely straight path. It starts with a value on the x-axis of 50. At the next snapshot, it has a value of 54, and at the final snapshot one of 52. Nevertheless, on the conceptual level, it is desirable to consider this movement as straight. For this example, a triple of PES is generated that corresponds to the following referential net:

(3)

$$
\begin{array}{lll}
\text{object} \longrightarrow & r1 & \longleftarrow \eta x \, plane(x) \\
\text{plane} & & \searrow \eta x \, chpos(r2, x, r3) \\
pe(o) & &
\end{array}
$$

$$
\begin{array}{lll}
\text{situation} \longrightarrow & r2 & \longrightarrow \eta x \, chpos(x, r1, r3) \\
pe(1) & & \\
at\_time(1, 3) & &
\end{array}
$$

$$
\begin{array}{lll}
\text{path} \longrightarrow & r3 & \longleftarrow \eta x \, chpos(r2, r1, x) \\
pe(2) & & \searrow \eta x \, straight(x)
\end{array}
$$

(See appendix B for the exact format of PES.) The direction information is currently not used. The at_time attribute serves to synchronize INC to the points in time when the events occurred. This is necessary, because INC reads its input from a file (chap. 13). Note that the number identifying the object in the 5-tuples is a different number than the one given in the pe attribute (the object with ID 1 becomes pe(o)). The former is generated by the program with which the planes are displayed on the screen and enables the PPU to identify the objects. The latter is used on the interface between PPU and INC for referring to PES, for example, if the PPU must inform INC about an update of a PE.

   For an example of an update, assume that the third 5-tuple is (3, 1, 56, 127, 92). The PPU may still classify the movement as straight. Yet, because the PPU must work incrementally (otherwise INC could not operate incrementally), at a given point in time, not all information is available that may be necessary for the correct and complete computation of an output. If the next 5-tuple is (4, 1, 60, 142, 94), the path should be classified as curved, because the evidence for a curved movement is now much stronger, whereas the justification for assuming a straight movement got weaker. The value on the x-axis increased starting from time frame 1; thus, the curved movement does not start at the current time frame 4 but at frame 1. This means that corresponding corrections must be made, which is done by updating PES.

The PPU segments movements according to two criteria:

1. An object changes between moving and not moving.
2. The shape of the path changes.

An example of the first case is given in the introductory example. When the plane stops, the situation in which it moved ends, and a new situation starts in which it is not moving but standing. An example of the second case is a plane that moves on a straight path and then begins to follow a curved path. The point where the plane commences the curved movement is the segmentation point between the two situations (cf. the example discussed in §52).

I assume another idealization apart from the sharp distinction between perception and conceptualization, namely the unidirectionality of information flow. That is, no information is given back from INC to the PPU. This limits the cognitive adequacy of the proposed model, because there are clear influences from cognition to perception. For example, priming effects occur on the perceptual as well as on the cognitive level. Cast in INC terminology, this means two things. First, expected elements in the conceptual representation are processed faster than nonexpected elements. Second, the PPU must be sensitive to results of INC's computations. Therefore, INC should be extended to give feedback to the PPU. However, because I concentrate on the data-driven aspects of conceptualization, INC gives no feedback to the PPU. Support that this is a valid idealization comes from Barsalou (1999, p. 588–589). He emphasizes the fact that although the interrelation between perception and cognition is bidirectional, the bottom-up (data-driven) information, in most cases, dominates over top-down information. That is, information from perception to cognition exerts more influence than information flowing in the opposite direction.

A final remark on the term *perceived entity*. I chose this term—especially in contrast to *basic entity*—to make clear that these entities are actually perceived and do not belong to a fixed level of granularity. For example, a motion event can be perceived as consisting of subevents or as a whole. INC is designed in a way that it can deal with both. That is, it is able to segment one motion event into subevents on the basis of conceptual knowledge, and it is able to group motion events to more complex events. Currently, however, only the second possibility is implemented.

$$\sim \quad 9 \quad \sim$$

CURRENT CONCEPTUAL REPRESENTATION (CCR)

T HE CURRENT CONCEPTUAL REPRESENTATION (CCR) is INC's central storage device. Together with the concept storage (CS), it constitutes INC's model knowledge. Here, I describe its functions in more detail (§40). The CCR contains two specialized structures: the traverse buffer (§41), which contains the event refOs that have been selected for verbalization but are not yet verbalized, and the traverse (§42), which contains all the refOs that were sent to the formulator as part of an incremental preverbal message. The CCR is a shared memory that contains INC's knowledge of the current external state of affairs. Although this may also be called a blackboard, I use the term *shared memory*, because this emphasizes the fact that it models a part of human memory as an integrated representation used by all processes of INC's cascade.

§ 40   *The representation*

The CCR contains the conceptual representation for a perceived state of affairs represented as a referential net. The knowledge on how to construct the conceptual representation is stored in the CS (§44). The name *current* conceptual representation emphasizes the fact that the CCR is permanently changing. Its function is comparable to working memories of unified cognitive architectures (§36).

The CCR is an internal representation (§19), so it is not a one-to-one representation of the external world. On the one hand, it contains some entities (more precisely, representations of entities) that are not present in the external world (e.g., expectations). On the other hand, it lacks entities that are present in the external world but did not "make it" into the CCR, because they were not attended to or because they were filtered out in previous processing steps, for example, in the PPU. The same is true for attributes of entities and relations between entities. Examples of actual states of the CCR are given and discussed in the context of how they are processed (cf. the referential nets given in figs. 4.2 and 13.3.

The CCR is constructed from the input increments of construction: Each PE received by construction is added to the CCR. The construction process—with the help of the concept matcher—builds up the CCR in an interplay between PEs, rules in the CS, and the current state of the CCR. Each time construction modifies the

CCR, the selection process evaluates whether the changed element is verbalized (i.e., whether an utterance describing it is generated), and linearization checks whether the elements selected for verbalization should be reordered. PVM-generation uses the knowledge in the CCR for the generation of incremental preverbal messages. All knowledge that is part of a preverbal message is also stored in the *traverse*, which is the memory of what has been said (cf. §42; chap. 12). This knowledge can be used in the generation of subsequent preverbal messages, for example, for generating reduced or anaphoric expressions.

The CCR is implemented as separate process, which is connected to the cascade's processes via increment streams. Increment streams are unidirectional, and so there are two increment streams between the CCR process and each of the processes of the cascade. This way, each process has its own view on the CCR; that is, each process can access only part of the representation. This is implemented by restricted access functions that the CCR process executes on the referential net, depending on the cascade process that requests an operation.

There are three main motivations for using only one data structure:

1. It is more efficient in terms of storage capacity, because it reduces unnecessary redundancies.
2. It is compliant with the principles of unified cognitive architectures. One reason is that—especially in the more central components of cognition—the informational encapsulation is not strict (cf. the discussion of quasi-modules, p. 31).
3. It allows indirect feedback. In INC, this is mainly done via the traverse buffer. Other possibilities, which are not used yet, include that selection and linearization can make their choices dependent on the verbalization refOs, which are generated by PVM-generation and stored in the traverse.

These reasons are not imperative, and the internal conceptual representation can be organized differently so that each process has an internal storage. However, this requires converting the indirect feedback to explicit feedback. The disadvantage of this solution is that it significantly increases the cost for maintaining these storages.

The CCR contains two special substructures: the traverse and the traverse buffer. Figure 9.1 contains a symbolic depiction.*

---

* The traverse buffer was originally considered a part of the traverse (Guhe & Habel, 2001; Guhe et al., 2000; Guhe & Huber, 2000). This is fine if event and object structures are more or less isomorphic, as in sketch generation events (Guhe & Habel, 2001), but it causes problems when they are not. Additionally, the traverse was considered simply a path through the CCR. A problem with this is that this information structure is not rich enough for a discourse memory, because different verbalizations of different states of an object or event are not preserved and cannot be referred to. Among other things, it is impossible to determine whether an entity can be referred to by a reduced referring expression like a pronoun. Although these terms have lost some of their original motivation, I keep them for continuity's sake.

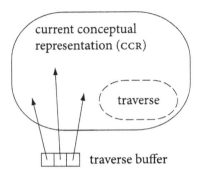

Figure 9.1: The CCR, including traverse and traverse buffer

TERM 26: TRAVERSE
The traverse is the path through the CCR consisting of the verbalization refOs in the order in which they were generated.

Verbalization refOs are generated by PVM-generation from refOs in the CCR. Each time it sends a refO to the formulator as part of an incremental preverbal message, it creates a new verbalization refO, which is appended to the traverse. The verbalization refO contains all information given to the formulator in the current preverbal message (term 30, p. 155). Additionally, the traverse preserves the sequence in which the verbalization refOs were generated. The traverse is the basis of the discourse memory, as it contains all information that has been verbalized.

TERM 27: TRAVERSE BUFFER
The traverse buffer is an increment buffer that contains pointers to all refOs that were selected for verbalization but are not yet verbalized. If a refO is appended to the traverse buffer when it is filled, the first element (the head of traverse buffer*) is deleted.*

Each time a refO is verbalized, that is, a verbalization refO is generated for it, the pointer is removed from the traverse buffer. As only the head of traverse buffer is accessible to PVM-generation, it is the only pointer that PVM-generation can remove. Otherwise, only selection can add or remove the elements stored in the traverse buffer by appending and replacing elements. (Linearization can only change the order of elements.)

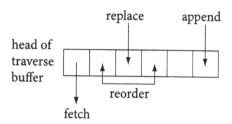

Figure 9.2: Operations on the traverse buffer

§ 41   *Traverse buffer*

The traverse buffer is an increment buffer that is accessed by the processes selection, linearization, and PVM-generation. Its length is specified by the parameter LOTB (§ 38). When selection chooses a refO for verbalization, it inserts a pointer to the refO into the traverse buffer. The pointer stays in the buffer until PVM-generation produces a preverbal message with the referenced refO as its starting point (cf. Guhe, 2003; chap. 12, this vol.). The traverse buffer contains pointers (and not copies of refOs like the traverse), because PVM-generation requires the current knowledge stored with a refO when it generates a preverbal message, and this knowledge may change while the pointer is in the buffer. (Because all other refOs are directly retrieved from the CCR by PVM-generation, only the refO the verbalization starts with would be out of date, which would be an odd distinction. And updating the refOs in the traverse buffer each time they change in the CCR would be unnecessarily complex.)

The traverse buffer can only be changed by few operations. Selection can append an element to the buffer or replace an existing element (but not simply delete one), linearization can reorder elements, and PVM-generation can fetch elements, in particular, the head of traverse buffer. These operations are symbolically depicted in figure 9.2.

Because the number of elements is limited, an append operation can cause the loss of an element: When the buffer is filled and selection appends an element, the head of traverse buffer is deleted. Observe that this need not be the element that is in the buffer for the longest time, because linearization may put an element in head position that is newer; thus, even the most recent element can be pushed out of the buffer.* Because selection has no access to the fill level of the traverse

---

* For cognitive adequacy, it might be better to delete the element with the lowest activation. However, since activation is not yet fully integrated in the INC model, this is an idea for future versions.

buffer, IN C does not "notice" that the head of traverse buffer gets lost. (It is just recorded in the log file during a simulation.) Although this possesses some cognitive justification—we usually do not notice that we forget something—selection could make its choices dependent on the number of elements in the traverse buffer. If the buffer is in danger of being filled, selection can adapt its strategy accordingly.

The length of the traverse buffer can be considered proportional to the size of the part of working memory that is available for this temporary storage function. Yet, the CCR itself functions as simple working memory; so this does not mean that the working memory has a capacity of the number of items specified by LOTB (perhaps even like the "magical number seven plus or minus two" of Miller, 1956). Instead, LOTB is only a relative measure of the memory size for this temporary storage function in one simulation versus another one.

The second parameter relevant for the traverse buffer is LT (latency; §38). It determines how long an element must remain in the traverse buffer before PVM-generation can take it out. This gives linearization time to make its computations and reorderings, and it allows selection to revert choices. (Due to Extended Wundt's Principle, there are many revisions.) It is not ascertained, however, that directly after LT has expired, the element is taken out of the traverse buffer. Because PVM-generation only has access to the head of traverse buffer, and elements can be reordered by linearization, an element can be in the traverse buffer as long as IN C is running—provided it never becomes head of traverse buffer after its latency expired.

IN C does not keep track of cases in which a speaker remembers wanting to say something, without actually doing so. Because the traverse buffer is only a temporary memory, such information is lost. While there are settings in which retaining such cases would be useful or even necessary, my solution is in accordance with the view that working memory is not capable of storing information permanently (Eysenck & Keane, 1995, 129–134).

42   Traverse

The traverse is a path through the CCR that contains all verbalization refOs in the temporal order in which they were created (term 26). Thus, it contains all information IN C sent to the formulator. In this way, the traverse serves as a basic discourse memory. However, it must be distinguished from another part of the discourse memory: By recording what is sent to the formulator, the speaker/conceptualizer keeps track of what he *wants* to say; by recording what comes in from the language comprehension system via the monitoring component, he knows what he actually *said*. As I do not consider information from other interlocutors here, these are the only kinds of information available. The traverse contains only refOs of the first kind. That is, the traverse is that part of the discourse memory with the information of what the speaker intended to say. The information of what he actually said is represented in the *monitored traverse* (term 31, p. 191), where the information received by the monitor is stored (chap. 14).

When PVM-generation hands on a refO to the formulator, it has to decide which knowledge from the refO is used for the utterance it currently generates; that is, it has to choose the refO's designations and attributes. When the head of traverse buffer is deleted, a verbalization refO for the refO is created, and the verbalization refO is appended to the traverse. This verbalization refO contains the information that is used in this particular verbalization of the original refO.

The information of a refO used in a verbalization is not simply duplicated. The references of a verbalization refO to other refOs always refer to other verbalization refOs, not to the original refO. This is necessary for using the traverse as discourse memory. Consider a short, abstract example in which the CCR contains the following two refOs:

(1)

$$\begin{array}{c} \text{sort}_1 \longrightarrow \\ \text{att}_1 \nearrow \end{array} \text{r5} \begin{array}{c} \longleftarrow \text{'NAME'} \\ \searrow \eta x\, p_1(x) \end{array}$$

$$\begin{array}{c} \text{sort}_2 \longrightarrow \\ \text{att}_2 \nearrow \end{array} \text{r7} \longrightarrow \eta x\, p_2(x, \text{r5})$$

A sequence of verbalization refOs generated by PVM-generation out of this CCR may look as follows:

(2)

$$\begin{array}{c} \text{sort}_1 \longrightarrow \\ \text{att}_1 \nearrow \\ \text{verb\_of(r5)} \nearrow \end{array} \text{v1} \longrightarrow \text{'NAME'}$$

$$\begin{array}{c} \text{sort}_2 \longrightarrow \\ \text{att}_2 \nearrow \\ \text{verb\_of(r7)} \nearrow \end{array} \text{v2} \longrightarrow \eta x\, p_2(x, \text{v1})$$

$$\begin{array}{c} \text{sort}_2 \longrightarrow \\ \text{att}_2 \nearrow \\ \text{verb\_of(r7)} \nearrow \end{array} \text{v3} \longrightarrow \eta x\, p_2(x, \text{v4})$$

$$\begin{array}{c} \text{sort}_1 \longrightarrow \\ \text{att}_1 \nearrow \\ \text{verb\_of(r5)} \nearrow \end{array} \text{v4} \longrightarrow \eta x\, p_1(x)$$

There are two verbalizations of r5 (v1 and v4) and two verbalizations of r7 (v2 and v3). In the first verbalization of r5, the 'NAME' designation is used; in the second, the description $\eta x \, p_1(x)$. The important point here is that there are the two verbalizations of r7. Both use the same original description, $\eta x \, p_2(x, r5)$. For the system to know, for example, which verbalization of r5 the description belonging to v3 refers to, the original reference to r5 is replaced by the corresponding verbalization refO (v4) during the generation of the incremental preverbal message.

This implies that forward references have to be used (and resolved). At the point of time when v3 is created by PVM-generation and $\eta x \, p_2(x, r5)$ is chosen to verbalize the refO, the reference to r5 must already be replaced by the corresponding verbalization refO. The reason is that immediately after its creation, the verbalization refO (v3 in this case) is sent to the formulator. Yet, in the way PVM-generation operates this is no problem, because deciding on one designation means that all refOs that the designation refers to must be verbalized as well. For the example, this means that another refO for the verbalization of r5 must be created as soon as PVM-generation decides to use $\eta x \, p_2(x, r5)$ for verbalizing r7. This happens during the creation of v3. The automatic refO numbering mechanism decides at this point to call the verbalization refO v4. If no designation is found for verbalizing r5 later on, v4 will be generated as an empty verbalization refO, that is, a verbalization refO containing no designation. The underlying idea is that such verbalization refOs may be encoded as pro-forms by the formulator, for example, as pronouns. (See chap. 12 for further details.)

CONSTRUCTION

C ONSTRUCTION IS THE first process in INC's cascade. It builds up the current conceptual representation (CCR) by reading perceived entities (PEs) from the preprocessing unit (PPU) and calling the concept matcher to find more complex concepts. Depending on the concept matcher's results, construction modifies the CCR and sends a notification to selection. As the concept matcher interacts exclusively with construction, it could also be modeled as part of the construction task. Due to this close connection, I not only describe the construction process (§ 43) but also the concept matcher (§ 44) and the concept storage (§ 45) in this chapter.

In this and the following chapters, I discuss INC's algorithms in detail and provide pseudo-code. I assume the reader is familiar with such notations, and I presuppose a set of common operations—especially list operations—like Append*, Filter, Replace, Delete, and so forth. These operations are particularly important, because increment streams and increment buffers are implemented as lists.

§ 43 The process

The construction process receives PEs and builds up the CCR from them.† It is supported by the concept matcher. Constructions sends lists of refOs, called *candidate lists*, to the concept matcher. A candidate list contains refOs from the CCR; that is, PEs as well as refOs that were generated as results of previous matches. The concept matcher returns the best match, namely the concept in the concept storage (CS) that has the highest degree of agreement (DOA) with the refOs in the candidate list. If the DOA is greater than or equal to the degree of agreement threshold (DOAT), construction updates the CCR accordingly; otherwise, the match is ignored. Construction is the process most similar to anytime algorithms, because it tries to find more complex concepts until no new candidate list can be assembled or a new PE is

---

* Append will stand for appending a list to a list as well as appending an element to a list. Furthermore, I will not distinguish the Append operation on an increment buffer, which includes the deletion of an element if the buffer is full, from the Append operation on an increment stream, where this restriction does not exist. In the actual implementation, these operations are, of course, realized by different functions. *Mutatis mudandis* this holds for the other functions.

† More precisely, the basis of the CCR consists of refOs that are generated by construction for the PEs it receives from the PPU. For simplicity's sake, I simply refer to these refOs as PEs.

```
var pe,  #the PE received from the PPU
    fe,  #focused element
    candidate_list,  #candidate list (local context)
    best_match, match_list, doa  #return values of the concept matcher
    doat  #the value of the parameter DOAT
wait input_stream ≠ ⟨⟩
fe ← pe ← Fetch(input_stream)
Insert(pe, ccr)
repeat
    candidate_list ← ComputeCandidateList(fe)
    best_match ← (match_list, doa) ← ConceptMatcher(fe, candidate_list)
    if doa ⩾ doat then
        Update(match_list, ccr)
    endif
    if input_stream = ⟨⟩ then
        fe ← ComputeNewFE(best_match, fe)
    else
        fe ← pe ← Fetch(input_stream)
        if Type(pe) = new then
            Insert(pe, ccr)
        elsif Type(pe) = update then
            Update(pe, ccr)
        endif
    endif
until pe = eof
```

Figure 10.1: The construction process

available. In the first case, it suspends itself until it receives a new PE.

Because the concept matcher only interacts with construction and the CS is only accessible by the concept matcher, both could also be seen as part of construction. However, the CS represents INC's long-term memory, that is, the knowledge that is available independently from the currently observed scene. Thus, the concept matcher can be seen as an interface between working memory and long-term memory. Viewing the concept matcher as separate process helps to keep these memories apart.

The pseudo-code for the construction process is given in figure 10.1. Variables are lowercased, and functions uppercased. Roughly, the incremental algorithm of construction (in the sense of term 16, p. 84) consists of calling the concept matcher and evaluating the match result.

Construction waits until the first pe is available in the input_stream (the wait statement). As soon as this is the case, the pe is fetched and inserted into the ccr. It is also the new focused element (fe). Then construction loops until the PPU signals that no more input will follow by sending eof.* The first operation in the loop consists of taking fe and computing the candidate_list for the call of the concept matcher (cf. figure 10.3).† So, the local contexts of construction are candidate lists.‡

The return value of the function calling the concept matcher is a pair consisting of match_list and doa; this is the best_match. The *match list* contains pairs of refOs. Each pair consists of a CS refO and its matching CCR refO (if the CCR contains such a refO). If the best_match is good enough, that is, if doa $\geq$ doat, then the ccr is updated accordingly. The Update operation takes into account that refOs that are part of the best match can already be in the CCR. There are three critical cases for this operation. First, the DOA can be smaller than 1; that is, the match contains refOs for which the CCR contains no corresponding ones that were already perceived. In this case, new refOs are created and inserted into the CCR for the ones without counterpart in the match list. These refOs are marked expected.

Second, the best match can be different from the previous one. For example, it may turn out that the PLANE that is expected to move toward GATE-B21 is not moving there but toward RUNWAY-3. In this case, the expected CCR refOs must be discarded, here the expected situation and path refOs.

Third, there may already exist an expected refO in the CCR for a newly received PE. This case is quite complex, because there are now two refOs for the new PE: the expected refO inserted by the earlier match and a refO representing the PE.§ The best match makes it possible to establish the identity of these two refOs, and the refOs are fused. Put informally, in the fusion, the old refO changes its status from expected to regular, and the newly perceived entity contributes the information of how the refO actually "looks."

Figure 10.2 shows the five most important stages of the construction of the first part of the event structure for the example in chapter 1. This is the part in which the PLANE moves toward the GATE and stops, which corresponds to the first two phases of the scene. In stage 1, only the PE MOVEp is present, which is short for the refO representing the situation in which the plane moves. Assume that the best match resulting from the call of the concept matcher leads, in stage 2, to the

---

* Calling eof a PE is a bit misleading, but it simplifies the model.
† Executing the loop can be made dependent on the fact whether the pe is already present in the ccr as an expected refO. If this is the case, the status of the expected refO is changed to regular. This way it would be possible to model a real priming effect, because expected PEs are integrated directly without calling the concept matcher, whereas removing an expectation requires extra effort.
‡ Because the available knowledge of the concept matcher consists of the cs and the candidate list, it has no third argument as is usually required for an incremental algorithm. In other words, the concept matcher cannot modify a representation that exists independently from it.
§ The match involving the PE must yield the same complex concept as the last one, because otherwise the expectations would have been discarded already.

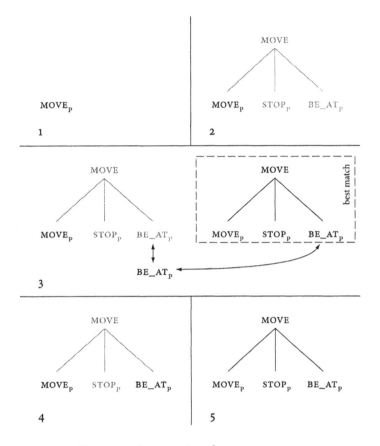

Figure 10.2: Construction of an event structure

insertion of three expected refOs, depicted in gray. In stage 3, the next PE is read by construction. This is the left black BE_ATp node. The concept matcher is then called with the two (black) concepts MOVEp and BE_ATp as candidate list. Note that before the call of the concept matcher, the two left BE_ATp nodes are in no way related; that is, the relation indicated by the bidirectional arrow is not present before the concept matcher is called. The resulting best match, given on the right side in stage 3, is the same as the previous one. With the help of the best match, it can now be established that the two BE_ATp nodes must be identical and, therefore, fused.*
The result of the fusion results in stage 4. Finally, as all concepts for the match are

---

* The identity of the MOVEp in the CCR and the MOVEp of the best match also must be established again. The corresponding arrow is left out of the figure for better readability.

present ($\mathrm{DOA} = 1$), the status of the other two expected nodes changes to regular, shown as stage 5. CS rules and the functioning of the concept matcher are discussed in § 44 and § 45. The representation in this example includes only the event structure. Similar computations have to be carried out for the substructures containing the spatial and object information.

After the CCR is updated, the next call of the concept matcher is prepared. The first step is to check whether the input_stream is empty. In this case, the new fe is computed from the old fe and the best_match. The one possibility is that the new fe is the old one. Then a different local context must be determined for the call of the concept matcher.* The other possibility is that it is an element of the best match. In particular, after a successful match, that is, if $\mathrm{DOA} \geqslant \mathrm{DOAT}$, the new focused element is a complex concept of the best match. Because the concept matcher can give back multiple complex concepts in a match (§ 45), the new focused element in these cases always is the situation refO. (If multiple complex concepts are computed by the concept matcher, one concept always *is* a situation refO.) The reason for making this simplification is, again, that INC is a model of event conceptualization.

If a new input increment is present in the input_stream, it is fetched and becomes the new focused element of construction. If it is a new pe, it is inserted into the CCR; if it is an update increment, the old pe that is already in the CCR is updated. If also pe $\neq$ eof, the next iteration of the loop starts with the computation of the candidate_list.

The part of construction handling the suspension of the process is not given here, for reasons of brevity. The process considers suspending itself after the candidate_list of the next iteration is computed. If the values of best_match, fe, and candidate_list are identical to the previous ones, construction suspends itself until a new pe is available in the input_stream. Furthermore, figure 10.1 does not show the notifications, which are sent to selection each time construction modifies the CCR, eg by inserting a new refO.

The function computing the candidate lists is given in figure 10.3. (This is the function for the motion events domain; the one for sketch maps is essentially the same.) Its computations depend on whether the focused element (fe) is of the sort situation, object, or spatial_entity. In the first case, the largest local contexts are generated, which is due to the central role that situation refOs play in the domain

---

* This is currently not done by INC, because construction can deal with all examples investigated so far without determining different local contexts. Consequently, the heuristic computing candidate lists (ComputeCandidateList) does not do this. It is necessary in the general case, though, because the candidate list yielding the highest DOA may not have been found yet. The idea of increasingly broadening local contexts originated in the analysis of drawings of complex sketch maps, which consist of up to 150 PEs for events and for objects (300 *in all*).

```
fun ComputeCandidateList(fe)
   if Sort(fe) = situation then
     return Append(
        ExtractRefOs(Filter(DescriptionPreds(fe), Member([chpos, be_at, ...]))),
        ExtractRefOs(Filter(AttributeNames(fe), Member([temp_rels]))))
   elsif Sort(fe) = object then
     return nil  #currently, objects are not matched
   elsif Sort(fe) = spatial_entity then
     return ExtractRefOs(Filter(DescriptionPreds(fe),
        Member([finalpoint, startpoint, ...])))
   endif
endfun
```

Figure 10.3: Construction's heuristic for establishing the candidate list

and the representations used here. Informally speaking, these refOs are the glue of the conceptual representation. The designations of the fe are searched for those that have a predicate linking the situation refO to other refOs participating in the situation, mostly chpos, be_at, start, and stop. Additionally, the situation refOs directly connected to fe by a temporal relation become part of the local context.

In the second case, that is, if the sort of fe is object, no matching takes place, because the structure of objects has no direct influence on the conceptualization of motion events. (As example could be considered that objects moving on parallel paths can be grouped. But even in this case, the grouping is due to the parallelism of the paths, not because of properties of the objects.) Matching of objects is quite important for resultative events though, in the domain of sketch maps (Guhe & Huber, 2000).

The third case, finally, captures refOs of sort spatial_entity. In particular, paths and locations are grouped with calls of the concept matcher that use such local contexts.

§ 44   Concept storage (CS)

The CS is INC's second knowledge representation besides the CCR. In contrast to the CCR, it does not change over time; in particular, nothing is added, which would correspond to learning of categories. The CS corresponds to INC's long-term memory and can exclusively be accessed by the concept matcher. Hence, there are no different views on the CS. Like the CCR, the CS is a referential net. It consists of production-like rules of how simple concepts are related to more complex concepts.

This allows the concept matcher to make inferences about concepts on one level of the part-of hierarchy on the basis of knowledge about concepts on a neighboring level. The rules partition the cs; that is, they are not interconnected. A very simple rule for connecting two paths is as follows:

(1)
$$
\begin{array}{l}
\text{path} \longrightarrow r1 \longrightarrow \iota x\ endpoint(r3, x) \\
part\_of([r4])
\end{array}
$$

$$
\begin{array}{l}
\text{path} \longrightarrow r2 \longrightarrow \iota x\ startpoint(r3, x) \\
part\_of([r4])
\end{array}
$$

$$
\begin{array}{l}
\text{location} \longrightarrow r3 \longleftarrow \iota x\ endpoint(x, r1) \\
\qquad\qquad\qquad\qquad \iota x\ startpoint(x, r2)
\end{array}
$$

$$
\begin{array}{l}
\text{path} \longrightarrow r4 \\
concat([r1, r2]) \\
no\_of\_refOs(3)
\end{array}
$$

In this rule, r1 and r2 represent two PATHS that meet at the LOCATION represented by r3. The concat attribute of r4 is a special version of the parts attribute, which not only says that the listed refOs are parts of the refO but also that the subsumed refOs are concatenated in the sequence in which they are given in the list. Thus, in this rule, the refOs r1–r3 are matched onto a complex path, r4. The attribute no_of_refOs specifies the number of refOs that must be present for a DOA = 1. The concept matcher computes the DOA as ratio of the number of refOs present to the number of refOs specified in the rule (equation 3, p. 144). In this rule, two PATHS and the LOCATION connecting them must be present; thus, no_of_refOs = 3.

In a more detailed version of this rule, the PATHS each contain a description of their form.

(2)
$$
\begin{array}{l}
\text{path} \longrightarrow r1 \longleftarrow \iota x\ endpoint(r3, x) \\
part\_of([r4]) \qquad\qquad\quad \eta x\ straight(x)
\end{array}
$$

$$
\begin{array}{l}
\text{path} \longrightarrow r2 \longleftarrow \iota x\ startpoint(r3, x) \\
part\_of([r4]) \qquad\qquad\quad \eta x\ curved(x)
\end{array}
$$

$$
\begin{array}{l}
\text{location} \longrightarrow r3 \longleftarrow \iota x\ endpoint(x, r1) \\
\qquad\qquad\qquad\qquad \iota x\ startpoint(x, r2) \\
\qquad\qquad\qquad\qquad \eta x\ transitionpoint(x, r4) \longrightarrow *
\end{array}
$$

$$\begin{array}{l} \text{path} \longrightarrow \\ \text{concat}([r1, r2]) \\ \text{no\_of\_refOs}(3) \end{array} \quad r4 \quad \begin{array}{l} \longleftarrow \eta x \; \text{p\_curved}(x) \\ \longleftarrow \eta x \; \text{transitionpoint}(r3, x) \end{array}$$

This rule takes two refOs representing a straight PATH (r1) and a curved PATH (r2). The complex refO that is generated by applying this rule differs from the one above in that it contains an additional description specifying the form of the concatenated PATH (p_curved stands for *partially curved*) and in that the LOCATION where the two PATHS meet is a TRANSITIONPOINT. The special designation attribute ∗ marks those designations that have to be added to refOs already present in the CCR. So, if construction uses the match result of an application of this rule, it inserts a refO corresponding to r4 into the CCR, say r20, and adds the $\iota x \; \text{transitionpoint}(x, r20)$ description to the refO that has been matched onto r3.

The rules given so far have an illustrating purpose. Among other things, their results consist of only one complex refO. A rule for connecting two PATHS that is actually used by INC is shown in figure 10.4 (cf. the worked example in § 52*). This rule not only matches the two PATHS but also the bearer of motion, which must be an object—a PLANE, for example—and the SITUATIONS in which the movements along the PATHS take place. These three kinds of refOs are bound together by the chpos descriptions.

45   *Concept matcher*

The main function of the concept matcher is, from a general perspective, to access the knowledge stored in long-term memory. From a more technical perspective, the concept matcher accesses the CS. However, these accesses are not "simple find-and-fetch" (Dietrich, 2000, p. 277), but are intertwined with the categorizations task (Goldstone, 1994; Murphy, 2002). The concept matcher uses a mainly classical approach to categorization, concepts, and similarity by using features and feature vectors (E. E. Smith, 1995). However, there are two special points about the concept matcher. First, it enables construction to generate *expectations*, that is, it is capable of computing incomplete matches (categorizations). Second, the concept matcher is an *n:m-matcher*; that is, it can find m more complex concepts for n simpler ones within one match.

The rules stored in the CS can also be used to find simpler concepts for more complex ones. In particular, it is possible to segment a (complex) concept into

---

* This is not completely correct. The rule used in § 52 also includes the handling of spatial reference systems. I illustrate this when discussing the example.

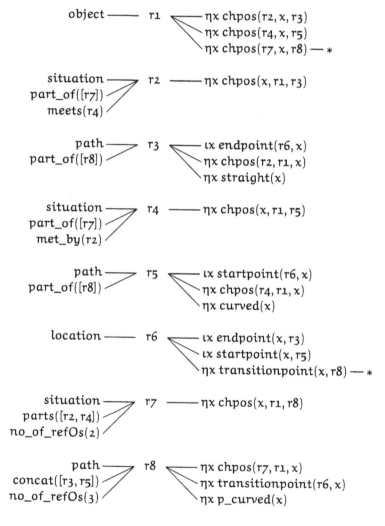

Figure 10.4: A rule of the cs

```
var candidate_list, #the candidate list received from construction
    doa, #the degree of agreement of the best match
    match_list #the match list given back to construction
repeat
  wait input_stream ≠ ⟨⟩
  input_increment ← Fetch(input_stream)
  if input_increment ≠ terminate then
    candidate_list ← input_increment
    (doa, match_list) ← MatchCandidateList(candidate_list)
    Append((doa, match_list), outputStream)
  endif
until input_increment = terminate
```

Figure 10.5: The concept matcher process

multiple simpler ones. This is necessary to connect INC to a PPU that produces not only the simplest concepts, as I assume in the following, but also concepts of a higher granularity. A second assumption the concept matcher currently makes is that the refOs in the candidate list must be on the same level of granularity; that is, they must not be related by parts or part_of relations.

Figure 10.5 shows the main loop of the concept matcher process. After initialization, it waits until a new input_increment is available in the input_stream. The loop ends when the input_increment is the termination signal. Otherwise, the input increment contains a candidate_list, for which the matching function MatchCandidateList is called. This is the incremental algorithm of the concept matcher. It returns the best match, which is a pair consisting of the match_list of refO pairs (those consisting of a CCR and a CS refO) and the corresponding doa of the match. The best match is appended to the outputStream.

The concept matcher has no access to the CCR. That is, the available knowledge of the concept matcher's incremental algorithm consists of the CS and the candidate list it obtained from construction. Thus, the concept matcher cannot change available knowledge of any kind.

The function MatchCandidateList is shown in figure 10.6. It takes the candidate_list sent by construction and searches the CS for the best matching concept, the best match. The function consists of two nested for-loops. The outer loop runs over all refOs that are in the start_refOs list, the inner loop over the refOs in the candidate_list. Each rule in the CS has start_refOs with which matching can be started. For example, the rule in figure 10.4 has three such refOs: r1, r2, r3. (The refOs are not marked as start-refOs in the figure.) By using start_refOs the concept matcher does not have to try all possible combinations of refOs in the rule

```
fun MatchCandidateList(candidate_list)
    var doa,
        start_refOs,  #list of refOs the matching starts with
        match,  #a match of the candidate list onto a rule of the cs
        list_of_matches,  #list of all matches
    for all r_s ∈ start_refOs do
      for all r_c ∈ candidate_list do
        if InitialMatch(r_s, r_c) then
          match ←
            BuildFinalMatchList(
              BuildPartsList(
                BuildPartOfList(
                  BuildBasicMatchList(r_s, r_c))))
          doa ← ComputeDoA(match)
          list_of_matches ← Append((match, doa), list_of_matches)
        endif
      endfor
    endfor
    return FindBestMatch(list_of_matches)
endfun
```

Figure 10.6: The function MatchCandidateList

and refOs in the candidate_list. This increases efficiency, in particular, if the rule is symmetric, for example, a rule that groups together two planes moving in parallel, where it makes no difference whether PLANE$_A$ is matched onto r_x of the cs rule and PLANE$_B$ onto r_y or vice versa.

All refOs in the candidate list are compared whether they can be matched onto one of the start_refOs. Only if the InitialMatch is possible is the DOA for the rule computed. If the same rule can be applied to a candidate list more than once, the match with the highest DOA is taken.

The matching proper is done in four distinct steps. Before I describe these steps, however, I give some examples of how the DOA is determined. The DOA could be determined in many different ways, but because measuring the similarity of concepts is not in the focus of this book, I simply use the following equation:

$$(3) \quad \text{DOA} = \frac{\text{number refOs present}}{\text{number of refOs required by rule}}$$

A better similarity measure may be required in the future, for example, one that also accounts for how similar a CCR refO is to the corresponding CS refO, but for the present purposes of the model, this one suffices.

Consider the simple rule (1) given in §44. It requires three refOs in the candidate list that correspond to r1–r3 in order to yield a DOA = 1. That is, the DOA of this rule is computed as DOA = $^x/_3$, where x is the number of matching refOs in the candidate list. Consider that this rule is used for matching the following two candidate lists, each consisting of only one element:

(4)   spatial_entity ——— r30

(5)   path ——— r31

In both cases, DOA = $^0/_3$ = 0, because none of the simpler refOs in the rule (r1–r3) can be matched onto the one in the candidate lists. The reason in the first case is that not even the sorts of the refOs match—spatial_entity is not specific enough. In the second case, r31 has no common designation with one of the CS refOs, which is the minimal condition for two refOs to be matched onto each other.
     For the following candidate list, DOA = $^1/_3$.

(6)   path ——— r32 ——— ɩx endpoint(r40, x)

Here, the refO in the candidate list and the CS refO have the same designation. Thus, r32 can be matched onto r1. Observe, however, that this is a very strange candidate list, because it contains no corresponding refO for r40/r3. Hence, construction should not produce such a list, and the actual implementation does not do it.
     Finally, the candidate list

(7)   path ——— r32 ——— ɩx endpoint(r40, x)

              location ——— r40 ——— ɩx endpoint(x, r32)

yields DOA = $^2/_3$. The corresponding match list is

(8) [(ccr(r32), cs(r1)), (ccr(r40), cs(r3))]

This means that r32 of the CCR is matched onto r1 of the CS, and r40 onto r3. It is also the basic match list of this example, the first of the four steps in computing a match (cf. figure 10.6). Computing a match consists of a sequence of building up the following four lists:

1. Basic match list
2. Part-of list
3. Parts list
4. Final match list

The first step in computing a basic match list is to find an initial match, which is done by the function InitialMatch by comparing the start_refOs to the refOs in the candidate list. Due to the two nested for-loops, all permutations are tried; that is, all refOs of the candidate list are matched onto all start_refOs of the cs rule. According to the initial match, the other refOs in the candidate list are matched onto refOs of the rule so that each refO of the candidate list is matched onto a refO of the cs rule.*

With the basic match list, no hierarchical relations have been established yet. The next step, therefore, is to construct the part-of list. It contains the possible complex refOs for each refO in the basic match list. This step is necessary, because a simpler refO can be part of multiple complex refOs. Although this case is rare in the domain of motion events, it frequently occurs in the domain of sketch maps, where, for instance, one line can belong to multiple objects. In those cases, the part_of attribute of the simple refO contains more than one element. For the example at hand, the part-of list is the following:

(9) $[(\text{complexes}([r4]), \text{part}(\text{ccr}(r32), \text{cs}(r1)))$,
    $(\text{complexes}([r4]), \text{part}(\text{ccr}(r40), \text{cs}(r3))))]$

From the part-of list the *parts list* is constructed, which can be imagined as a part-of list upside down: For each complex refO in the part-of list, its parts are determined. For the example, it is a list of only one element:

(10) $[(\text{complex}(r4), \text{parts}([(\text{ccr}(r32), \text{cs}(r1)), (\text{ccr}(r40), \text{cs}(r3))]))]$

This list is almost in the format that is given back to construction. The *final match list* is computed from the parts list by extending each pair in the parts list (consisting of complex and parts) by the information about the refOs that are still missing for a complete match:

(11) $[(\text{complex}(r4), \text{parts}([(\text{ccr}(r32), \text{cs}(r1)), (\text{ccr}(r40), \text{cs}(r3))]), \text{missing}([r2]))]$

For the final match list, the doa is determined. Because the final match list can contain multiple complex concepts (complex-refOs), the doa of the list is computed as mean of the doa of each complex concept. For the example, it is

(12) $\text{DOA} = \frac{\frac{2}{3}}{1} = \frac{2}{3} \approx .67$

For a more interesting example, assume that for each of of the complex refOs of the rule given in figure 10.4 (r7 and r8), one part-refO was found. The doa for this final match list then is

---

* An issue not further discussed here is that the match must be consistent. That is, if r40 of the ιx endpoint(r40, x) description is matched onto r3 of the cs rule, this match must hold in all cases. If another refO contains a description ηx p(x, r40), this occurrence of r40 must also be matched onto r3.

$$(13) \quad \text{DOA} = \frac{\frac{1}{2} + \frac{1}{3}}{2} = \frac{\frac{5}{6}}{2} = \frac{5}{12} \approx .42$$

All of these matches (all final match lists) are collected together with their doa in the list_of_matches. If no match was found, the empty list (nil) with a doa of 0 is taken instead. After all rules in the cs have been tried, the match with the highest DOA is chosen from the list_of_matches. This is the best match, which is the result of the function MatchCandidateList and given back to construction by the concept matcher. The final match list that is given back to construction as part of the best match is referred to as *the match list* in the rest of this book. If matching was not successful, the best match consists of the match list nil with DOA = 0. If multiple matches with identical DOA compete to be the best match, the first match in the list_of_matches is given back to construction. Another possibility would be to return all matches and let construction decide which one it takes as best match. Another one is to let construction pursue multiple possibilities in parallel. A third possibility is to ascertain that this case cannot occur, by introducing a decision function that can be made dependent on further factors.

11

SELECTION AND LINEARIZATION

S ELECTION AND LINEARIZATION are linked so closely that they may really just form one integrated process. (However, linearization needs to be realized first.) Therefore, I describe them both in this chapter. Selection decides which event refOs are verbalized by adding those event refOs to the traverse buffer (§ 46). Linearization can reorder the refOs while they are in the traverse buffer to produce better verbalizations (§ 47).

§ 46   *Selection*

Selection evaluates each element (refO) of the CCR that is added or changed by construction. The information processed by construction, including the increment construction passes on to selection, is in the focus of attention. It is information that was either just received from the PPU or created with the help of the concept matcher. That this approach is cognitively adequate is shown in § 53, where INC is tested against empirical data (see also Guhe & Habel, 2001; Guhe, Habel, & Tschander, 2003b).

The outer loop of selection is shown in figure 11.1. The loop runs until construction signals that it terminates, in which case selection does so as well. Construction indicates its termination via a special increment that is sent by construction when it terminates. (Similarly, selection sends such an increment to linearization when it terminates, which is not shown in the figure.)

Each iteration of the loop waits until a new input increment is available, which is then fetched from the input_stream. Selection only considers situation refOs for verbalization.* Hence, input increments of another sort than situation are ignored.† For these situation-refOs, three cases must be distinguished:

---

* This limitation is, as already pointed out repeatedly, due to the fact that I am only concerned with *event* conceptualization. In general, refOs of all sorts can be selected. The difference in selecting, say, an object refO is that the resulting utterance is about the object, not the situation the object is in. In other words, the focus (topic) of the resulting preverbal message generated by PVM-generation is different.

† I make a simplification in these formulations. The increments between construction and selection—like the increments stored in the traverse buffer—are actually pointers to refOs in the CCR. Thus, the full formulation would be: *Input increments that are pointers to refOs in the CCR that have another sort than* situation *are ignored.*

```
repeat
   wait input_stream ≠ ⟨⟩
   input_inc ← Fetch(input_stream)
   if input_inc ≠ terminate then
      if Sort(input_inc) = situation then
         if Type(input_inc) = new or Type(input_inc) = update then
            MakeDecision(input_inc)
         elsif Type(input_inc) = expectation_discarded then
            Delete(input_inc, traverse_buffer)
         endif
      endif
   endif
until input_inc = terminate
```

Figure 11.1: The selection process

```
fun MakeDecision(input_inc)
   parts ← Simpler(input_inc, traverse_buffer)
   part_of ← Complex(input_inc, traverse_buffer)
   if parts ≠ ⟨⟩ then
      Replace(parts, input_inc)
   elsif part_of = ⟨⟩ then
      Append(input_inc, traverse_buffer)
   endif
endfun
```

Figure 11.2: The standard selection algorithm

1. A new refO has been added to the CCR.
2. An existing refO has been updated.
3. An expected refO has been discarded.

The third case occurs when an expectation no longer holds, for example, because the concept matcher found a new best match for the elements under consideration. If there is a pointer to this refO in the traverse buffer, selection deletes it. The first two cases are treated identically up to now by calling MakeDecision, which decides whether the situation refO under consideration is selected. It differs depending on the selection strategy that is used. (The selection strategy is set before INC is started; cf. chap. 13.) INC's standard selection strategy is to select the most complex situation refO for verbalization that is currently not selected (figure 11.2). Thus, the decision is made with regard to the part-of hierarchy. There are three cases:

1. If a more complex refO is already in the traverse buffer nothing is done.
2. If simpler refOs are already selected, they are replaced.
3. Otherwise, the refO is appended to the traverse buffer (this is the default).

In other words, this strategy evaluates the hierarchical relations between the refO under consideration and the refOs that are currently in the traverse buffer. At first, it tests whether the refO under consideration has parts refOs in the traverse buffer, that is, refOs that are lower in the part-of hierarchy.* If the refO has parts (simpler) refOs in the traverse buffer, then the first of these refOs, that is, the headmost refO, is replaced by the refO under consideration; the others are deleted.† Both operations are carried out by only one operation, which is called Replace in figure 11.2. This is necessary, because otherwise inconsistencies might arise if linearization exchanges refOs in the traverse buffer while selection is performing this operation.‡

After this, it is tested whether the refO under consideration is part_of traverse buffer refOs. If this is not the case, then it is appended to the traverse buffer.§ Thus, the three cases to consider are condensed to just two cases in the implementation. The local context of this selection strategy is the traverse buffer. No other information from the CCR is used.

Each modification of the traverse buffer by the operations Replace, Append, or Delete includes a notification of the linearization process by an output increment, which is not given in figure 11.2 for reasons of brevity.

An alternative selection strategy is given in figure 11.3. Its aim is to keep the level of the selected refOs on the same level of granularity. As in the other selection strategy, the level of granularity is not explicitly fixed in advance but is a result of INC's computations. It uses the additional function Granularity to identify the level of granularity of a refO.‖ A refO is selected in two of three possible cases:

1. If the traverse buffer is empty, the refO is selected.
2. If the refO has the same granularity as a refO in the traverse buffer, the refO is selected as well.
3. Otherwise, the refO is not selected.

---

* The parts attributes are expanded as far as necessary; the underlying relation is transitive.
† This operation causes no gaps in the traverse buffer, because the traverse buffer is defined as a sequence of increments. This means that it is implemented as a list, not as an array.
‡ In fact, in the implementation I was even more cautious in that the complete selection algorithm is encapsulated in a critical section so that such inconsistencies can never arise.
§ The Append operation ascertains that the head of traverse buffer is deleted if the maximal length of the traverse buffer has been reached before the operation is applied.
‖ Currently, it uses a rather simple method, namely using the part-of hierarchy to count the number of edges that the refO is away from the PEs from which it is built up. This method fails, however, if the number of edges to different PEs is not the same.

```
fun MakeDecision(input_inc)
  if traverse_buffer = ⟨⟩ then
    Append(input_inc, traverse_buffer)
  elsif ∃e(e ∈ traverse_buffer and
    Granularity(input_inc) = Granularity(e) then
    Append(input_inc, traverse_buffer)
  endif
endfun
```

Figure 11.3: An alternative selection algorithm

In other words, the effect of this selection strategy is that only refOs of the same granularity are present in the traverse buffer. A change of granularity can occur only if the traverse buffer is empty.

§ 47   *Linearization*

Because linearization has been considered only scarcely and theoretically in the context of INC up to now, it is not implemented yet (apart from a dummy function). Reordering events is expendable for the moment, because the strictly sequential order of the input information means that only one *event thread* is conceptualized.

TERM 28: EVENT THREAD
An event thread is a sequence of events that have the same bearer.

(The bearer of motion is the entity that is moving. It can be different from the *actor*, the entity that caused the motion of the moving entity (cf. Eschenbach et al., 2000.) The only consequence of this limitation is that INC generates no verbalizations that describe events in an order different from the one in which they occurred. Therefore, I only point out some important issues in this section that are important for adequately modeling and implementing the linearization process.

First of all, linearization performs a linearization of utterances (subintentions, situations, events), not of phrases. A method of how phrases can be linearized incrementally within a model of the formulator is Performance Grammar, described in Kempen (1997) and Kempen and Harbusch (2002, 2003). This method depends on the sequence in which the increments arrive in the formulator, that is, the sequence in which PVM-generation produces output. (Note that PVM-generation contains no computations of the linear order of increments but produces increments as soon as they become available.)

Linearization in the online description of events can be investigated by an extension of the setting used here in which the participants have to verbalize concurrent events (see Guhe et al., 2004 and §50 for a first proposal). The term *concurrent* means that in the scene, the participants observe more than one event happening simultaneously, for example, multiple planes moving simultaneously. A case in which linearization must be performed is if selection alternatingly appends events of different event threads to the traverse buffer, say event threads A and B. In this case, linearization should reorder these events in such a way that not one event of thread A, then one of B, then again one of A, then again one of B, and so on is verbalized. (Because selection always decides whether an event is verbalized after it was introduced or updated by construction, such a ordering of events in the traverse buffer is quite likely, in particular if the event threads proceed with a similar pace.) Instead, some events belonging to event thread A should be verbalized, then some belonging to B, and so on. This could be captured by a new parameter for INC, an event thread retention (§59).

Like the selection strategies described in §46, linearization should be able to work according to different linearization strategies. One of these strategies can be to order the events according to their importance so that the most important event is mentioned first. The importance of an event can, for instance, be determined on the basis of its perceptual prominence. Another strategy might consist in uttering contrasting events first so that utterance (1) is preferred over (2), which would be preferred by the first strategy. The second linearization strategy would work especially well with a selection strategy that prefers contrasting information.

(1) *Plane A and plane B move straight ahead. Plane A stops, and plane B continues.*
(2) *Plane A and plane B move straight ahead. Plane B continues, and plane A stops.*

In §13, I argued that all deviations from the chronological order must be overtly marked. That means, if the order in which events are verbalized is different from the one in which they occurred, this must be made explicit in the utterance. The task that has to ascertain this is PVM-generation. Thus, developing linearization means that PVM-generation has to be extended as well.

12

PREVERBAL MESSAGE GENERATION

*P*VM-GENERATION CORRESPONDS to Levelt's (1989) microplanning. It would be more accurate to speak of microselection, because there is no micro-linearization within the conceptualizer—this is done by the formulator. A model that takes care of microlinearization is, for example, Kempen's Performance Grammar. In INC, the selection of utterances is done by the selection process, and PVM-generation selects the means to express the utterance. This division of labor is analogous to the one between *what-to-say* and *how-to-say* that distinguishes conceptualizer and formulator (de Smedt et al., 1996).

Precursors of the ideas presented in this chapter have been previously published. Guhe et al. (2000) and Guhe (2003) introduce and discuss the idea of incremental preverbal messages (§ 48). Guhe, Habel, and Tschander (2003a); Guhe et al. (2003b) describe the incremental algorithm that generates the incremental preverbal messages (§ 49). I close this chapter with showing how referential nets can be used to establish coreferential relations between entities of subsequent incremental preverbal messages (§ 50).

§ 48   *Incremental preverbal messages*

The term *incremental preverbal message* emphasises the incremental mode of generating preverbal messages.

TERM 29: INCREMENTAL PREVERBAL MESSAGE
An incremental preverbal message is a preverbal message that is generated incrementally.

The preverbal messages produced this way are equivalent in their expressive power to nonincremental semantic structures proposed by linguists, especially those by Jackendoff (1990, 1997, 2002). Jackendoff's semantic representations are on the level of abstractness that Levelt proposes when he speaks of *preverbal message*. These semantic structures are rather close to conceptual representations compared to other approaches, for example, the one by Bierwisch and Schreuder (1992). In fact, they are regarded as special conceptual representations. PVM-generation is similar to Wiese's (2003b) account of how a semantic representation is computed from a conceptual one.

The incremental mode of generation implies that an incremental preverbal message is complete only when a new one is started. In other words, the fact that an incremental preverbal message is completed is established in retrospect. The reason for this is that preverbal messages (semantic structures) can be extended incrementally ad infinitum: "In an incremental mode of sentence generation ... a sentence which is in principle complete may often be extended by adding another modifier or even a case relation" (de Smedt, 1990a, p. 83) This can be done by three mechanisms in incremental grammatical encoding: expansion, coordination, and correction (p. 16). The latter two were already discussed in connection with underspecification formalisms in §27. The first one is the normal mode of operation when generating a preverbal message incrementally.

Incremental preverbal messages, as they are produced by PVM-generation, can be rewritten so that they conform to semantic representations as they are proposed by Jackendoff (Guhe, 2003). The basic idea is that the increments belonging to one incremental preverbal message are collected until the preverbal message is complete. Then this representation is rewritten so that it is equivalent to a representation that was not generated in an incremental fashion but *en bloc*. One can imagine this as having two different views on the same representation: a temporal and a nontemporal view. In the temporal (incremental) view, the emphasis lies on the succession of increments; that is, the generation of the representation is emphasized. In the nontemporal view, which is traditionally taken in linguistics, all increments belonging to an incremental preverbal message are considered simultaneously. While the processing mechanism is the main interest in the first view, it is the information required for an adequate semantic representation in the second view.

Both views can profit from each other. One result of considering the processing mechanism is that the focus and perspective of a semantic representation can be encoded by the order of the representation's components. Considering the nontemporal properties of a semantic representation makes it possible to concentrate on its informational content so as to formulate the goal representation of the generation process. A model like INC can then be tested whether the generated preverbal messages are equivalent to these semantic representations. In §6 and §15, I proposed as a working hypothesis that the first element is the item that is in the focus of the utterance. Additionally, each time an element is chosen for verbalization, the perspective of the utterance is narrowed down.

PVM-generation must meet two crucial conditions (§10). First, for each increment of an incremental preverbal message, it must be ascertained that it fits to the increments already generated. This is the *consistency condition*. Second, all increments of an incremental preverbal message taken together must form a complete semantic representation as it is required by accounts like Jackendoff's. This is the *completeness condition*. Meeting these conditions is a result of the functioning of INC. There are no explicit computations whether they are fulfilled; that is, there are no consistency and completeness checks. This is a further point in favor of INC's cognitive adequacy: Humans do not perform explicit reasoning about whether a sentence is complete. This knowledge is implicit. The only way to detect inconsistencies and incompleteness in an utterance is via self-monitoring (Levelt, 1989).

There are two important differences between a sequence of increments like an incremental preverbal message and a dynamic representation like the CCR. First, a sequence of increments is a richer representation in that it contains information about the temporal order in which increments are generated. This is not stored in a dynamic representation.*† Second, in contrast to the knowledge stored in the CCR, which simply exists as long as INC is running (remember that there is no "forgetting mechanism"), incremental preverbal messages have a twofold character. Seen as a succession of increments between conceptualizer and formulator, they are nonpersistent representations, whereas in the traverse, which is part of the CCR, they are permanent representations as well.

To keep track of what it already produced as part of the preverbal message that is currently generating, PVM-generation uses an additional data structure, the *current preverbal message*.

TERM 30: CURRENT PREVERBAL MESSAGE
The current preverbal message is the preverbal message that is currently produced by PVM-generation. The increments contained in the current preverbal message are accessible by PVM-generation so that it can (a) keep track of still missing parts of the incremental preverbal message and (b) compute extensions, modifications, and self-corrections.

Current preverbal messages are used to keep track of what has already been said. This is important, for example, when PVM-generation decides which designations to use for verbalizing a refO (see the next section). Additionally, they allow detecting the need for self-corrections in the case of conceptual changes. These are changes to elements in the conceptual representation that are part of the current preverbal

---

* Note that there is a difference between storing information about when a refO is generated and the information about when a situation represented by the refO takes/took place. The latter can be part of both representations; the former is only present in a sequence of increments.
† Dynamic representations can also be seen as a succession of states of the representation. However, under this perspective, the order in which the elements of the representation were inserted or modified is not preserved either. Only the succession of the states of the representation contains this information (which is not preserved in INC).

message. In other words, if PVM-generation detects that a refO that is used in the current preverbal message changed after it was sent to the formulator, it can initiate a self-correction. For instance, if the PPU computes that the plane of the introductory example does not move toward GATE-B21 but toward GATE-B23, the following utterance could result (cf. example (2), p. 90):

(1) *Flug CK-314 bewegt sich auf Gate B21 zu ... äh nein ... auf Gate B23.*
     'Flight CK-314 moves toward gate B21 ... uh no ... gate B23.'

For reasons of brevity, I do not discuss the detection of conceptual changes here.

§ 49   *Incremental generation of preverbal messages*

Before describing how incremental preverbal messages are generated by PVM-generation, I want to make some introductory remarks. According to de Smedt (1990a), the following information is required by the formulator:

1. Semantic concepts (that refer to entities, events)
2. Case relations ("deep" case, i.e., semantic roles between concepts)
3. Features (definiteness, number, etc.)

The algorithm presented in the following only generates the first two kinds of information. Features required by a formulator must be added to PVM-generation when INC is actually connected to one, because this will depend on the requirements of the formulator and on the language specificity of the preverbal message. For example, a formulator generating in a language that not only makes a singular/plural distinction but also knows a dual needs a threefold distinction of number in the preverbal message whereas in other languages a twofold distinction suffices. In fact, using a threefold distinction may even be disadvantageous in the latter case, because it adds unnecessary information, which may increase run-time.

Similarly, the problem of encodability (also called the *generation gap problem*; Meteer, 1990) is not considered in the following. Encodability means the conceptualizer must ascertain that the formulator is able to encode a preverbal message linguistically. It can be easily achieved if only a small subset of natural language is used, but it is difficult if the system is to use the full productivity and complexity of a natural language. A conceptualizer may, therefore, profit from a formulator that uses "productive lexical rules which derive categories from other ones, e.g. nominalization and passivization" (de Smedt, 1990a, p. 148–149).

PVM-generation's algorithm bears some resemblance to the so-called incremental algorithm by Dale and Reiter (Dale & Reiter, 1995; E. Reiter & Dale, 1992, 2000). (However, this is only a single algorithm, not a class of algorithms as I defined it in part B.) The Dale and Reiter algorithm is the first incremental algorithm of a whole series for the generation of referring expressions. Thus, PVM-generation's algorithm is much more general. One of the main advantages of this algorithm for the purposes at hand is that it possesses some psychological plausibility, because its results are in accordance with empirical findings, for example, the ones by Pechmann (1984), and because it implicitly observes the Gricean maxims (Grice, 1975). Extensions proposed by van Deemter (2002) and Krahmer and Theune (2002) describe a variant for the generation of reduced expressions in a discourse context. For example, *the tiny, red, cute dog* may be referred to simply as *the dog* when it is mentioned for a second time. A multimodal variant is given in van der Sluis and Krahmer (2001) and van der Sluis (2005), where the generation of the referring expression is supported by a pointing gesture of variable precision. A proposal of how this algorithm may be cast into graph-theoretical terms is given by Krahmer, van Erk, and Verleg (2003). The latter allows the use of results from the study of graphs for improving the algorithm. The Dale and Reiter algorithm has more or less become the baseline algorithm for this task in the NLG field. In INC, a version of the algorithm can be used for generating referring expressions, in particular for verbalizing object refOs, but this has not been done up to now.

The fact that PVM-generation does not perform a linearization of any kind is in agreement with assumptions of models of incrementally working formulators. Such formulators, for example, IPF (de Smedt, 1990a, 1990b) or Performance Grammar (Kempen, 1997; Kempen & Harbusch, 2002, 2003), explicitly acknowledge that input increments do not come in a prespecified order. The latter uses a slot–filler model for the positioning of increments (phrases/segments); the generation of an element is delayed if some grammatically required element is still missing.

The last precursory remark is that deciding on a verbalization is always a two-step process in INC: Frst it decides to verbalize a refO and only then how to verbalize it. This is true for the division of labor between selection and PVM-generation as well as for PVM-generation's incremental algorithm. After a refO is selected for verbalization, PVM-generation chooses the designations to verbalize it. Because refOs usually contain lots of designations, constraints for choosing them are indispensable: Not all information provided by the designations are needed in a verbalization. This is the microselection problem proper. Because some designations refer to other refOs, these refOs are selected for verbalization when the designation is selected. Following the selection of the designation, therefore, the referenced refOs with further designations (with further refOs and so on) are verbalized.

var head_of_TB,   #*the head of traverse buffer*
   current_pvm,   #*the current preverbal message*
   used_desigs   #*designations used in preverbal messages*
repeat
   wait Latency(head_of_TB) ⩾ lt
   Fetch(head_of_TB)
   new current_pvm
   Verbalize(head_of_TB)
until linearization terminates **and** coordination with monitor allows termination

Figure 12.1: The outer algorithm of PVM-generation

The PVM-generation process consists of three main parts. Apart from the outer loop that has the same function as the ones in the other processes (figure 12.1), there is the procedure Verbalize (figure 12.2) and the function SelectDesignations (figure 12.3). The outer loop watches the head of traverse buffer (head_of_TB) and waits for the defined latency (parameter LT) to expire. Then it fetches the head of traverse buffer and starts a new current preverbal message with the refO the head of traverse buffer is pointing to as first refO. (For reasons of brevity I, again, do not distinguish the pointers in the traverse buffer from the actual refOs in the CCR that the pointers refer to.) Finally, the procedure Verbalize is called, which generates the verbalization for the head of traverse buffer. This loop runs until the linearization process terminates and PVM-generation can synchronize with the monitor process that nothing remains to be done. This synchronisation is necessary, because the monitor process interacts directly with PVM-generation when it detects the need for a self-correction.*

This algorithm implies that an incremental preverbal message (a verbalization) must be finished before the next head of traverse buffer can be taken. This means two things. First, it is not ascertained that the head of traverse buffer is verbalized immediately after the latency expired. What is more, this means that the head of traverse buffer can be removed from the traverse buffer by an operation of the selection process without being verbalized even after its latency expired. Second, the generation of an incremental preverbal message cannot be interrupted; that is, selection cannot decide *not* to verbalize a situation (stop the verbalization) after the generation of the corresponding preverbal message has commenced. After PVM-generation has initiated an incremental preverbal message, it can be interrupted only in two cases: when the monitor process detects an error and inserts a self-correction or when PVM-generation detects a conceptual change and makes the corresponding

---

* Because the monitor process is only implemented very sketchily (because formulator and language comprehension system are missing), I do not discuss the exact termination conditions.

```
proc Verbalize(refO)
    var verbalization_refO,  #the newly created verbalization refO
        selected_desigs  #designations selected for verbalization of the refO
    Append(refO, current_pvm)
    verbalization_refO ←new refO
    selected_desigs ← SelectDesignations(refO)
    AddDesigs(selected_desigs, verbalization_refO)
    Append(selected_desigs, used_desigs)
    Append(verbalization_refO, output_stream)
    Append(verbalization_refO, traverse)
    for all r ← RelatedRefOs(selected_desigs) do
        Verbalize(r)
    endfor
endproc
```

Figure 12.2: The procedure Verbalize

self-correction or extension (§ 27).* To keep the description of the functioning of PVM-generation simple, neither possibility is discussed here.

The procedure Verbalize (figure 12.2) generates a verbalization for a refO. In its initial call, it receives the head of traverse buffer as argument. Because the verbalization of a head of traverse buffer involves the verbalization of further refOs, Verbalize calls itself recursively. Its first operation is to append the refO it is currently verbalising to the current preverbal message (current_pvm).† Then it creates a new verbalization refO, which initially only contains the attributes of the original refO and the information of which refO it is a verbalization. Of the designations only those actually used in the verbalization are added to the verbalization refO.

The selection of designations is performed by SelectDesignations. The result is stored in selected_desigs so that subsequent calls of SelectDesignations do not select these designations again. (Because the list selected_desigs is defined in Verbalize, it is also visible within SelectDesignations.) If a selected designation is a description, it is stored in its resolved form in the list. For example, if $\eta x\, chpos(x, r2, r3)$ is a description of $r1$, it is stored as $chpos(r1, r2, r3)$. This way it will not be selected if it is considered again when designations for refOs $r2$ and $r3$ are selected. The selected designations are added to the verbalization refO. With this,

---

* This is no claim that humans cannot interrupt the production of a preverbal message, which they obviously can do. This is a limitation of the model.

† The current preverbal message does not contain verbalization refOs but pointers to the refOs in the CCR, which is the prerequisite for detecting conceptual changes. (Conceptual changes are detected by comparing the refOs in the CCR to which the pointers in the current preverbal message refer to and the corresponding verbalization refOs that are stored in the traverse.)

the verbalization refO is complete. It is sent to the formulator as next increment of the incremental preverbal message and appended to the traverse. Finally, Verbalize calls itself for the refOs that the verbalized designations refer to.

PVM-generation uses three kinds of constraints for selecting designations: structural, activation, and conceptual constraints. Of these, the structural constraints are most important; they form the "backbone" SelectDesignations. See §52 for a worked example that demonstrates the interplay of these three constraints in detail. Before I describe SelectDesignations, I first illustrate the constraints in more detail.

The *structural constraint* says that only grounded designations are verbalized. If designations refer to no other refO they are directly grounded, for example, names or the description $\eta x\ plane(x)$. Designations pointing to other refOs, for example, $\eta x\ chpos(x, r2, r3)$, must be tested whether they are groundable. In the grounding chain, all refOs that the designation contains are checked whether they have a grounded designation. In the example, this must be done for $r2$ and $r3$. If a designation is groundable by a grounding chain, the designation is indirectly grounded. If a designation that is evaluated in the grounding chain has already been used in this chain it is cyclic, which lets the grounding attempt fail. For an example of a cyclic designation, assume that the description $\eta x\ chpos(x, r2, r3)$ has been chosen for the verbalization of $r1$. This means it is now part of the current preverbal message, and it was appended to the selected_desigs list in its resolved form, $chpos(r1, r2, r3)$. In the next step, a designation for $r2$ must be found. One possibility would be to select $\eta x\ chpos(r1, x, r3)$. However, choosing this description would add no new information to the current preverbal message, because it can also be reduced to $chpos(r1, r2, r3)$. For this reason, it is a cyclic designation that is not selected. This also holds for $r3$ and $\eta x\ chpos(r1, r2, x)$. Note that this use of the term *grounding* is totally unrelated to H. H. Clark's (1996).

The *activation constraint* evaluates the activation values assigned to the designations in question. It checks whether the activation of a designation is above the activation threshold (parameter AT). However, if a designation is needed to produce a semantically complete preverbal message, it may be chosen despite an activation value below AT. In the motion events domain, this constraint can be violated in the selection of designations for situation refOs. The reason is that situation refOs must have at least one designation for the generation process to function, whereas for refOs of other types verbalization refOs without designations are viable. Such "empty" refOs occur if, for example, they have been verbalized before, that is, if they were used in previous preverbal messages (§50).

The *conceptual constraints* evaluate whether a designation is conceptually consistent with the designations chosen so far. Up to now, there is only one conceptual constraint, the *homogeneous-part-of constraint*. If a refO is tested in the grounding

```
fun SelectDesignations(refO)
   var desigs, #designations of refO
      dg_desigs, #directly grounded designations
      non_cyclic_desigs, #designations without cyclic ones
      selected_desigs, #designations selected for verbalization; return value
      sit_desig_preds, #designation predicates for a situation refO
   desigs ← Designations(refO)
   non_cyclic_desigs ← AllNotCyclic(desigs, refO)
   if Sort(refO) = situation then
      selected_desigs ← Filter(non_cyclic_desigs, sit_desig_preds)
   else
      dg_desigs ← Filter(non_cyclic_desigs, DirectlyGrounded)
      for all d ∈ dg_desigs do
         if Activation(d) and ConcConsistent(d) and d ∉ used_desigs then
            Append(d, selected_desigs)
         endif
      endfor
      Append(Filter((non_cyclic_desigs \ dg_desigs \ used_desigs),
             (Groundable and Activation and ConcConsistent),
         selected_desigs)
   endif
   return selected_desigs
endfun
```

Figure 12.3: The function SelectDesignations

chain that is part of another refO in the current preverbal message and the refOs in question are of a homogeneous sort, no designation from the refO will be used in the verbalization. An entity is of a homogeneous sort if its parts are of the same sort as the entity. An example is path, because parts of paths are paths.*

The function SelectDesignations evaluates these constraints (cf., figure 12.3). It first copies all designations of the refO under consideration to a list† and collects the noncyclic designations of the refO. In the next step, the function distinguishes between the verbalization of a refO having sort situation and a verbalization of a refO having another sort. In the first case, the designation must be noncyclic, and it must have a predicate that can be used for describing a situation (situation refOs

---

* I regard paths as extended entities, and points lying on a path are not formalized as *parts* of a path but as *coinciding* with a path (Eschenbach et al., 1999, 2000). Thus, a point (e.g., a location) cannot be part of a path, but a path can have multiple subpaths.
† Apart from the fact that this enhances performance, it also ascertains that the function does not operate on a changing refO. This means, for instance, that if a designation is added while SelectDesignations is running, it is not considered.

can also have other designations). As situation refOs currently contain only few designations, a simple Filter operation suffices to find an appropriate one, and the constraints need not be evaluated further. This changes when the scenes become more complex.

If the refO to be verbalized has a sort other than situation, the directly grounded designations (dg_designs) are filtered from the noncyclic designations of the refO. All of these designations must also conform to the activation constraint and the conceptual constraints. Additionally, they must not be used in a previous preverbal message; that is, they must not be in the used_designs list. This list is stored at the topmost level of PVM-generation (figure 12.1). Thus, a designation can be used only once as long as INC is running.* The selected designations are appended to the used_designs list in the function Verbalize (figure 12.2). The designations that meet these conditions are selected for verbalization; that is, they are appended to the selected_designs list.

After this, the remaining designations, that is, the noncyclic, not directly grounded designations, are evaluated whether they are groundable, conform to the activation and conceptual constraints, and whether they were not already used in a verbalization before. The designations conforming to these conditions are appended to the selected_designs list as well. The list containing all selected designations is returned as result of the function.

§ 50   *Sequences of incremental preverbal messages*

The previous section described how PVM-generation produces incremental preverbal messages. This is the current state of the implementation. However, a verbal description of a scene like the one in chapter 1 usually requires a sequence of multiple preverbal messages. This raises two questions:

1. How are preverbal messages related to each other?
2. How are the parts of preverbal messages related?

In the context of online descriptions of events, a partial answer to the first question is that the preverbal messages must reflect the *temporal relations* between the described situations. In other words, the temporal relations that are represented

---

* situation refOs are not tested for this condition, because otherwise a situation could not be verbalized more than once, which is, for example, necessary when it is verbalized as an expected situation and then again after the situation actually took place. Allowing a designation to be verbalized only once is a strong simplification, which must be discarded in the next INC version but which causes no problems is short scenes. This assumption was needed to "get the implementation running."

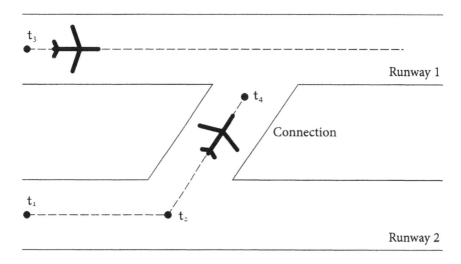

Figure 12.4: Scene with two moving planes

as refO attributes in the CCR can interrelate preverbal messages. Referential nets themselves offer a partial answer to the second question, because they facilitate the generation of coreferences between increments of preverbal messages. Because the increments of preverbal messages are refOs, the verbalization refOs referring to the same CCR refO are coreferential.

In this section, I present a proposal of how the current version of INC can be extended to accomplish this. It mainly affects the PVM-generation process. The proposal is published in more detail in Guhe et al. (2004).

Consider the scene shown in figure 12.4. The spatial background of the scene consists of another part of the maneuvering area already used in the example in chapter 1. It contains two parallel runways (RUNWAY-1 and RUNWAY-2) and a way connecting them (CONNECTION). In this scene, two planes are moving. Their movements become observable at different points of time, indicated in the figure by the time-stamps t1 and t3. The time-stamps depicted in figure 12.4 are numbered according to their temporal ordering (t1 ≺ t2 ≺ t3 ≺ t4). They also correlate with the positions of the planes during their movements that subdivide the scene into different situations. In extension of the segmentation points used so far—starting points and endpoints of movements—the PPU identifies the segmentation points for this scene where

1. A plane appears in the scene.
2. The direction of a movement changes.
3. A movement ends.

In this scene, a plane appears on RUNWAY-2 at t1 and moves straight until it reaches the CONNECTION way between RUNWAY-1 and RUNWAY-2, where it turns off at t2. While the plane is moving on the CONNECTION, a second plane appears on RUNWAY-1 at t3 and moves straight ahead. At t4, finally, the first plane stops. A verbalization of this scene is given in (2).

(2)   a. *Ein Flugzeug fährt auf Runway 2.*
          'A plane is moving on Runway 2.'
      b. *Nachdem es auf die Verbindung abgebogen ist,*
          'After it has turned off onto the Connection,'
      c. *fährt ein anderes Flugzeug auf Runway 1.*
          'another plane is moving on Runway 1.'
      d. *Dann stoppt das erste Flugzeug,*
          'Then the first plane stops,'
      e. *während das Flugzeug auf Runway 1 weiterfährt.*
          'while the plane on Runway 1 is moving on.'

This example is made up; the participants' verbalizations in the empirical studies are much noisier; for example, they produce incomplete sentences or make hesitations. The verbalizations for scenes that are very similar to the one discussed here are given in appendix C. They show that the means of verbalization discussed here are indeed used, but not in this concise and "literate" form. However, one aspect of the recorded verbalizations is not captured in this example or by INC, namely that the participants make statements about the causal relations within the scene. The most prominent point is that they believe that the first plane stops *in order to* let the second plane pass. INC could infer such relations by extrapolating the movements of both planes, which reveals that they will crash into each other if they continue their current movements. So, in order that this does *not* happen, one plane has to stop, which establishes the causal relation. Reasoning of this kind, especially reasoning about future states that will or should not occur is beyond INC's current inferential capabilities. INC builds up complex representations for the only reason that there is a corresponding rule in the CS.

I only comment on, and do not go into the details of, the conceptual representation, but see figure 12.5 for the event structure. The events with index P1 are the movements of the first plane (the one moving on RUNWAY-2 and the CONNECTION); the events with index P2 are the movements of the second plane. Thus,

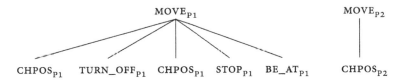

Figure 12.5: Event structure of scene with two moving planes

in this scene there are two event threads (cf. term 28, p. 151) that partition the event structure of the conceptual representation. TURN_OFF is a new situation type, namely the punctual event when the plane changes its direction and turns off onto the connection. Viewing turning off as a punctual event requires a slight abstraction, because in fact it consists of the point where the path initially changes its curvature, the movement along the curved path, and the point where the movement becomes straight again (§ 52), but I will not elaborate on this substructure here. Although it would be more accurate, it would also add a lot of details. Furthermore, the participants indeed regularly use the abstracted TURN_OFF; that is, they use the verb *abbiegen* 'turn off' (cf. appendix C).

INC requires three extensions to generate a verbalization like (2):

1. Construction must keep track of the temporal relations between the ongoing events,
2. PVM-generation must verbalize the temporal relations, and
3. PVM-generation must express the coreferences.

Extending construction is necessary, because it must establish the temporal relations between the currently ongoing events of different event threads. Otherwise, the utterances in (2b)–(2c) and (2d)–(2e) cannot be generated so that they explicitly mention the temporal relations between the events, which are expressed by the temporal connectives *nachdem* 'after', *dann* 'then', and *während* 'while/during'. The temporal relations can be expressed by a constraint net. The end state of the net for the example is given in figure 12.6. Relations in gray denote continuations of the scene that were once possible but did not occur. Remember that the relations differ with respect to whether they hold between extended situations, between punctual situations, or between punctual and extended ones (§ 20).

When PVM-generation generates a temporal relation, it must distinguish whether the relation connects the preverbal message with a previous or a following preverbal message. For the first case, INC's current mode of operation must only be extended by a computation that determines the temporal relation of the situation to be described with a previously generated preverbal message. This step is necessary, because there

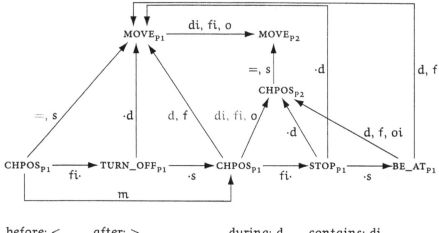

before: <   after: >   during: d   contains: di
equal: =   equal: =   starts: s   started_by: si
meets: m   met_by: mi   finishes: f   finished_by: fi
overlaps: o   overlapped_by: oi

Figure 12.6: The constraint net for the ongoing events

can be more than one relation between the two situations. Assume that the incremental preverbal message for utterance (2a), which describes CHPOS$_{P1}$, starts with the verbalization refO v_1. The skeleton of the corresponding refO sequence is given in (3).

(3)
$$\text{situation} \longrightarrow v_1 \longrightarrow \eta x\ \text{chpos}(\dots)$$
verb_of(CHPOS$_{P1}$)

$$\vdots$$

$$\text{discourse} \longrightarrow v_4 \longrightarrow \text{finished\_by}\cdot(v_1, v_5)$$

$$\text{situation} \longrightarrow v_5 \longrightarrow \eta x\ \text{turn\_off}(\dots)$$
verb_of(TURN_OFF$_{P1}$)

The next preverbal message for utterance (2b) that verbalizes TURN_OFF$_{P1}$ is connected to the previous one by discourse refO v_4. It starts with v_5, and the temporal relation, which can be encoded by the formulator as a temporal connective, is given as functional expression finished_by·(v_1, v_5) at the discourse refO. As there is no way to connect whole incremental preverbal messages (because there is no refO for the complete preverbal message), the temporal relation is given between the first increments.

However, this is only the first step in generating the preverbal messages for (2b)–(2c), because the temporal relation between both must be known in advance. Otherwise, *nachdem* 'after' cannot be generated at the beginning of the utterance.* Whereas the other mechanisms discussed in this section only extend IN C, this problem requires changing it, because PVM-generation needs access to more elements of the traverse buffer than just the head of traverse buffer. To generate (2b)–(2c), the traverse buffer must contain pointers to TURN_OFFp1 and CHPOSp2, and both must be verbalized together. The three incremental preverbal messages are generated as follows.

(4)

$$\text{situation} \longrightarrow v1 \longrightarrow \eta x\, \text{chpos}(\ldots)$$
$$\text{verb\_of}(\text{CHPOSp1})$$

$$\vdots$$

$$\text{discourse} \longrightarrow v4 \longrightarrow \text{finished\_by} \cdot (v6, v1)$$

$$\text{discourse} \longrightarrow v5 \longrightarrow \cdot \text{before}(v6, v7)$$

$$\text{situation} \longrightarrow v6 \longrightarrow \eta x\, \text{turn\_off}(x, v8, v9)$$
$$\text{verb\_of}(\text{TURN\_OFFp1})$$

$$\text{object} \longrightarrow v8 \longrightarrow \ldots$$
$$\text{verb\_of}(\text{PLANE-1})$$

$$\text{location} \longrightarrow v9 \longrightarrow \ldots$$
$$\text{verb\_of}(\ldots)$$

$$\text{situation} \longrightarrow v7 \longrightarrow \eta x\, \text{chpos}(\ldots)$$
$$\text{verb\_of}(\text{CHPOSp2})$$

As in the simpler case (3), $v4$ connects the forthcoming preverbal message with the previous one, whereas $v5$ connects the next two. Both must be planned together, because the temporal relation $\cdot\text{before}(v6, v7)$, which can result in the temporal connective *nachdem* 'after', must be available before the first incremental preverbal

---

* (2d)–(2e) can be generated without this, because *dann* 'then' connects (2d) to the previous utterance.

message is started. A consequence of this generation method is that $v7$ is announced rather early, and several other verbalization refOs are generated before it is actually generated. With regard to the distinction of linear and hierarchical incrementality (pp. 76–77), this means that not only does generating an incremental preverbal message involve hierarchical incrementality but also that the sequences of incremental preverbal messages add another level to the hierarchy.

I now turn to the issue of interrelating parts of incremental preverbal messages by coreferences, which can result in anaphora or ellipses. The referential nets formalism makes this task rather easy. Because coreferences are important primarily for generating referring expressions, an approach similar to the algorithm of Dale and Reiter (1995) and extended by Krahmer and Theune (2002) can be used. Three different verbalization refOs can be generated form the $\eta x\ plane(x)$ description of $r3$, given as $v1$ to $v3$. The verbalization refOs given in the following will only contain the information that is important for the examples, although the verbalization refOs actually generated may require more information.

(5) $plane$ ——— $r3$ ⟨ ——$\eta x\ plane(x)$
                                            $\eta x\ chpos(\text{CHPOS}_{P1}, x, \dots)$
                                            $\eta x\ chpos(\text{TURN\_OFF}_{P1}, x, \dots)$

(6) a. $plane$ ——→ $v1$ ——— $\eta x\ plane(x)$
            $verb\_of(r3)$

    b. $plane$ ——→ $v2$ ——— $\iota x\ plane(x)$
            $verb\_of(r3)$

    c. $plane$ ——→ $v3$
            $verb\_of(r3)$

$v1$ corresponds to a verbalization of the referring expression *ein Flugzeug* 'a plane'; $v2$ to *das Flugzeug* 'the plane'. The coreference of both verbalization refOs is expressed by $verb\_of(r3)$. That is, the CCR refO from which both verbalization refOs were generated is $r3$. Thus, both verbalizations refer to the same entity. $v3$ shows the case that no designation was chosen, which currently happens if the designation was already used (§49). Thus, in (2b) a verbalization refO like $v3$ is used, because the $\eta x\ plane(x)$ description, from which the alternative $\iota x\ plane(x)$ would be computed, was already used in (2a).

If there is more than just one possible referent of a (reduced) referring expression, for example, both planes are possible referents in (2c)–(2e), it is sometimes necessary to suppress coreferences. Linguistic means to do this are to use expressions like *ein anderes Flugzeug* 'another plane' (v4; assume that the second plane is represented by r20), *das andere Flugzeug* 'the other plane' (v5), and *das erste/zweite Flugzeug* 'the first/second plane' (v6). The indefinite variant is chosen in the first mentioning, the definite ones afterward.

(7)   a.

$$\text{plane} \longrightarrow \text{v4} \longleftarrow \begin{array}{l} \eta x\,\text{plane}(x) \\ \eta x\,\text{different}(x, v1) \end{array}$$
$$\text{verb\_of}(r20) \nearrow$$

b.

$$\text{plane} \longrightarrow \text{v5} \longleftarrow \begin{array}{l} \iota x\,\text{plane}(x) \\ \iota x\,\text{different}(x, v1) \end{array}$$
$$\text{verb\_of}(r20) \nearrow$$

c.

$$\text{plane} \longrightarrow \text{v6} \longleftarrow \begin{array}{l} \iota x\,\text{plane}(x) \\ \iota x\,\text{first}(x, v1) \end{array}$$
$$\text{verb\_of}(r3) \nearrow$$

Another possibility for referring to an entity is used in (2e), where the plane is identified by its position in the world, *das Flugzeug auf Runway 1* 'the plane on Runway 1'. This is accomplished by generating additional verbalization refOs from the spatial structure given in the CCR that locate the referent (the plane).

With these extensions, PVM-generation can already generate naturally sounding online descriptions of events. However, it still has many possibilities for generating utterances describing a scene. INC would, therefore, profit from integrating a more elaborate activation model, which would indicate the prominent elements of the CCR that are good candidates for verbalization.

13

SIMULATIONS

SIMULATIONS ARE THE means to establish IN C's cognitive adequacy. Up to now, my description of IN C has concentrated on its architecture and algorithms. This chapter presents its implementation and how this is used for simulations. Central to this task is accounting for the great variability of the data as well as for the default mode of operation that reproduces the most common verbalizations. IN C does this by using different settings of its parameters; the default behavior is determined by finding default values for the parameters. In this chapter, I first describe the interface of IN C's implementation (§51). The data presented in the remainder of this chapter were published previously. Guhe et al. (2003a, 2003b) presents data on simulations in the motion event domain (§52), and Guhe and Habel (2001) present the data for simulations in the domain of drawing sketch maps (§53).

§ 51 *The IN C simulator*

IN C is implemented in Mozart/Oz.* IN C itself is a Mozart/Oz module that can interact with other modules. The *IN C simulator* is a graphical interface that facilitates carrying out the simulations. It is shown in figure 13.1, just before the start of a simulation for the example discussed in the next section.

In the top left of the simulator window, the four parameters for a simulation are specified. Next to this, the domain is chosen. Apart from the two domains I discuss here (motion events and the generation of sketch maps), users can define their own domains. This mainly affects the concept storage; thus, to use one's own domain, a file containing the CS must be supplied. The logging output can be sent to a window, a file, or both. The rightmost field determines whether IN C will run in a simulated real time condition. This option is required, because currently the PPU does not send its output directly to IN C but writes it to a file. IN C needs to synchronize to the output of the PPU, because the PPU does not generate perceived entities (PEs) at a constant rate; that is, the time intervals between the produced PEs vary. If no real time behavior is required, this option can be switched off. (The simulations

---

* Information about Mozart/Oz can be found at http://www.mozart-oz.org.

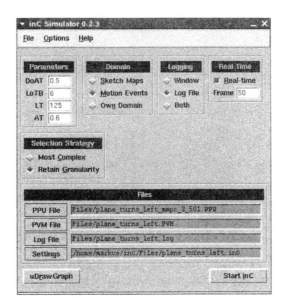

Figure 13.1: The INC simulator

showed that this has only little influence on INC's behavior.) The field below the checkbutton specifies the time of one frame of the PPU, usually 50 ms. Below these fields, the selection strategy is set. *Most Complex* stands for the standard selection strategy (see figure 11.2), *Retain Granularity* for the alternative one (see figure 11.3).

The bottom fields specify the files that are used by INC. The *PPU file* is the output of the PPU (thus, the input to INC), the *PVM file* is a text file containing the incremental preverbal messages (the output of INC), and the *log file* contains a log of INC's decisions and results. Because INC is indeterministic, this is a valuable means for reproducing the actual sequence in which INC performed its computations in a simulation. The *settings file*, finally, is used to store all the values just described.

The left of the two buttons at the bottom of the simulator window opens another window (not shown here) in which the settings for the visualization of the referential nets of the CCR and the CS are specified. The visualizations are done by the graph-drawing tool *uDraw(Graph)*.* Among other things, the window allows the filtering out of certain kinds of refOs (e.g., all verbalization refOs), because even simple referential nets are quite complex when visualized as graph. (This is due mainly to the many interrelations by attributes and designations.) uDraw(Graph) is also able

---

* This tool was formerly known under the name *DaVinci*. It can be obtained for all usual platforms at
http://www.informatik.uni-bremen.de/uDrawGraph/en/home.html.

Figure 13.2: A plane turning left

to draw the referential nets incrementally, that is, adding and updating nodes and edges as they become available. A graph drawn by uDraw(Graph) for the example discussed in the next section is given in appendix B.4. The button in the lower right corner starts the INC simulation.

§ 52   *A worked example*

The example simulation I present in this section is taken from Guhe et al. (2003a, 2003b). I use the example depicted in figure 13.2 instead of the one from chapter 1, because it is simpler (but complex nevertheless) and suffices for the purpose at hand. It consists of a plane taxiing straight forward and then, starting at the position indicated by the dot, moving to the left. (The participants in the corresponding verbalization study see neither the dot nor the dashed line.) The plane moves before a white background. The continuous movement is subdivided at the position of the dot; there is one subsituation where the plane moves forward and one where it moves to the left. The final state of CCR for the scene is given in figure 13.3. The system's actual output for this example is given in appendix B. Because it consists of text files, which are less readable than the drawn referential nets, I continue to use the graphical mode of presentation.

There are many possible verbalizations of this motion event. Some are given in (1) to (3). Utterance (1) describes the whole scene without going into the details of the event structure, whereas (2) and (3) take into account the subevents. The latter two verbalizations also express the temporal order of the subevents.*

---

* The incremental preverbal messages described in this section were produced without the extensions

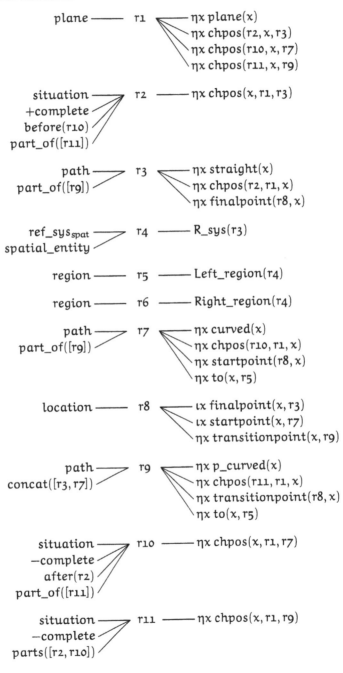

plane ——— r1 $\longleftarrow$ ηx plane(x)
$\qquad$ ηx chpos(r2, x, r3)
$\qquad$ ηx chpos(r10, x, r7)
$\qquad$ ηx chpos(r11, x, r9)

situation ——→ r2 ——— ηx chpos(x, r1, r3)
+complete
before(r10)
part_of([r11])

path ——→ r3 $\longleftarrow$ ηx straight(x)
part_of([r9]) $\qquad$ ηx chpos(r2, r1, x)
$\qquad$ ηx finalpoint(r8, x)

ref_sys$_{spat}$ ——→ r4 ——— R_sys(r3)
spatial_entity

region ——— r5 ——— Left_region(r4)

region ——— r6 ——— Right_region(r4)

path ——→ r7 $\longleftarrow$ ηx curved(x)
part_of([r9]) $\qquad$ ηx chpos(r10, r1, x)
$\qquad$ ηx startpoint(r8, x)
$\qquad$ ηx to(x, r5)

location ——— r8 $\longleftarrow$ ιx finalpoint(x, r3)
$\qquad$ ιx startpoint(x, r7)
$\qquad$ ηx transitionpoint(x, r9)

path ——→ r9 $\longleftarrow$ ηx p_curved(x)
concat([r3, r7]) $\qquad$ ηx chpos(r11, r1, x)
$\qquad$ ηx transitionpoint(r8, x)
$\qquad$ ηx to(x, r5)

situation ——→ r10 ——— ηx chpos(x, r1, r7)
−complete
after(r2)
part_of([r11])

situation ——→ r11 ——— ηx chpos(x, r1, r9)
−complete
parts([r2, r10])

Figure 13.3: Final state of the CCR for the plane turning left

(1) *Ein Flugzeug fährt nach links.*
     'A plane moves to the left.'
(2) *Ein Flugzeug bewegt sich geradeaus und fährt eine Linkskurve.*
     'A plane moves straight ahead and follows a left curve.'
(3) *Ein Flugzeug fährt und biegt nach links ab.*
     'A plane moves and turns off to the left.'

❧ PARAMETERS.   The default values for INC's parameters are:

- DOAT = 0.5
- LOTB = 6
- LT = 125 ms
- AT = 0.5

With these values INC exhibits "normal" behavior. The value for DOAT ascertains
that expectations are only generated if a substantial amount already has been perceived. The value for LOTB makes sure that nothing is lost due to the size limitation
of the traverse buffer. This usually only happens with values of 1 or 2. An LT of
125 ms has the effect that the situations that were selected by the selection process
are indeed verbalized. The only exception is if INC reads in a new PE and creates a
complex concept containing this new PE. The standard selection strategy replaces
the simpler element of the traverse buffer by the more complex one. Finally, an AT
of 0.5 means that only rather prominent designations are chosen for verbalization.

❧ CONSTRUCTION.   There are two points in time when construction obtains
information about new PEs; all other information sent by the PPU updates already
existing PEs. The first point is when the plane becomes visible. Then the PPU sends information about three PEs consisting of the triple of refOs about object, situation,
and spatial_entity (cf. p. 125), which results in the creation of r1–r3. The second
point is when the plane starts moving to the left, which brings about r7, r8, and r10.
r9 and r11 are inserted because of the concept matcher's matching results.
     Each path induces a spatial reference system, which I did not elaborate on in
chapter 10. It is introduced by three additional PEs coming from the PPU. The first
one introduces r4 of sort ref_sys$_{spat}$. It is linked to r3—the path generating the
reference system—by a functional relation. It is a functional relation, because r4 is
the only spatial reference system of r3.* At the same time, the path subdivides the
space into two half-planes with respect to its reference system: the left region (r5)

described in §50. Thus, temporal relations and coreferences are not computed explicitly.
* As the implementation cannot yet deal with functional expressions, it uses a ι-abstracted description
  instead.

and the right region (r6).

When the plane starts moving to the left, the PPU sends the second set of new PES. The new PES result in the creation of the path refO r7, which represents the curved part of the movement, the location refO r8, where the two paths meet, and the corresponding situation refO r10. According to the rule given in figure 10.4, the two path refOs are grouped to r9 for the overall path and the two situations to r11 for the overall situation.

❧ SELECTION.   The event structure of this example consists of only three situation refOs (r2, r10, r11); thus, the selection process selects one of two event sequences when the parameters are set to the default values. Using the standard selection strategy select the first situation refO (r2) and the situation refO encompassing the whole movement (r11). The alternative selection strategy, which retains the level of granularity as far as possible, selects the two simple movements (r2 and r10).

❧ PVM-GENERATION.   Compared to the previous two processes, PVM-generation has to perform rather complex computations. To simplify matters in the following, I assume that the scene has been completely perceived and that the parameters are set so that only the complex situation r11 is verbalized. This requires the most complex computations by PVM-generation for this scene. The required setting is LT $\geqslant$ 6050 ms, because r11 must be generated by construction before the first simple situation representing the movement along the straight path (r2) has been taken out of the traverse buffer by PVM-generation.* Only for LT = 0 ms are all situations including r10 verbalized; for values 0 ms < LT < 6050 ms, r2 and r11 are selected. The parameter values for the simulation I describe in the following are DOAT = 0.5, LOTB = 6, LT = 6050 ms, AT = 0.5. See appendix B for INC's actual output.

PVM-generation starts the generation of the incremental preverbal message for r11 with choosing description ηx chpos(x, r1, r9). No other designations have been generated so far, so it cannot be cyclic. Hence, it is chosen, sent to the formulator, and appended to the traverse.

Then, the two refOs referred to must be described. r1 contains four descriptions. ηx chpos(r11, x, r9) is cyclic, because—like the first description—it can be reduced

---

* The value is explained by the difference between the times that r2 and r10 inserted into the CCR. The PPU file given in appendix B.1 shows that PE number 2, which results in r2, is inserted after 200 time frames. This is the point of time when the first triple of PE is read in by INC. PE 7 (resulting in r10) follows after 320 time frames total, that is, 120 time frames or 6000 ms later. (Remember that a time frame is 50 ms.) Because matching and inserting the complex occurs almost instantaneously, r11 is inserted only a little later. So, for r2 *not* to be verbalized (i.e., in order that selection will replace it with r11), the LT must be longer than this time, or at least 6050 ms.

to chpos(r11, r1, r9). Therefore, it is not used. ηx plane(x) is directly grounded and conforms to the other constraints, for which reason it is chosen. When trying to ground ηx chpos(r2, x, r3) and ηx chpos(r10, x, r7), refOs r2 and r10 come up in the grounding chain. Neither has a groundable designation, because the chpos descriptions are cyclic, and neither contains any other designations. Consequently, neither designation can be grounded, and neither is chosen.

Examining the second refO (r9) yields that it has a directly grounded description, ηx p_curved(x), which is chosen immediately, because it violates no constraints. ηx chpos(r11, r1, x) is cyclic and, consequently, filtered out. The description ηx transitionpoint(r8, x) leads to the investigation of r8. Apart from the cyclic ηx transitionpoint(x, r9), refO r8 contains only descriptions with low activation values. The rationale is that the location is perceived mainly as a transition point and not as starting or endpoint, because at this point the orientation of the plane starts changing. Because the plane does not stop at this position, the latter two descriptions receive a very low activation value. Thus, they are only used if AT has a low value. Assume that the activation is below the activation threshold (INC sets these activations to 0.1), and no description of r8 can be used for grounding. Then, the grounding of ηx transitionpoint(r8, x) of r9 fails.

Transition points seem to play a special role in describing motion events. They are verbalized primarily if a landmark is close by. (This is not the case in the example at hand.) If the transition point is, for example, close to a TOWER, it can be referred to easily, as in (4). What is more, selecting the transition point means that the resulting verbalization can contain the verb *abbiegen* 'turn off' (Eschenbach et al., 1999, 2000). However, *abbiegen* already incorporates the transition point, so the additional phrase is optional, as in (5).

(4) *Ein Flugzeug biegt am Tower ab.*
     'A plane turns off at the tower.'
(5) *Ein Flugzeug biegt ab.*
     'A plane turns off.'

Vice versa, if the transition point is not chosen, the verbalization will not contain the verb *abbiegen* (and this is the reason the current example is *fäht nach links* 'moves to the left' and not *biegt nach links ab* 'turns off to the left'). Note that this is a working hypothesis on the basis of the theoretical analysis I describe here. Initial results from the corresponding subsequent verbalization study later corroborated this hypothesis.

Finally, the description, ηx to(x, r5) is checked. r5 is the left region of the reference system created by the straight path r3. Therefore, it contains the functional expression Left_region(r4). r4 refers to r3, which contains the directly grounded description ηx straight(x). Thus, ηx to$(x, r5)$ is grounded and, hence, chosen. However, because $r3$ is also part of a refO in the current preverbal message ($r9$), the homogeneous-part-of constraint brings about that none of $r4$'s descriptions is actually chosen when it is generated. This is a case in which a groundable designation is not chosen. In other words, ηx straight(x) serves to ground the designation ηx to$(x, r5)$ but is not verbalized, because it is ruled out by another constraint.

With this, the verbalization of the situation represented by $r11$ is finished. The preverbal message created this way will result in an utterance like (1), repeated here as (6a).

(6)   a.   *Ein Flugzeug fährt nach links.*
          'A plane moves to the left.'

   b.
$$\text{situation} \xrightarrow{\quad} v1 \xrightarrow{\quad} \eta x \, \text{chpos}(x, v2, v3)$$
$$\text{verb\_of}(r11)$$

$$\text{plane} \xrightarrow{\quad} v2 \xrightarrow{\quad} \eta x \, \text{plane}(x)$$
$$\text{verb\_of}(r1)$$

$$\text{path} \xrightarrow{\quad} v3 \begin{cases} \eta x \, \text{p\_curved}(x) \\ \eta x \, \text{to}(x, v4) \end{cases}$$
$$\text{verb\_of}(r9)$$

$$\text{region} \xrightarrow{\quad} v4 \xrightarrow{\quad} \text{Left\_region}(v5)$$
$$\text{verb\_of}(r5)$$

$$\text{ref\_sys}_{\text{spat}} \xrightarrow{\quad} v5$$
$$\text{verb\_of}(r4)$$

Two similar examples of incremental preverbal messages and corresponding verbalizations can be generated with an AT > 0.5, resulting in (7), and an AT $= 0.4$, resulting in (8). For more details, see the system output in appendix B.2.

(7)   a.   *Ein Flugzeug fährt eine Kurve.*
          'A plane follows a curve.'

   b.
$$\text{situation} \xrightarrow{\quad} v1 \xrightarrow{\quad} \eta x \, \text{chpos}(x, v2, v3)$$
$$\text{verb\_of}(r11)$$

$$\text{plane} \xrightarrow{\quad} v2 \xrightarrow{\quad} \eta x \, \text{plane}(x)$$
$$\text{verb\_of}(r1)$$

$$\text{path} \longrightarrow \text{v3} \longrightarrow \eta x \; p\_curved(x)$$
$$\text{verb\_of(r9)} \nearrow$$

(8) a. *Ein Flugzeug biegt ab.*
    'A plane turns off.'

b.
$$\text{situation} \longrightarrow \text{v1} \longrightarrow \eta x \; chpos(x, v2, v3)$$
$$\text{verb\_of(r11)} \nearrow$$

$$\text{plane} \longrightarrow \text{v2} \longrightarrow \eta x \; plane(x)$$
$$\text{verb\_of(r1)} \nearrow$$

$$\text{path} \longrightarrow \text{v3} \quad \begin{array}{l} \longleftarrow \eta x \; p\_curved(x) \\ \searrow \eta x \; transitionpoint(v4, x) \end{array}$$
$$\text{verb\_of(r9)} \nearrow$$

$$\text{location} \longrightarrow \text{v4}$$
$$\text{verb\_of(r8)} \nearrow$$

Coming back to the idea that the perspective of an utterance arises from the sequence in which the increments are generated, it is now clear how PVM-generation can produce utterances with different perspectives. To take just one example, consider the case that $to(r7, Left\_region(r4))$ is generated directly after the situation refO. This leads to a topicalized utterance like

(9) *Nach links bewegt sich etwas.*
    'To the left something moves.'

Currently, however, PVM-generation visits the refOs in the order in which they occur in the designation that is just verbalized. As this limits the number of possible verbalizations, a computational mechanism should be added that results in different orderings, for example, additional constraints. Note that this additional computational mechanism should also not perform an explicit linearization, for the reasons already laid out. Instead, it should depend on factors like activation, focus, or attention.

Concluding this example, remember that selection plays a crucial role for the utterances generated by PVM-generation. For example, a lower value for LT (a shorter latency) has the effect that PVM-generation takes out the head of traverse buffer earlier so that not only the refO representing the whole situation (r11) is verbalized. The alternative selection strategy furthermore has the effect that rather than the most complex situation (r11), the two simpler ones (r2 and r10) are taken. This results in the generation of two preverbal messages, for which a corresponding verbalization is

(10)   *Ein Flugzeug fährt geradeaus. Es fährt nach links.**
       'A plane is moving straight forward. It is moving to the left.'

The preverbal messages underlying such an utterance is

(11)

$$
\begin{array}{l}
\text{situation} \longrightarrow v_1 \longrightarrow \eta x\,\text{chpos}(x, v_2, v_3) \\
\text{verb\_of}(r_2)
\end{array}
$$

$$
\begin{array}{l}
\text{plane} \longrightarrow v_2 \longrightarrow \eta x\,\text{plane}(x) \\
\text{verb\_of}(r_1)
\end{array}
$$

$$
\begin{array}{l}
\text{path} \longrightarrow v_3 \longrightarrow \eta x\,\text{straight}(x) \\
\text{verb\_of}(r_3)
\end{array}
$$

$$
\begin{array}{l}
\text{situation} \longrightarrow v_4 \longrightarrow \eta x\,\text{chpos}(x, v_5, v_6) \\
\text{verb\_of}(r_{10}) \\
\text{after}(v_1)
\end{array}
$$

$$
\begin{array}{l}
\text{plane} \longrightarrow v_5 \\
\text{verb\_of}(r_1)
\end{array}
$$

$$
\begin{array}{l}
\text{path} \longrightarrow v_6 \longleftarrow \eta x\,\text{curved}(x) \\
\text{verb\_of}(r_7) \qquad\quad \eta x\,\text{to}(x, v_7)
\end{array}
$$

$$
\begin{array}{l}
\text{region} \longrightarrow v_7 \longrightarrow \text{Left\_region}(v_8) \\
\text{verb\_of}(r_5)
\end{array}
$$

$$
\begin{array}{l}
\text{ref\_sys}_{\text{spat}} \longrightarrow v_8 \\
\text{verb\_of}(r_4)
\end{array}
$$

After v_3, the verbalization of the first situation is completed, and v_4 starts a new preverbal message. The second verbalization of the plane (v_5) contains no designation, because $\eta x\,\text{plane}(x)$ was already used in the first verbalization (v_2). (The first verbalization adds the description to the used_desigs list; cf. § 49.)

---

* Although using unconnected utterances may sound unusual, it is in fact predominant in the verbalizations given in appendix C.

❧ WHAT HAPPENS NEXT.   The designations of a refO are closely related to lexical items. For example, the description ηx to(x, r5) corresponds to lexical items of
prepositions specifying a goal. Yet, a direct correspondence between designation
and lexical item is not always given: The lexical item for *abbiegen* 'turn off' contains not only a transition point but also a component for motion, corresponding
to a propositional formula like chpos(r11, r1, r9). Each increment of a preverbal
message that is received by the formulator triggers a lexical access—the selection
of a lemma, to be precise—which is the first step in the generation of the syntactic
structure. Which lexical item is accessed depends mainly on which designations are
chosen. The details, however, are beyond the scope of this book.

❧ EVALUATION.   Instead of providing a statistical evaluation, I present some
additional incremental preverbal messages that INC can generate by using different
settings to give an impression of the range of output it generates. There are two main
reasons for not making a statistical evaluation. First, the variability in the observed
verbalizations and in the output of INC make this a daunting undertaking. Second,
there is not yet an adequately large corpus of verbalizations available to do this.

The three resource parameters DOAT, LOTB, and LT will be discussed extensively
in the next section. Therefore, I mainly discuss how the parameter AT and the
selection strategy cause different behavior of INC, that is, how different incremental
preverbal messages are generated. I only use the activation values of descriptions
and no activations of refOs. Figure 13.4 shows the incremental preverbal messages
generated by INC for DOAT = 0.5, LOTB = 6, LT = 125, AT = 0.6, and the alternative
selection strategy that retains the level of granularity.

Because the numbers of refOs are assigned by the system, the numbering can
be different in each simulation. In this notation, <<. . . >> stands for the activation
value of a designation. The attribute at_time represents the time interval of the
situation; for example, at_time(0 200) says that the situation represented by
r8 happened in time frames 0 to 200. Given that each time frame spans 50 ms,
this means that it lasted 10 s. Two situation refOs, r8 and r16, are selected in this
simulation. As they must now be verbalized, PVM-generation uses their designations
although the activation is below AT (cf. chap. 12). The other refOs have designations
above AT. The incremental preverbal message may result in an utterance like

(12)   *Ein Flugzeug fährt geradeaus. Es fährt eine Kurve.*
       'A plane moves straight ahead. It moves on a curve.'

For AT = 0.5, the incremental preverbal message is continued as shown in figure 13.5; see appendix B.2 for the full output of this and the following simulations. In
this simulation, the eta x: to(x, 24) designation is chosen by PVM-generation

```
=======================================================
This is the PVM file of inC version 0.2.2 (build 077)
DoAT=0.5; LoTB=6; LT=125; AT=0.6
Domain: motionEvents
Selection Strategy: retainGranularity
Real-Time: true; Time Frame: 50


------------------------------------------------------
New PVM starting with ref0 8

situation ----------- r13  ---- eta x: chpos(x 14 15)   <<0.5>>
verb_of(8)
at_time(0 200)
status(regular)
pe(2)


object -------------- r14  ---- eta x: plane(x)   <<0.9>>
verb_of(7)
plane
status(regular)
pe(1)


path ---------------- r15  ---- eta x: straight(x)   <<0.6>>
verb_of(9)
status(regular)
pe(3)


------------------------------------------------------
New PVM starting with ref0 16

situation ----------- r21  ---- eta x: chpos(x 22 23)   <<0.5>>
verb_of(16)
part_of([19])
met_by(8)
at_time(201 320)
status(regular)
pe(7)


object -------------- r22  ----
verb_of(7)
plane
status(regular)
pe(1)


path ---------------- r23  ---- eta x: curved(x)   <<0.6>>
verb_of(17)
part_of([20])
status(regular)
pe(8)
```

Figure 13.4: An incremental preverbal message generated by INC for DOAT = 0.5, LOTB = 6,
LT = 125, AT = 0.6

```
path ---------------- r23  ---- eta x: to(x, 24)       <<0.5>>
verb_of(17)                     eta x: curved(x)       <<0.6>>
part_of([20])
status(regular)
pe(8)

region -------------- r24  ---- iota x: Left_region(x 25)   <<0.5>>
verb_of(11)
status(regular)
pe(5)

ref_sys_spat -------- r25  ----
verb_of(10)
spatial_entity
status(regular)
pe(4)
```

Figure 13.5: Continuation for AT = 0.5

as well, which means that r24 and, consequently, r25 must also be generated. This preverbal message is similar to the one in (6).

Another verbalization arises if the standard selection strategy is used. The first incremental preverbal message, describing the straight movement, is identical to the one in figure 13.4. For the second preverbal message, however, the situation refO representing the whole movement is selected (r19 in figure 13.6). The output given in figure 13.6 was generated using an AT = 0.4, but it would be the same for 0.1 < AT < 0.5. These AT values mean that eta x: transitionpoint(24 x) is generated as well, which will have the proposed impact on the selected lexemes later on: With this additional designation, a lexeme like *abbiegen* 'turn off' is chosen.

(13) *Ein Flugzeug fährt geradeaus. Es biegt ab.*
      'A plane moves straight ahead. It turns off.'

If AT is set to 0.1, even more designations and refOs are generated. The (rather strange) output is given in appendix B.2. It is unlikely that these incremental preverbal messages reflect human verbalizations.

Summing up, for the discussed example, two factors mainly influence the generated output. The selection strategy decides whether the two simple situations are described, or the first simple one and the complex situation. If, additionally, LT ⩾ 6050 ms, only the complex situation is generated. The value of AT influences which designations are used in the incremental preverbal messages; AT > 0.1 ensures that no spurious designations are chosen.

```
--------------------------------------------------
New PVM starting with ref0 19

situation ---------- r21  ---- eta x: chpos(x 22 23)    <<0.5>>
verb_of(19)
parts([8 16])
at_time(0 320)
status(regular)

object -------------- r22  ----
verb_of(7)
plane
status(regular)
pe(1)

path --------------- r23  ---- eta x: transitionpoint(24 x)   <<0.4>>
verb_of(20)                    eta x: p_curved(x)    <<0.6>>
concat([9 17])
status(regular)

location ----------- r24  ----
verb_of(18)
status(regular)
pe(9)
```

Figure 13.6: The second incremental preverbal message for AT = 0.4 and the standard selection strategy

§ 53   A worked example for the generation of sketch maps

The first phase of INC's development did not use the domain of motion events but the domain of the verbalization of dynamic sketch maps. Additionally, descriptions of sketch maps have a more complex event structure, which makes it easier to demonstrate the effects of different values for the three parameters DOAT, LOTB, and LT. The simulations reported in the following were carried out with a precursor of the current implementation, which was done in Prolog. One insight gained by these simulations was that Prolog needs a lot of resources for INC's algorithms—run-time as well as memory. This was the main reason for switching to Mozart/Oz, which directly supports INC's process-based architecture. As a consequence, the current version of INC is much more efficient. The older implementation contains no parameter AT. However, since this parameter is mainly used in the selection of designations in PVM-generation, which is not required in the following, this has no effect on the data discussed here.

For this domain, drawings of sketch maps were recorded with a drawing tablet in the first phase of the empirical studies. These sketch maps were then presented to

Figure 13.7: A simple sketch

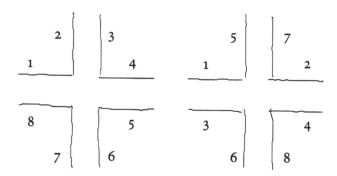

Figure 13.8: Different sequences of drawing the lines of the crossing

participants of verbalization studies, who were instructed to describe what they saw. The sketch maps were shown to them as they developed on the screen. In technical terms, each 50 ms a pixel was added at the coordinates where the drawing pen was registered during the recording. Depending on whether the pen was up or down, a white or a black pixel was added. As in the other study, the participants did not describe the resulting sketch map but how it was drawn. So, again, this study focused on investigating the conceptualization of events.

An example of a very simple sketch is shown in figure 13.7, a crossing consisting of eight lines. The numbers in figure 13.8 indicate two different sequences in which the eight lines of this crossing were drawn. A closer look reveals that the two crossings also differ in the shape of the lines. For example the lines annotated by 1 and 5 in the right crossing do not meet at their endpoints, whereas in the left drawing they do. These differences are due to the fact that the sketches were drawn free-hand. Because such deviations from ideal straight lines are handled by the PPU for this domain,

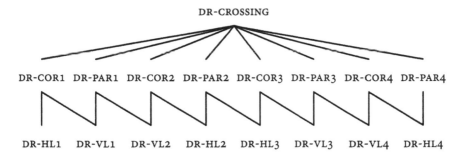

Figure 13.9: The event structure of the first crossing (the connection between DR-PAR4 and DR-HL1 is left out for better readability)

they will concern us no further. On the conceptual level, they can be regarded as ideal, straight lines. The crucial point here is that the lines are read by INC in different sequences. Thus, although the object structure is identical in both cases, the event structure differs. In the following, I mainly consider the left crossing.

The hierarchical event structure of the left crossing is given in figure 13.9. In this figure, DR-HL stands for the event of drawing a horizontal line, DR-VL for drawing a vertical line. DR-PAR represents the drawing of two parallel lines (e.g., the ones annotated by 1 and 8 in the left crossing in figure 13.8), DR-COR that of a corner, that is, two lines meeting at their endpoints (e.g., 1 and 2). DR-CROSSING denotes the event of drawing the whole crossing. In figure 13.9, the line linking DR-PAR4 to DR-HL1 is left out for better readability. The temporal order of the events corresponds to their positions from left to right. The structure of the object representation is isomorphic to the event representation, except for the temporal ordering.

The sketches were presented to 12 participants. Their verbal descriptions were recorded and transcribed. Ten of the participants used the following pattern to describe the drawing of the left crossing:

· Frst segment (DR-HL1)
· Intermediary complexes (DR-COR1, DR-PAR1, DR-COR2)
· Crossing expected (DR-CROSSING)
· Intermediary complexes (DR-COR3, DR-PAR3, DR-COR4)
· Crossing complete (DR-CROSSING)

One of the remaining two participants kept silent until the sketch was complete and then said:

```
TB: hline1                        TB: crossingE
TB: hline1, vline1                Gen: crossingE
Gen: hline1                       TB: corner3
TB: corner1                       Gen: corner3
TB: corner1, vline2               TB: vline4
Gen: corner1                      TB: parallel3
TB: parallel1                     TB: parallel3, hline4
TB: parallel1, hline2             Gen: parallel3
TB: parallel1, corner2            TB: corner4
Gen: parallel1                    Gen: corner4
TB: corner2                       TB: parallel4
TB: corner2, hline3               TB: crossingR
Gen: corner2                      Gen: crossingR
TB: parallel2
```

Figure 13.10: Log-output for the verbalization of the crossing

(14) *eine Kreuzung oder 'n Kreuz*
      'a crossing or a cross'

The 12th participant uttered no expectations but only described the emerging lines before naming the result. The other 10 differed only slightly in how much of the crossing was visible when they produced the expectation, but all named it before it was fully visible. The verbalizations of the other crossing stick to a similar standard pattern:

· The first two segments (DR-HL1, DR-HL2)
· Intermediary complexes (DR-PAR1, DR-PAR2, DR-COR1)
· Crossing expected (DR-CROSSING)
· Intermediary complexes (DR-PAR3/DR-COR2, DR-PAR4/DR-COR3)*
· Crossing complete (DR-CROSSING)

The output of a simulation for the first crossing with DOA = 0.5, LOTB = 6, and LT = 125 ms is given in figure 13.10. The following notation is used: Lines starting with TB contain the state of the traverse buffer at that point in time; they are generated as soon as the content of the traverse buffer changed. Lines starting with Gen indicate that this refO is verbalized, that is, sent to the formulator by PVM-generation. Entries like hline1 stand for the corresponding node in the event structure, here: DR-HL1. crossingE is an expected crossing, crossingR a completely perceived one. So,

---

* Here, DR-PAR and DR-COR are generated at the same time. As there is no temporal criterion for selecting one of the two, the choice is random.

here preverbal messages are not generated completely but only their "core." For example, Gen: hline1 can be understood as a preverbal message that leads to an utterance like

(15) *Ein horizontaler Strich wurde gezeichnet.*
      'A horizontal line has been drawn.'

❧ EVALUATION.   The output of the simulations is close to the observed human verbalizations. In other words, the sequence of preverbal messages (Gen lines) corresponds structurally to the sequences of utterances of the human verbalizations.

The values for LT and the run-time of the program in the following are machine dependent and possess only limited cognitive adequacy, because this implementation of INC can only read prefabricated input files and does not have the ability to simulate real time behavior. Thus, the simulations were faster than real time, albeit directly proportional to it. The values for DOAT and LOTB certainly come closer to being psychologically real.

DOAT was set to 0.5 and 0.9, LOTB to values between 2 and 6, and LT was varied between 50 ms and 2000 ms. The run-time of the program is split into two phases: (a) 1400 ms for the initialization of program and the concept storage and (b) the run-time of the conceptualization. The second value, which is the important one here, is 2700 ms to 3000 ms for the first crossing and 2500 ms to 2800 ms for the second one. The differences in run-time are due to the fact that several preprocessing files per sketch were used, all of which yielded equivalent output but took a different run-time. The values of the parameters for both crossings resulting in the simulation of the human verbalizations sketched previously were determined as INC's default values: DOAT = 0.5, LOTB = 6, LT = 125 ms.* (These values are the same that the Mozart/Oz implementation uses, and the new implementation structurally produces the same output as the Prolog implementation. This corroborates the similarity of both implementations.) Varying these default parameter values creates the following effects.

The maximum DOA for the crossings before they are complete is 0.81. Therefore, the maximum value of DOAT that has the effect that an expected crossing is introduced into the CCR is 0.8. Thus, using DOAT = 0.9 instead of 0.5 means that no expectation is inserted into the CCR.

A value for LOTB > 5 is never needed. LOTB = 5 is required for LT ⩾ 800 ms, if no elements of the traverse buffer get lost. LOTB = 3 suffices for most settings; only with LT ⩽ 125 ms does a value of 2 suffice. Other settings (LOTB < 3 with 125 ms < LT

---

* In fact, each value of LT > 1 suffices for the default case, but this way it is ascertained that no element of the traverse buffer gets lost.

< 800 ms or LOTB < 5 for LT ⩾ 800 ms) have the effect that elements are lost. A value of LOTB = 1 means that elements are lost, and in almost all cases, only the complete crossing is verbalized. (In this case, the output sequence shows considerable gaps, which corresponds to verbalizations in which the participant did not keep up with the ongoing events. In the recorded verbalizations, however, there were no such cases.)

As in the case discussed in §52, decreasing the value for LT means that more preverbal messages are produced; increasing it leads to the production of less. From an LT ⩾ 800 ms on, no simple elements and no intermediary complex refOs (parallels, corners) are verbalized but only the expected and the complete crossing (crossingE and crossingR). The maximum value that still leads to the production of a preverbal message for the expected crossing is around 500 ms for the first crossing and around 1000 ms for the second crossing. (Both values should be more or less the same. The gap is an artefact that arises because the simulations were carried out with preprocessed files as input.) So, using these values produces the verbalization of participant 11 given in (14). With LT < 125 ms, more simple events and some intermediary complex ones, which are otherwise replaced by selection before they are generated, are verbalized. With LT = 50 ms, each selected node is verbalized. This is the pattern observed with participant 12.

Thus, INC produced all types of verbalizations present in the verbalization corpus. The different verbalizations are produced by varying the parameters. The main class of verbalizations is produced by setting the parameters to their default values. (Vice versa, the default values were determined by evaluating the corpus.) But INC can also generate the more unusual cases of participants 11 and 12.

14

MONITORING AND SELF-CORRECTIONS

*M*ONITORING AND MESSAGES GENERATION are the two subcomponents of the conceptualizer. The monitor compares a speaker's actual utterances with the planned ones. That is, it compares the output of the language comprehension system for the speaker's own utterances to the corresponding utterance plans. Although INC is mainly a model of the message generation component, in this chapter I lay the foundation of extending it by a monitoring component. I first explain the problem of detecting errors in the conceptualizer and the consequences this has for INC (§54). Then, I describe the implementation of a rudimentary monitor for INC (§55).

§54   Detecting errors

Because INC is not connected to a formulator and a language comprehension system, the monitor only detects artificially generated errors, which dramatically limits the conclusions that can be drawn. Figuratively speaking, one cannot ascertain that detecting such errors is more than pulling the rabbit out of the hat one has previously placed just there. However, the main purpose of this prototypical component is to explore the ways in which INC can be extended by a monitoring component (cf. figure 14.1).*

In conceptualization, there are two main sources for errors: performance errors, usually detected by self-monitoring, and what I call conceptual changes (Guhe & Schilder, 2002a). *Performance errors* are errors that are caused by a malfunction of the system, for example, accessing the wrong lexeme for a lemma. *Conceptual changes* are changes in the conceptual representation that affect a part of the representation that has just been uttered. Whereas for performance errors it can be argued that NLG systems should not make such errors (which is usually the goal in noncognitively motivated NLG research), it is impossible to avoid conceptual changes in an incrementally working system. There are two ways to detect errors:

---

* Calling the INC implementation with the monitor in operation requires closing the loop from preverbal messages to parsed speech. This is done by calling the INC module directly from a Mozart/Oz program that contains this loop. This program reads the preverbal messages generated by INC, inserts errors, and sends these modified "post"verbal messages back to the INC monitor as "parsed speech."

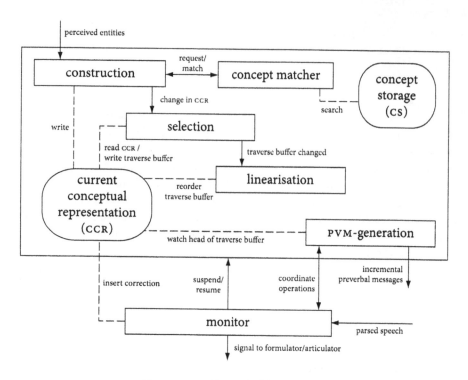

Figure 14.1: IN C extended by a monitor

1. Comparing the planned with the produced utterances and
2. Comparing the planned (and produced) utterances with the current state of affairs.

Whereas the first method requires a monitoring component, the latter can be used at different points of conceptualization by different processes:

1. PVM-generation compares the content of the current preverbal message to the content of the CCR. If a refO in the CCR changes and the refO is used in the current preverbal message, a self-correction is generated.
2. PVM-generation detects "dead ends," that is, situations where the speaker "talked himself into a corner" (de Smedt, 1990a, p. 29). (PVM-generation can do this only for semantic errors; if the dead end is due to the grammatical structure, a cooperation of monitor and language comprehension system is required.)
3. Construction compares the content of the traverse (or the complete CCR) with its focused element. Because construction's focused element is the element of the CCR that it used—and perhaps changed—most recently, it is the best starting point to find

changes in the CCR.* In this case, the contradiction must be explicitly represented in the CCR's referential net in order to be selected and verbalized.

4. The monitor compares what was said (what is in the traverse) with the current state of affairs stored in the CCR.

Only two of these cases are currently realized. The monitor compares planned with produced refOs (case 4), and PVM-generation compares the refOs in the current preverbal message with the current state of these refOs in the CCR (case 1). The functioning of the monitor requires a *monitored traverse*.

TERM 31: MONITORED TRAVERSE
The monitored traverse is the part of the CCR that contains the information that has been received by the monitor from the language comprehension system. This information is correlated with the information in the CCR and the traverse. In the ideal case, this is a one-to-one correspondence of refOs.

The refOs in the monitored traverse are linked to other CCR refOs—in particular, those in the traverse—by computing similarities between monitored refOs and the other CCR refOs. If there are no errors, each refO in the monitored traverse has a corresponding refO in the traverse.

§ 55   *The exploratory monitor implementation*

Figure 14.2 shows the overall structure of the monitor process. The monitor process loops until no more parsed speech will follow that corresponds to preverbal messages generated by the message generation component. Technically, for the termination, the monitor and PVM-generation follow a synchronization protocol that ascertains that (a) the monitor will send no further instructions to PVM-generation to generate corrections and that (b) equally makes sure that PVM-generation does not generate any output that the monitor will have to check against the traverse. The details of this protocol are of no interest here.

In the loop, the monitor waits for an increment of parsed speech. When one is available, it is appended to the monitored traverse. Then, the monitor checks if the increment has a corresponding increment in the traverse or if there is some

---

* The knowledge that is corrected by such a verbalization must not necessarily have been uttered overtly. Having planned the utterance suffices. An example is:

  (i) *The ball is red. I thought it was orange.*

  Thus, the corrected utterance (*The ball is orange*) was never uttered. However, this not what I consider a self-correction here.

```
var monitored_traverse,
    traverse,  #traverse in the CCR
    parsed_speech_stream,  #input stream containing the parsed speech
    pvm_gen_stream  #increment stream for coordination with PVM-generation
while coordination for termination with PVM-generation fails do
    wait parsed_speech_stream ≠ ⟨⟩
    input_inc ← Fetch(parsed_speech_stream)
    Append(input_inc, monitored_traverse)
    if input_inc ∉ traverse or
        Mismatch(monitored_traverse, traverse) then
        suspend message generation component
        signal [formulator, articulator]
        correction ← ComputeCorrection(input_inc)
        Insert(correction, ccr)
        Append(correction, pvm_gen_stream)
        resume message generation component
    endif
endwhile
```

Figure 14.2: The monitor process

other new mismatch between the monitored traverse and the traverse. If an error is detected, the message generation component is suspended and a signal is sent directly to formulator and articulator. (Hartsuiker & Kolk, 2001, show that humans can almost instantly stop utterance production on detection of an error.) Then, the correction is computed, inserted into the CCR, and sent to PVM-generation. Finally, the message generation component is resumed. Note that chapter 12 does not describe the corresponding part of PVM-generation. In each iteration of its loop, PVM-generation checks whether the monitor sent a correction, and, if so, it generates the required increments.

The current implementation is actually a bit simpler. The monitor only tries to find a refO in the traverse that was not yet received as parsed speech and that is identical to the input increment (input_inc). If this fails, ComputeCorrection searches for the refO that is the one most similar to input_inc. This refO is assumed to be the refO that should have been verbalized. The correction information sent to PVM-generation consists of

· Which refO to correct,
· Which information is to be deleted from the refO, and
· Which information is to be added to the refO.

One problem in particular is not addressed by this: The parsed speech need not be subdivided into refOs in the same way as the preverbal messages. (After all, language comprehension is not simply language production backward.) Hence, finding correspondences between the monitored traverse and the traverse is a quite complex task.

The interleaving of message generation and monitoring is a central aspect of the incrementality of generation: How far apart are conceptualization and receiving the corresponding parsed speech? This is a twofold question. The first is what time intervals (how many ms) there are between generating the increments of preverbal messages and receiving the corresponding increments as parsed speech. The second is how many increments message generation is ahead of the corresponding parsed speech. Answering these questions depends on the following points:

1. How long does it take for an increment of an incremental preverbal message to be encoded into language and decoded again into parsed speech?
2. How long does it take for an increment to be generated? (At what rate does the conceptualizer generate increments of preverbal messages?)

A good assumption is that both proceed at roughly the same speed. But these are difficult questions, in particular because identifying increments is difficult to establish experimentally so high in the language production system. There are a few empirical findings and computational models that give first clues (see, e.g., Hartsuiker & Kolk, 2001). These will have to be considered for developing INC further, but I do not discuss this here. It seems clear, though, that self-corrections are generated rapidly as can be seen from the face that utterance production— including articulation—is often interrupted even while the flawed segment is being uttered (Levelt, 1983). This means, feedback is rapidly available, and there is only a short delay between generating the increment of a preverbal message and perceiving the corresponding verbalization—provided the increment is immediately generated by the formulator, that is, no reordering takes place. The very least that can be said is that this delay is so short that generation of an increment, parsing it again, and interrupting one's own speech can all occur during the production of the increment that is corrected.

❦ 15 ❦

EVALUATION AND ENHANCEMENTS

*M*ODELS LIKE INC can never be complete, and I already pointed out some of INC's limitations and possible enhancements. In this chapter, I review what INC has already achieved and point out ways in which it can and should be extended and improved. I, start by recapitulating the main points of this book (§56) and compare the approach I take with INC to Levelt's original conception (§57). I then describe general enhancements that will improve INC (§58) and give a number of additional parameters that add more flexibility to future versions of the implementation (§59).

§ 56   *Main points of this book*

With INC, I present the first cognitive computational model of a conceptualizer. AI systems that perform similar tasks include text summarization systems or systems that generate language from a knowledge base. However, INC is the first model of a psycholinguistically plausible conceptualizer.

Methodologically, conceptualization is difficult to investigate, because a "surface modality" has to be employed, and the computations on the conceptual level can only be inferred. The online description of events allows us to observe conceptualization more directly: Due to its temporal proximity, the input can be correlated with the verbal output, and it is much easier to capture the (relevant part of the) conceptual representation at that point in time. The conceptualizer consists of four main processes that (1) construct the conceptual representation, (2) select the concepts that will be verbalized, (3) bring the selected concepts into an appropriate linear order, and (4) generate an incremental preverbal message for each selected concept. The conceptual representations in the domain of motion events, which I used as example domain, consist of three different kinds of concepts: situations, objects, and spatial entities.

To generate online descriptions, the system simulating the human verbalizations must operate incrementally. Based on an overview of different kinds of incremental processing that are proposed in the relevant literature, I presented an overview of different kinds of incrementality and dimensions along which it can vary. Based on this general account of incremental processing, I developed a general specification (a "blueprint") for building cascaded incremental models. For this purpose, I specified a class of incremental models and incremental algorithms that are capable of exhibiting incremental behavior. The conceptualization task that I discussed in this book, the online description of events, requires a particular kind of incrementality; see § 34 for details. In addition to the particular kind of incrementality, the conceptualization task requires a particular kind of representations: dynamic representations, that is, representations that can change over time.

The *incremental conceptualizer* (inC) combines conceptualization and incrementality and integrates the two issues into a coherent model. In addition to this, inC brings together research from different disciplines that very often work in isolation and integrates their approaches, methods, and findings. Furthermore, the validity of inC is supported by the fact that it was tested and compared to empirical data—although fitting empirical data is not its main purpose. In this sense, this book is a contribution to cognitive science, more specifically a contribution to computational cognitive modeling. Only very few models of the human language faculty using this approach exist. Although my emphasis lies on the modeling part and not on analyzing empirical data, inC is detailed and powerful enough to be used in future empirical studies.

§ 57   Comparison with Levelt's model

inC is a model within Levelt's (1989) account of language production. It extends his work in a number of ways; I mention the three most ones important here.

First, Levelt only gives a general account of language production and conceptualization, not a working implemented/executable model. (But see Levelt et al. (1999) for such a model of formulator and articulator.) Focusing on the online setting in which the conceptualizer operates allows more detail on a number of points while deemphasizing others. Getting to this level of detail is necessary to produce an executable model. Yet, while inC covers a lot of important points, it is still only a first version, providing a framework for many possible extensions.

Second, apart from stating that different knowledge representations are used, Levelt does not explain from where and how the conceptualizer receives its input.

This makes it difficult to determine what knowledge is actually present and can be used for language production. The data-driven online setting—including the PPU as interface to the outside world—makes this explicit.

Third, I give an account of incremental processing, explore some of its consequences, and identify the particular kinds of incrementality that work smoothly with Levelt's conception of language production. I took the idea of the unidirectionality of the information flow and pushed it to its extreme. This showed that although language production can work without direct feedback, some form of indirect feedback facilitates the coordination of processing. The results from my analyzes are encouraging and indicate a solution for the main problem of investigating conceptualization: its high complexity. The "one-shot decision making" approach that only has limited options for corrections and alterations I am advocating does not have this problem. At the same time, this means that the system does not have properties like truth-maintenance or absence of contradictions in the representation, which enhances its cognitive adequacy. In this context, I extended Wundt's Principle as it is proposed by Levelt to a processing principle where processing is not only triggered by an input increment but also uses massive incrementality as principle for when to generate output. This principle emphasizes a key property that models of cognitive systems should have: The processes of which the system consists should be as simple as possible; the complexity of behavior comes from the interaction among these processes.

§ 58   *Future enhancements*

Despite all accomplishments, INC still is only a simple model of the conceptualizer. I comment on a few necessary enhancements in this section. The first one is to develop and implement the *linearization* process. Although it is the most dispensable of INC's four main tasks, it is important, which is shown by the fact that there is a substantial amount of literature on this topic (§ 13).

Because INC is a model of the message generation part of conceptualization only, the *monitor* should be added, as described in chapter 14. Monitoring is especially relevant because self-corrections are a well-studied and valuable source for investigating conceptualization.

INC must be able to detect *decision cues* in the represented knowledge. For example, I described two different selection strategies in § 46. Currently, the decision of which one to use is made before the simulation starts. This shifts part of the selection problem: Which algorithm should be used? Therefore, it is desirable to decide on one strategy or switch strategies on the basis of cues from the environment or the current state of the model.

A related issue is that new *heuristics* should be developed and the existing
ones should be extended. In particular the "simple heuristics that make us smart"
approach (Gigerenzer et al., 1999; Todd & Gigerenzer, 2000) could be applied to the
conceptualization tasks. As these are general decision making heuristics, they must
be adapted to conceptualization issues. (Note that the term *heuristic* as it is used
by Gigerenzer et al. is what I call *selection strategy*, not the heuristics that establish
local contexts.)

IN C's static *activation* model must be refined to include decay and reactivation.
Additionally, it must be elaborated under which conditions the activation constraint
in PVM-generation can be violated. Furthermore, I hinted at the possibility of modeling priming effects by preactivating elements of the available knowledge that
become the local context for the next execution of the incremental algorithm (p. 70).
Because a large body of psychological studies relies on priming, this would be a
major source for new insights. Activation would be especially useful for the case
that the traverse buffer is filled: Instead of always deleting the head of traverse buffer,
the element with the lowest activation can be taken.

IN C can be extended to a more autonomous *agent* model, for which the notion
of an incremental agent could be used (p. 89). (According to the classification of
agents in Luck and d'Inverno (2001) IN C in its current form is a deliberative agent,
which is rather low in the "agent hierarchy.") This provides the groundwork for two
major enhancements. First, multiple instances of IN C can interact with each other;
in particular, they can communicate on the level of preverbal messages. Because
preverbal messages are represented as referential nets, they can be easily processed
by a modified construction process. Second, IN C would not only react to the environment but could also act. For example, it could navigate through the environment
on the basis of a conceptual representation similar to the representations used for
the description of motion events.

Finally, IN C can be extended to process knowledge in *modalities* other than
language. A multimodalIN C would use the CCR not only for generating preverbal
messages but for actions in other modalities as well (Habel, 2003; Reithinger, 1991,
1992). Of particular interest is the generation of gestures. Previous work in this
direction has been carried out by van der Sluis and Krahmer (2001) and De Ruiter
(2000).

§ 59   *Additional parameters*

An aim in developing cognitive models is to make claims about cognition that are
as strong as possible. Strength of a cognitive model is often taken to mean that the
model should have only few parameters, which can be used to fit model behavior to

empirical data. However, INC's parameters have the additional function of showing how different factors, which are not under the control of the model, influence the model's behavior. These factors pull out into the open what otherwise might stay hidden in the model's functionality. For this reason, INC also should be extended by additional parameters. For example, a parameter like *maximal PVM idle time* can model the time span that a speaker can "bear it" to keep silent. To model this explicitly is quite different from finding values for the available parameters that evoke the desired behavior. For instance, to get INC to simulate the behavior of talking continuously, it is possible to use a value for LOTB that is high enough to ascertain that there always is something to be verbalized. Equally, LT can be increased so that output is slow (but not so slow as to produce silences longer than the maximal PVM idle time), or it is possible to lower DOAT to generate lots of (mostly implausible) expectations. All of these methods obscure the actual aim of the simulation, namely to produce output without gaps longer than the maximal PVM idle time.

With regard to this issue, then, it actually pays off to have a model specialized to a particular task, rather than a model of general cognitive principles, such as a unified cognitive architecture. What follows is a list of possible additional parameters.

· *Length of preprocess buffer.* The preprocessing unit also works incrementally (§39). Using the standard 50 ms interval in which the PPU records changes in the observed environment, this parameter determines how many intervals can maximally be stored until the PPU sends information to INC. It specifies the maximal number of elements, because when a situation ends during the interval, the PPU passes it on to INC. So, this parameter influences at which rate the PPU sends information about perceived entities to INC.
· *Length of perceived entity buffer.* The increment buffer between PPU and INC currently is unlimited in size. This parameter determines how many elements can be stored in the buffer.
· *Expectation retention threshold.* Construction can be equipped with a "reluctance" to change an existing expectation. For instance, if the previous DOA was 0.6 and the current one is 0.63 but for a different best match, it may be useful not to change the existing expectation but to retain the existing one. For this example, a value greater than 0.02 would have this effect. This parameter is motivated by the fact that changing the conceptual representation requires resources.
· *Fill rate of traverse buffer.* Selection can be extended so that it keeps the traverse buffer filled to a desired degree. For example, if the traverse buffer contains two elements and this parameter is set to 2, selection would not (normally) replace these elements by another one, because that would contradict the parameter value.
· *Event thread retention.* One function of linearization is to avoid descriptions of concurrent event threads that quickly switch between the event threads (§47). Instead,

one thread should be described for a time before switching to another one. An event thread retention parameter models the preference to stick to an event thread.

- *Output refO rate.* Producing language fluently means that its parts (syllables, words, phrases, sentences, utterances) are generated at a relatively constant rate. To induce the formulator to work at a constant speed, the conceptualizer should produce output increments at a steady rate. A parameter can determine the target rate with which refOs are produced by PVM-generation. (A second parameter could state the maximal deviation from this value.)

- *Maximal PVM idle time.* Similarly, a parameter can specify the maximal amount of time that PVM-generation produces no output increment. When this time span has passed, PVM-generation must generate output even if the LT for the head of traverse buffer is not over or even if the traverse buffer is empty. In the latter case, PVM-generation could produce a hesitation or a fixed phrase like *Let's see.* This parameter could also be integrated into the selection process.

- *Idle time of processes.* On a more general level, if an increment stream or an increment buffer is empty when the reading process tries to retrieve an element, the process has three options: First, it can continue processing available information so as to improve previous output. Second, it can suspend itself until the next element is available. Third, it can suspend itself for a certain idle time. IN C uses the first two methods. For the third method, a parameter can determine the suspension time of the process. This method requires less supervision of increment streams and buffers, which speeds up processing.

THIS BOOK'S THESES

*T*HROUGHOUT THIS BOOK, I pursued a number of theses. This chapter lists them in a concise form. Not all of these theses are controversial or new, but a result of this book is that they form a coherent, interconnected whole. They are a reference for future research that will show whether they are correct.

1 *Language production is incremental.*
Although it is obvious that humans produce and understand language incrementally, that is, as a sequence of increments (§1), this is often not reflected in the scientific discussions, in particular in noncognitive approaches to language. However, some phenomena of language can only be understood properly with respect to their temporal dimension. Examples are that the perspective of an utterance depends on the sequence in which increments are generated (§6) or that the uttered content depends on the point in time when it is generated. For example, for generating self-corrections it is important to know how far the utterance production has progressed. This is important not only for generating a suitable correction but for actually generating a *correct* correction (§28).

2 *To understand conceptualization, one must understand its incremental nature.*
Extending thesis 1, incrementality is not just one of many different ways in which conceptualization works. A proper understanding of conceptualization is interwoven with a proper understanding of its incrementality. There are two prime examples for this. First, understanding the temporal interleaving of reading input and generating output is central to understanding conceptualization. Only those situations that are in the conceptual representation can be verbalized; thus, verbalizations depend on the point in time when they are initiated (§52). Second, preverbal messages are not generated as whole propositions but incrementally; they are sequences of well-formed propositional structures on a subpropositional level (§12). Seeing preverbal messages as incremental representations has, for example, the benefit that perspect-ivization need not be modeled as a separate, transformational process. Instead, it is an effect of incrementality (§6).

3 *The conceptualizer is a quasi-module.*
The components carrying out the subtasks of conceptualization are modular only

to some extent, which means they are only partly independent of other cognitive faculties. Hence, the components of conceptualization and conceptualization as a whole are quasi-modules, which possess the domain specificity of modules but lack their strict informational encapsulation (§11). Additionally, conceptualization has many properties of an open-ended system. For example, logical inferences, gestures, consciousness, or multimodal representations play a role in conceptualization even if they do not lie at its core (§4, §9).

4 *Conceptualization can be investigated with an online setting.*
Conceptualization is a central cognitive component (although it is not the central executive). From this results the main methodological difficulty: It can never be observed directly. This means that an "interface modality" must be used to infer what happens on the conceptual level (§12). This problem can be alleviated by using an online setting: The temporal interleaving of the perceptual input and the generated verbal output makes it possible to correlate input and output (§2). This in turn makes it possible to identify the computations that transform the one into the other and the conceptual representations that are used for this. In an online setting, conceptualization can be investigated as a task in its own right, that is, a task independent from language. This is a prerequisite to be able to focus its core issues; for example, the issue of how communicative intentions and what I called subintentions (§11) are generated. The online setting has the additional advantages of allowing a focus on the conceptualization of events in contrast to the usually investigated conceptualization of objects. It also reduces the high complexity of conceptualization to a degree where it is possible to build a computational model.

5 *Conceptualization is prelinguistic.*
Although it is rather uncontroversial that conceptualization is a rather central cognitive task, it is often mixed with accounts of linguistic tasks. However, problems of conceptualization are different from linguistic problems. For example, the selection of the content to be verbalized is not a linguistic problem, and a lot of difficulties for understanding conceptualization originate in this disregard of the distinction between language and conceptualization (§12). This means that conceptualization is *pre*linguistic—separate from the language components. However, it is also pre*linguistic*, that is, its output is tailored to be the input for the subsequent components of language production. In particular, its output consists of semantic representations that are used as input by a subsequent formulator (§10).

6 *Conceptualization is a mediator between language and other cognitive faculties.*
When humans talk about what is happening in the world, they are perceiving the world in a modality different from language. Conceptualization is (among other

things) the mediator between nonlinguistic modalities and preverbal messages (§9). More specifically, conceptualization connects perceived entities (perceptual incre- ments) to existing knowledge, determines the content that will be verbalized, and generates semantic structures for this content (§13). In so doing conceptualization comprises or makes use of additional tasks, for example, the generation of expecta- tions or categorization. These tasks, in particular, serve to enrich the conceptualizer's knowledge by inferring new knowledge, for example, by making inferences about temporal relations in the conceptual representation.

7 *Conceptualization is language-specific to some extent.*
According to thesis 5 conceptualization is language-specific in the sense that it is pre*linguistic*. That is, although conceptualization is not a linguistic task, its output consists of semantic representations that are the input to a formulator. Whether it is language-specific in another sense, namely whether a conceptualizer can produce output for only a particular language, is a question of a longstanding debate: the issue of linguistic relativity (§1, §11). Although linguistic relativity is not a major concern of this book, INC allows us to ask this question in a more technical way that may facilitate finding an answer: Do speakers of all languages produce the same preverbal messages? If they do, how much and in what way do the conceptualization processes that produce the preverbal messages differ for speakers of different languages? As for the overall question, both extreme positions (identical conceptualization or entirely different conceptualization) are very unlikely, so the appropriate question is *how much* the processes and representations differ for different languages. For example, although it is likely that all speakers' conceptual representations distinguish between situations and objects, they probably do not specify number or tense in the preverbal message in languages that do not make these distinctions.

8 *Preverbal messages are produced incrementally.*
For the entire language production system to work incrementally, the conceptualizer and the formulator have to work incrementally. From this follows that the interface between them, the preverbal message, is also incremental (§12, §48). If a preverbal message had to be assembled completely before the formulator starts processing it, the steady flow of information would be interrupted and the whole system could not operate incrementally. This would also mean that the formulator must wait until all increments are available before it starts processing, which contradicts a central property of incrementality, namely that input is processed as soon as it becomes available (Wundt's Principle, §22).

9 *The increments of preverbal messages are concepts.*
Because semantic representations are linear conceptual representations, it follows

that its increments are concepts (§10, §49). In INC, concepts are represented by refOs, which are a very flexible and versatile means of representing preverbal messages and the relations between concepts that is particularly suited for incremental processing (§52).

10 *Subintentions can be captured by a computational process.*
Although the nature of intentions is a difficult issue, the notion of subintentions proves useful on the computational level. These are the communicative intentions that are computed by the conceptualizer's selection process (§46). They can be understood as sub-goals to realising the overall communicative intention to describe the observed scene, which is hardwired into INC (§11).

11 *Deciding on what-to-say differs from and precedes how-to-say it.*
Deciding *what-to-say* differs from deciding *how-to-say* it, and the former precedes the latter. This this formulation cannot only distinguish the functions of conceptualizer and formulator but can also describe the two processing stages within the conceptualizer, where the first one selects a concept for verbalization and the second one generates a semantic representation for it. This distinction has an important implication for INC, namely that after it has decided to verbalize something, the realization must necessarily follow (§49). The reason is that due to the massive incrementality that results from Extended Wundt's Principle (§22), the decision to verbalize something cannot be reversed.

12 *Incremental processing is the piecemeal processing of information.*
Despite the differences in what is meant by the term *incrementality* (thesis 13), the unifying property is that incremental processing is the piecemeal processing of information (§22). This stands in contrast to notions like qualitative incrementality, where the pieces are repetitions of the whole information, and to nonsymbolic approaches like connectionism (§23).

13 *Incrementality is no uniform concept.*
The literature distinguishes different kinds of incrementality, for example, massive and moderate incrementality (§23), and there are many dimensions along which incremental processing can vary, including monotonicity, buffering, lookahead, and feedback (§25). Generally, systems can use all kinds of incrementality and vary along all dimensions, but to understand the incrementality of cognitive systems and to understand how this shapes the cognitive processes, it is crucial to identify the kinds and dimensions that actually occur in natural cognitive systems. This does not mean that cognitive systems can employ only one kind of incremental processes—as cognitive processes possess a high degree of flexibility—but that it is

possible to identify the incrementality used for a particular task. This book describes the incrementality of the online verbalization of events (§34).

14 *Incrementality shares properties with anytime processing.*
Incrementality is similar to anytime processing in some respects (§31). Most important, both methods reduce the amount of the required resources and can model bounded rationality. They differ in that anytime processing is closer to Herbert Simon's notion of satisficing, because it calculates the trade-off between the time spent on a computation and how large the gain in quality is, whereas incrementality is better described by Gerd Gigerenzer's fast and frugal heuristics, because they describe how to make quick decisions based on cues retrieved from the environment. Due to the similarities between the two notions, it is interesting to build incremental models that exhibit anytime behavior (§30).

15 *Language production conforms to Extended Wundt's Principle.*
Extending the processing principle that Levelt termed *Wundt's Principle,* I propose that language production in general and conceptualization in particular conforms to massive incrementality, or Extended Wundt's Principle: *Each processing component will be triggered into activity by a minimal amount of its characteristic input and produces characteristic output as soon as a minimal amount of output is available* (§22). This means that the components involved in language production do not determine the best time for sending their results to the next component in the cascade but do this as soon as the output is available; they do not compute the *when-to-say* (§34). Controlling output is only possible via monitoring (§54).

16 *Indirect feedback preserves the unidirectionality of the information flow.*
The cascaded architecture of incremental models brings with it a unidirectional information flow that allows no direct feedback. Thus, an incremental process cannot send information to processes further up in the cascade. Although this no-feedback condition keeps the model simple and saves resources, it is also an error source, because, for example, there is no way to inform a previous process about how far the processing of its output has proceeded or whether an error has been detected. However, indirect feedback can be used without violating the strong no-feedback condition and without sacrificing the unidirectionality of the information flow. Indirect feedback means that no explicit information is sent but that the effects of computations can affect previous components. This can be realized by shared memories or increment buffers (§25).

17 *An incremental model consists of a cascade and exhibits incremental behavior.*
The two most important notions for incremental processing are incremental models

and incremental behavior. An incremental model is a computational model that (a) consists of a cascade of incremental processes and a representation of the model knowledge and (b) exhibits incremental behavior. A model behaves incrementally if it produces output while it reads input (§ 24).

18 *Incremental processing requires dynamic representations.*
Incremental processing requires representations that can change over time: dynamic representations. They are necessary to keep up with new input and allow seamless connections between components. For example, incremental preverbal messages connect the conceptualizer to an incremental formulator. In this book, I demonstrated how referential nets (§ 6, § 20) and semantic underspecification formalisms (in particular, their extendability property; § 27) can be used as dynamic representations.

19 *Incremental processing is a way to cope with limited resources.*
Cognition must cope with limited resources (§ 29), in particular with a limited time span to compute an answer. Incrementality is an elegant way to cope with this time pressure. It is particularly useful for online settings because it considers only the changes in the representation. In this way, a focused element is identified in the representation, which allows to reduce the knowledge considered in the computations to knowledge connected to the focused element—the local context. This reduction decreases the processing time further, because not all available knowledge is considered in the computation (§ 24).

20 *INC is cognitively adequate.*
Although the focus of this book is not to match INC to a set of data points, there are several points that demonstrate INC's cognitive adequacy. First, computing the focused element in relation to the available knowledge in a local context is an efficient way of processing, suited to cope with limited resources and to model attentional mechanisms and priming phenomena. Second, the piecemeal way of processing and the parallel processing of an information stream on multiple stages, which includes the simultaneous reading of input and production of output, are adequate ways to perform the given task of generating online descriptions of events. Third, Extended Wundt's Principle deals with the fact that deliberation time is short. Fourth, the particular incrementality used by INC models a suitable notion of bounded rationality. Finally, simulations carried out with the implementation of INC and comparing the behavior to human verbalization data show that INC is a realistic model of the human conceptualizer.

21 *Simple selection strategies suffice to produce realistic online verbalizations of events.*
Elaborating on thesis 20, support for INC's cognitive adequacy also comes from
INC's two selection strategies: a preference for complex events and a preference
not to change the granularity of the selected events. Despite their simplicity, they
successfully select the situations that humans used in their verbalizations of the
same scenes (§53).

22 *INC's resource parameters can account for the variability in the verbalization data.*
Setting INC's resource parameters (§38) to different values influences the generated
output. They are the means to produce verbalizations that cover the range of the
recorded human verbalizations. Verbalizations that were used by the majority of
participants are reproduced by default values for the parameters (§52, §53).

23 *Cognitive modeling is the "bionics of AI".*
This book is in the tradition of a computational modeling approach to cognition.
However, in contrast to comparable research, it is not so much concerned with
matching a set of empirical data points onto a computational model as with developing a model for an extensive cognitive task. To do so, and to fill the gaps that still
exist in the cognitive and psychological explanations of conceptualization, I used
AI and NLG methods. Although cognitive considerations usually play no role in the
mainstream of NLG/AI, these disciplines can strongly profit from using models of
natural intelligence. This can be described as *bionics of AI*, as research where results
from observing nature are transferred to applications (§5).

$$\sim$$

I used Slobin's notion of *thinking for speaking* in different forms throughout this book.
Thus, it is appropriate to conclude by applying it to different aspects of this book, as
conceptualization really *is* thinking for speaking. Thinking and speaking take place
simultaneously; that is, the thinking for speaking really is a thinking *while* speaking.
The incremental mode of processing requires certain kinds of *representations* for
speaking, in particular dynamic, conceptual representations. In this book, I covered
only one instance of thinking, namely thinking for *speaking*, as opposed to, for
example, thinking for *navigating*. Vice versa, I left out other language-related issues,
for example, grammatical encoding, which means that I considered *thinking* for
speaking.

The central point of this book is that thinking (conceptualization) and speaking
take place simultaneously and that this temporal overlap has significant influences on
how both work. This is crucial for a proper understanding of not only the problems
of conceptualization but also language in general.

≈ A ≈

REFERENTIAL NETS

R ERFERENTIAL NETS ARE the representational formalism INC uses for the CCR and the CS. RefNets are a way to represent knowledge that is particularly suited for the purpose at hand. RefNets consist of interrelated *referential objects* (refOs) representing entities (Eschenbach, 1988; Habel, 1982, 1986). Formally, a refO is a term.

There are three main reasons for choosing refNets for INC. First, refOs are the major means of structuring knowledge, which could be called an object-oriented way to represent predicate logic. Consequently, the representations focus on the knowledge about individual concepts. The conception of refNets was developed to model the structure and organization of human memory and the way it supports the processes of storing and remembering (Habel, 1986, p. 111–112). Second, refNets are especially suited to connect the different levels of representation used here. That is, it is possible to represent semantic and conceptual knowledge as well as to connect a refO to the perceptual information provided by the PPU. Additionally, refNets can integrate multimodal knowledge, for example, pictorial and gestural knowledge (cf. chap. 1). Third, refNets facilitate incremental processing, which I elaborate later on.

Consider the following part of a refNet, which might be used in the conceptual representation of the introductory example:

(1)
$$\text{plane} \text{———} \text{r1} \begin{cases} \text{'CK-314'} \\ \text{owner('LUFTHANSA')} \\ \eta x\,\text{plane}(x) \end{cases}$$

In this notation, r1 is the refO term. The lines leading toward r1 connect it to the expressions on either side. The ones to the left are *attributes*, the ones to the right *designations*. The basic inventory of which expressions are constructed consists of three sets: variables (VAR), operators (OP), and operator effects (EFF := {t, f}) (Habel,

1986, p. 59). The effect of an operator shows whether the result of its application is a term (t) or a formula (f). Operators are specified by the function TYP:

(2) $\text{TYP} = \text{OP} \rightarrow \text{EFF} \times \mathbb{N} \times \mathbb{N} \times \mathbb{N}$

The three $\mathbb{N}$ values stand for the number of variables bound by OP, and the terms and formulas OP has as arguments, respectively. In the shorthand notation

(3) $\text{TYP}(\text{op}) = \langle e, m, n, p \rangle$

e determines the effect, and m, n, and p the numbers of variables, terms, and formulas, respectively, that are bound by op. This notion of types is also used in the semantics of programming languages and logic, which goes back to Kalish and Montague (1964).

Expressions are sorted (Habel, 1986, p. 66), that is, the set SORT is a set of names of sorts, and each expression has a *sort frame*. The sort frame defines of which sort the arguments of an expression must be in order for the expression to be *sort-correct*. For example, the expression chpos (change of position), which represents the movement of an object along a path in a situation (see also §20), has the sort frame (situation, object, path). However, the formalism also allows *sort-incorrect* expressions (Habel, 1986, p. 66).

This basic inventory is used to form different kinds of expressions. Apart from refOs, which are of type $\langle t, 0, 0, 0 \rangle$, especially two kinds of terms play an important role: *names*, which have type $\langle t, 0, 0, 0 \rangle$, and *descriptions*, with type $\langle t, m, n, p \rangle$, with $n > 0$ or $p > 0$ (Habel, 1986, p. 117). Examples of names are 'DAVID', the proper name of a person, or 'CK-314', the flight number of the plane in the introductory example. Names are written in capital letters and quotation marks.

Descriptions are either functional expressions, or they are constructed with a description operator. An example of the former is owner('LUFTHANSA'), which states that the represented entity is owned by Lufthansa. Two points are important here. First, the owner relation expressed by the functional expression can refer to another refO, for example, owner(r2). Then, the owner of the entity is represented by r2, which has the advantage that additional knowledge about the owner can be represented. Second, because functional expressions are functions, they must uniquely refer to an entity; that is, they must constitute a many-to-one or a one-to-one relation. In the case of ownership, one can assume an entity has only one owner.* It must be determined for each representation individually what is to be represented as functional expressions, because this depends on the content of the representation.

---

* If there is a group of owners, this can be represented by a refO standing for the group. The functional expression then refers to the refO. It is not possible to have multiple refOs representing owners and refer to them with the same functional expression.

Descriptions that are constructed with a description operator are of the form op var formula, with the operators op $\in \{\iota, \eta, \text{all\_t}, \text{some\_t}\}$, the variables var $\in \{x, y, z, \ldots\}$, and formula being a formula of predicate logic. The operators reflect the cardinality of the refO and the definiteness of the designation (Habel, 1986, p. 137; cf. table 1.1, repeated here as table A.1). For example, $\eta x\ \text{plane}(x)$ stands for *a plane* and $\text{all\_t}\ x\ \text{plane}(x)$ for *all planes*.*

	DEFINITE	INDEFINITE
cardinality $= 1$	ι	η
cardinality > 1	some_t	all_t

Table A.1: Operators in referential nets

Names and descriptions form the two sets NAM (names) and DESCR (descriptions). The latter contains the subset of closed descriptions DESCR.cl. As usual, closed terms (here: descriptions) are defined as those terms that contain no free variables. The union of NAM and DESCR.cl constitutes the set of designations (written to the right of the refO term):

(4) DESIGN $=$ NAM $\cup$ DESCR.cl

Because refOs are also defined as terms, terms are members of one of the following sets (Habel, 1986, p. 117):

- Referential objects (REFO)
- Variables (VAR)
- Names (NAM)
- Descriptions (DESCR)

Whereas designations represent linguistic knowledge, especially about meaning, the attributes of a refO† represent inferential knowledge. Examples are the information about the sort of a refO, which is obligatory and always stands in first position (plane in example (1)). If the sort of an entity is unknown, the top-sort is used (cf. figure 4.1, p. 57). Because the sort hierarchy is formally a lattice, it also contains a bottom sort. Temporal relations between situation refOs, for example, are represented by attributes; for example, before(r3) as attribute of r2 represents the relation r2 before r3. Thus, attributes can have values. These values can be lists, written as

---

* These operators construct terms; thus, they are of type $\langle t, m, n, p \rangle$, whereas the well-known quantifiers $\exists$ and $\forall$ construct formulas; that is, they are of type $\langle f, m, n, p \rangle$.

† Designations can also have attributes. However, I only use them once in § 45.

[. . .]. An example of an important list attribute is parts.* Assume that r5 represents Oscar Peterson, r6 Ray Brown, and r7 Herb Ellis. Then the refO representing the The Oscar Peterson Trio, say r8, has the attribute parts([r5, r6, r7]).

The sort plane and the description ηx plane(x) both encode the fact that r1 is a plane. However, whereas the former stands for an essential property of the refO, from which, for example, it can be inferred that the entity is capable of flying, the latter says that it can be described as *a plane* (Habel, 1986, p. 156). This is the reason that mainly designations are used for the generation of preverbal messages.†

Although refNets are mainly used for representing propositional knowledge, they can also represent knowledge in other modalities, in particular spatial knowledge, for which the formalism was already extended by depictions (Habel, 1987, 1988). Similar extensions for other modalities are possible, which facilitates translations of other modalities into the propositional one. The perceived entities from which the conceptual representation is constructed are identified by nonlinguistic properties. Such properties as well as knowledge retrieved from long-term memory (in C's CS) need not be propositional. Yet, when a preverbal message is generated, only the propositional parts of a refO are used, that is, mainly names and descriptions.‡

I want to conclude the discussion of referential nets with two general remarks and two remarks concerning the suitability of referential nets for incremental processing. The first general remark is that a refNet need not be consistent but allows contradictions. This makes it possible to adequately represent cognitive knowledge, because humans (can) have inconsistent representations. Thus, contradictions must be resolved by the processes operating on the representations.§ The second general

---

* In previous publications and in Eschenbach (1988), this attribute was called sum. However, for events, this is problematic because what is regarded part of an event is not as well-defined as, say, that a cube is the sum of its six sides. In the docking example, the complexDOCKING event may be constructed even if the event representing the start of the walkway movement is missing.

† The difference between attributes and designations is close albeit not identical to the difference of semantic memory (attributes) and episodic memory (designations) (cf., e.g., Tulving, 1999). Properties of the kind used by Gärdenfors (2000), that is, properties tightly connected to perception, are represented mainly by attributes and only partly by designations. Properties connected to linguistic knowledge are represented mainly by designations and only partly by attributes. However, the decision whether to use attributes or designations must be made for each case individually. Because a representation always is an abstraction, this depends strongly on what the representation is used for.

‡ Not all knowledge about an entity is needed for a verbalization. For example, very often a name suffices to refer to an object (CK-314 in example (1)), and the other designations are not used. Consequently, an increment of an incremental preverbal message is determined by deciding that a refO will be verbalized. Then, in a separate step the knowledge about this refO that is needed for an adequate verbalization is determined. This is part of perspectivization (cf.§6, §13, and §15). The algorithm of how descriptions are selected is described in chapter 12.

§ One may ask whether a representation really is contradictory if a process operating on it can resolve the conflict. Thus, from a logical standpoint, it is more accurate to speak of conflicting representations.

remark is that it is possible to represent default knowledge (e.g., the famous case that penguins are birds, birds can fly, but penguins cannot), and so the default knowledge has to be overwritten.

The first reason refNets are suited for incremental processing is that all knowledge about a concept is localized, that is, stored in one spot. Thus, referential nets are highly redundant representations. This makes them costly in terms of storage capacity, because a description like chpos is stored thrice instead of only once, namely at the situation, the object, and the path refO (§20). Yet, refNets are highly efficient with regard to access time, because once a refO is accessed, all explicit knowledge about the entity is instantly available.* Because the main reason for using an incremental mode of processing for language production is to enable the human/system to speak fluently despite limited resources, incremental processing is mainly a means to save processing time, not storage capacity.

The second aspect is that refNets provide means to change the representation; that is, refOs, attributes, and designations can be inserted, deleted, or changed. For example, a name can be attached only temporally to the refO; for example, the name 'CK-314' standing for the flight number can be replaced by another name for the return flight. Or, if the members of The Oscar Peterson Trio, represented by r8, change so that Niels-Henning Ørsted Pedersen (r9) and Terry Clark (r10) instead of Ray Brown and Herb Ellis now belong to the trio then r8 has the attribute parts([r5, r9, r10]).

Examples are of the kind where a representation contains the propositions red(A) and green(A) and the knowledge that A can only have one color. For cognitive systems this is quite plausible; for example, one proposition may be due to perceived information while the other is inferred from previous knowledge. A system with such representations must be capable of dealing with the conflict in some manner.

* Additionally, knowledge may be retrieved by following links to other refOs, for example, knowledge about the owner of the plane in the earlier example. However, this only adds to the cognitive adequacy of referential nets.

SYSTEM OUTPUT OF INC

THE EXAMPLE DISCUSSED in chapter 13 is based on an actual simulation carried out with the implementation of INC. This appendix contains the corresponding system output. Note that the numbering of refOs differs, because the system automatically assigns numbers, whereas in the discussion, I used a different numbering for presentational reasons. The activation of designations is written as <<...>>, and the refOs are written as simple numbers, that is, without leading r (except in the headline of a refO).

B.1 The input coming from the PPU

The PPU generates PEs as a sequence of lines of text. The position of a line is meaningful, for example, it makes a difference whether the line comes third or fourth. The PPU can send two types of increments: new PEs or updates for existing PEs. For new PEs, the lines contain the following information:

1. The PE number with which the PE is identified by PPU and INC
2. new
3. Attributes for the refO
4. Designations of the refO

For updates of existing PEs, the lines specify

1. PE number
2. update
3. Attributes to be removed from the corresponding refO
4. Attributes to be added
5. Designations to be removed
6. Designations to be added

The input file for INC that was used in the simulations of chapter 13 has the following content:

```
1
new
object
plane
eta x: plane(x)
2
new
situation
at_time(0 200)
nil
3
new
path
nil
eta x: chpos(#2# #1# x);eta x: straight(x)
2
update
nil
nil
nil
eta x: chpos(x #1# #3#)
1
update
nil
nil
nil
eta x: chpos(#2# x #3#)
4
new
ref_sys_spat
spatial_entity
iota x: R_sys(x #3#)
5
new
region
nil
iota x: Left_region(x #4#)
6
new
region
nil
iota x: Right_region(x #4#)
7
new
situation
at_time(201 320);met_by(#2#)
nil
2
update
nil
meets(#7#)
nil
nil
8
new
path
nil
eta x: chpos(#7# #1# x);eta x: curved(x);eta x to(x #5#)
7
```

```
update
nil
nil
nil
eta x: chpos(x #1# #8#)
1
update
nil
nil
nil
eta x: chpos(#7# x #8#)
9
new
location
nil
eta x: finalpoint(x #3#);eta x: startpoint(x #8#)
3
update
nil
nil
nil
eta x: finalpoint(#9# x)
8
update
nil
nil
nil
eta x: startpoint(#9# x)
eof
.
```

B.2   *Examples of generated incremental preverbal messages*

This section contains the incremental preverbal messages that were generated in the simulations.

```
=====================================================
This is the PVM file of inC version 0.2.2 (build 077)
DoAT=0.5; LoTB=6; LT=6050; AT=0.5
Domain: motionEvents
Selection Strategy: mostComplex
Real-Time: true; Time Frame: 50


-------------------------------------------------------
New PVM starting with ref0 16

situation ----------- r18  ---- eta x: chpos(x 19 20)   <<0.5>>
verb_of(16)
parts([8 13])
at_time(0 320)
status(regular)

object -------------- r19  ---- eta x: plane(x)   <<0.9>>
verb_of(7)
plane
status(regular)
pe(1)

path ---------------- r20  ---- eta x: to(x 21)   <<0.5>>
verb_of(17)                    eta x: p_curved(x)   <<0.6>>
parts([9 14])
status(regular)

region -------------- r21  ---- iota x: Left_region(x 22)   <<0.5>>
verb_of(11)
status(regular)
pe(5)

ref_sys_spat -------- r22  ----
verb_of(10)
spatial_entity
status(regular)
pe(4)
```

```
========================================================
This is the PVM file of inC version 0.2.2 (build 077)
DoAT=0.5; LoTB=6; LT=125; AT=0.4
Domain: motionEvents
Selection Strategy: mostComplex
Real-Time: true; Time Frame: 50


----------------------------------------------------
New PVM starting with ref0 8

situation ----------- r13  ---- eta x: chpos(x 14 15)   <<0.5>>
verb_of(8)
at_time(0 200)
status(regular)
pe(2)

object ------------- r14  ---- eta x: plane(x)   <<0.9>>
verb_of(7)
plane
status(regular)
pe(1)

path --------------- r15  ---- eta x: straight(x)   <<0.6>>
verb_of(9)
status(regular)
pe(3)


----------------------------------------------------
New PVM starting with ref0 19

situation ----------- r21  ---- eta x: chpos(x 22 23)   <<0.5>>
verb_of(19)
parts([8 16])
at_time(0 320)
status(regular)

object ------------- r22  ----
verb_of(7)
plane
status(regular)
pe(1)

path --------------- r23  ---- eta x: transitionpoint(24 x)   <<0.4>>
verb_of(20)                    eta x: p_curved(x)   <<0.6>>
concat([9 17])
status(regular)

location ----------- r24  ----
verb_of(18)
status(regular)
pe(9)
```

```
=======================================================
This is the PVM file of inC version 0.2.2 (build 077)
DoAT=0.5; LoTB=6; LT=125; AT=0.6
Domain: motionEvents
Selection Strategy: retainGranularity
Real-Time: true; Time Frame: 50


-----------------------------------------------------
New PVM starting with ref0 8

situation ----------- r13   ---- eta x: chpos(x 14 15)   <<0.5>>
verb_of(8)
at_time(0 200)
status(regular)
pe(2)

object -------------- r14   ---- eta x: plane(x)   <<0.9>>
verb_of(7)
plane
status(regular)
pe(1)

path --------------- r15   ---- eta x: straight(x)   <<0.6>>
verb_of(9)
status(regular)
pe(3)


-----------------------------------------------------
New PVM starting with ref0 16

situation ----------- r21   ---- eta x: chpos(x 22 23)   <<0.5>>
verb_of(16)
part_of([19])
met_by(8)
at_time(201 320)
status(regular)
pe(7)

object -------------- r22   ----
verb_of(7)
plane
status(regular)
pe(1)

path --------------- r23   ---- eta x: curved(x)   <<0.6>>
verb_of(17)
part_of([20])
status(regular)
pe(8)
```

```
========================================================
This is the PVM file of inC version 0.2.2 (build 077)
DoAT=0.5; LoTB=6; LT=125; AT=0.5
Domain: motionEvents
Selection Strategy: retainGranularity
Real-Time: true; Time Frame: 50


----------------------------------------------------
New PVM starting with ref0 8

situation ----------- r13  ---- eta x: chpos(x 14 15)   <<0.5>>
verb_of(8)
at_time(0 200)
status(regular)
pe(2)


object -------------- r14  ---- eta x: plane(x)   <<0.9>>
verb_of(7)
plane
status(regular)
pe(1)


path ---------------- r15  ---- eta x: straight(x)   <<0.6>>
verb_of(9)
status(regular)
pe(3)


----------------------------------------------------
New PVM starting with ref0 16

situation ----------- r21  ---- eta x: chpos(x 22 23)   <<0.5>>
verb_of(16)
part_of([19])
met_by(8)
at_time(201 320)
status(regular)
pe(7)


object -------------- r22  ----
verb_of(7)
plane
status(regular)
pe(1)


path ---------------- r23  ---- eta x: to(x 24)   <<0.5>>
verb_of(17)                     eta x: curved(x)   <<0.6>>
part_of([20])
status(regular)
pe(8)


region -------------- r24  ---- iota x: Left_region(x 25)   <<0.5>>
verb_of(11)
status(regular)
pe(5)


ref_sys_spat -------- r25  ----
verb_of(10)
spatial_entity
status(regular)
pe(4)
```

```
========================================================
This is the PVM file of inC version 0.2.2 (build 077)
DoAT=0.5; LoTB=6; LT=125; AT=0.1
Domain: motionEvents
Selection Strategy: retainGranularity
Real-Time: true; Time Frame: 50


-----------------------------------------------------
New PVM starting with ref0 8

situation ----------- r13   ---- eta x: chpos(x 14 15)    <<0.5>>
verb_of(8)
at_time(0 200)
status(regular)
pe(2)


object -------------- r14   ---- eta x: plane(x)    <<0.9>>
verb_of(7)
plane
status(regular)
pe(1)


path ---------------- r15   ---- eta x: straight(x)    <<0.6>>
verb_of(9)
status(regular)
pe(3)


-----------------------------------------------------
New PVM starting with ref0 16

situation ----------- r21   ---- eta x: chpos(x 22 23)    <<0.5>>
verb_of(16)
part_of([19])
met_by(8)
at_time(201 320)
status(regular)
pe(7)


object -------------- r22   ----
verb_of(7)
plane
status(regular)
pe(1)


path ---------------- r23   ---- eta x: startpoint(24 x)    <<0.1>>
verb_of(17)                      eta x: to(x 27)    <<0.5>>
part_of([20])                    eta x: curved(x)    <<0.6>>
status(regular)
pe(8)


location ------------ r24   ---- eta x: transitionpoint(x 25)    <<0.4>>
verb_of(18)                      eta x: finalpoint(x 26)    <<0.1>>
status(regular)
pe(9)


path ---------------- r25   ----
verb_of(20)
concat([9 17])
status(regular)
```

```
path --------------- r26  ----
verb_of(9)
part_of([20])
status(regular)
pe(3)

region ------------- r27  ---- iota x: Left_region(x 28)   <<0.5>>
verb_of(11)
status(regular)
pe(5)

ref_sys_spat -------- r28  ----
verb_of(10)
spatial_entity
status(regular)
pe(4)
```

B.3   A final state of the CCR

There are two factors that influence the final state of the CCR. First, as the CCR
contains the traverse (i.e., it contains all verbalization refOs), the CCR differs in
the verbalization refOs that were inserted. Second, just as the verbalization refOs,
the refOs inserted into the CCR due to the concept matcher's matching results
differ for different parameter values. Otherwise, all other refOs are identical in
the simulations—apart from variations due to the indeterminacy of the system,
which affects, for example, the numbering of the refOs. Here follows the CCR for
the default parameter values: DOAT = 0.5, LOTB = 6, LT = 125, AT = 0.6 and the
alternative selection strategy that retains the level of granularity as far as possible.

```
object ------------- r7  ----- eta x: chpos(19 x 20)   <<0.5>>
plane                          eta x: chpos(16 x 17)   <<0.5>>
status(regular)                eta x: chpos(8 x 9)   <<0.5>>
pe(1)                          eta x: plane(x)   <<0.9>>

situation ----------- r8  ----- eta x: chpos(x 7 9)   <<0.5>>
part_of([19])
meets(16)
at_time(0 200)
status(regular)
pe(2)

path --------------- r9  ----- eta x: finalpoint(18 x)   <<0.1>>
part_of([20])                  eta x: straight(x)   <<0.6>>
status(regular)                eta x: chpos(8 7 x)   <<0.5>>
pe(3)

ref_sys_spat -------- r10  ---- R_sys(x 9)   <<0.5>>
spatial_entity
status(regular)
pe(4)
```

```
region -------------- r11  ---- Left_region(x 10)    <<0.5>>
spatial_entity
status(regular)
pe(5)

region -------------- r12  ---- Right_region(x 10)   <<0.5>>
spatial_entity
status(regular)
pe(6)

situation ----------- r13  ---- eta x: chpos(x 14 15)   <<0.5>>
verb_of(8)
at_time(0 200)
status(regular)
pe(2)

object -------------- r14  ---- eta x: plane(x)    <<0.9>>
verb_of(7)
plane
status(regular)
pe(1)

path ---------------- r15  ---- eta x: straight(x)    <<0.6>>
verb_of(9)
status(regular)
pe(3)

situation ----------- r16  ---- eta x: chpos(x 7 17)    <<0.5>>
part_of([19])
met_by(8)
at_time(201 320)
status(regular)
pe(7)

path ---------------- r17  ---- eta x: startpoint(18 x)    <<0.1>>
part_of([20])                  eta x: to(x 11)    <<0.5>>
status(regular)                eta x: curved(x)    <<0.6>>
pe(8)                          eta x: chpos(16 7 x)    <<0.5>>

location ------------ r18  ---- eta x: transitionpoint(x 20)    <<0.4>>
status(regular)                eta x: startpoint(x 17)    <<0.1>>
pe(9)                          eta x: finalpoint(x 9)    <<0.1>>

situation ----------- r19  ---- eta x: chpos(x 7 20)    <<0.5>>
parts([8 16])
at_time(0 320)
status(regular)

path ---------------- r20  ---- eta x: transitionpoint(18 x)    <<0.4>>
concat([9 17])                 eta x: p_curved(x)    <<0.6>>
status(regular)                eta x: chpos(19 7 x)    <<0.5>>

situation ----------- r21  ---- eta x: chpos(x 22 23)    <<0.5>>
verb_of(16)
part_of([19])
met_by(8)
at_time(201 320)
status(regular)
```

```
pe(7)

object -------------- r22  ----
verb_of(7)
plane
status(regular)
pe(1)

path --------------- r23  ---- eta x: curved(x)   <<0.6>>
verb_of(17)
part_of([20])
status(regular)
pe(8)
```

B.4   The uDraw(Graph) output window of the CCR

The window shown below is the output of the CCR given in the previous section. It is generated with the help of the uDraw(Graph) graph drawing tool. RefOs are represented by nodes, relations by edges. The different kinds of refOs and relations are kept apart by a color scheme. In this visualization, the relations chpos, startpoint, and finalpoint are not given to keep the graph simple. This results in a graph consisting of nonconnected subgraphs. The leftmost subgraph contains the situation refOs with the numbers 8, 16, and 19. The refOs with the numbers 13 and 21 are the two verbalizations that were generated for the two simpler situations. The next subgraph contains the refO representing the plane (7) and its two verbalization refOs. The rightmost subgraph represents the spatial entities: 9, 17, 20 are the three paths, 18 is the location where the simpler paths meet, 10 is the spatial reference system, and the 11 and 12 and the left and right region, respectively. 15 and 23 are the verbalization refOs of the simpler paths.

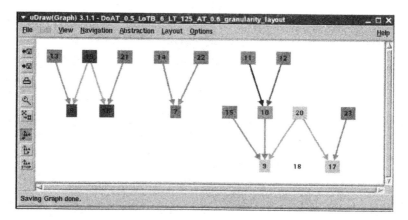

~ c ~

VERBALIZATIONS OF MOTION EVENTS

T HE VERBALIZATIONS GIVEN in this appendix are transcriptions of verbalizations of five speakers. The two scenes they describe are subscenes from a larger scene, which is similar to the scene discussed in §50. The first scene differs in that both planes come into view simultaneously, the second scene in that the first plane (the one turning off the runway) moves on Runway 1 (on the upper runway) and the other plane on Runway 2. Words in small caps were uttered with emphasis. A single period indicates a short pause, two periods a long pause. The length of the pauses was not measured; they were distinguished by the judgment of the transcribers. Double letters indicate a lengthening in the German originals, which is not preserved in the English translation. Unidentifiable material (e.g., "pf") was just repeated in the translation. The English translations try to capture the structure of the German originals as closely as possible, leading to some nonstandard, even ungrammatical word orderings, and do not use progressive forms.

❧ PARTICIPANT 1, SCENE 1.   jetzt kommn ZWEI Flugzeuge von links .. ÄH .. HEREIN und, ähm, auf Laufbahn eins und zwei, also parallel und dann, äh, ist das untere Flugzeug, das auf .. äh .. Laufbahn zwei war .. nach links abgebogen und hat dann geWARTET bis das .. Flugzeug auf der .. ERSTEN Laufbahn an ihm vorbeigefahren is

Translation: now come TWO planes from the left .. UHM .. INTO [the visible area] and, uhm, on runway one and two, [they move] in parallel and then, uhm, the other plane, which was on .. uhm .. runway two .. has turned off to the left and has then WAITED until the .. plane on the .. FIRST runway has passed it

❧ PARTICIPANT 1, SCENE 2.   jetzt kommt von LINKS ein Flugzeug, äh, reingefahren .. macht eine RECHTSBIEGUNG, auf der erstenn Rollbahn war das, jetzt kommt par, äh, GLEICHZEITIG ein .. äh, Flugzeug auf der zweiten Rollbahn von links, so m.deswegen muss das erste Flugzeug HALTEN .. und das, äh, zweite Flugzeug ist jetzt an dem .. haltenden Flugzeug vorbeigeFAHRN und fährt gradeaus weiter auf der zweiten Rollbahn

Translation: now comes from the LEFT a plane, uhm, moving into [the visible area] .. makes a RIGHT TURN, on the first runway that was, now comes par, uhm, AT THE SAME TIME a .. uhm, plane on the second runway from the left, so m.because of that the first plane must STOP .. and the, uhm, second plane has now the .. non-moving plane PASSED and moves on straight ahead on the second runway

✿ PARTICIPANT 2, SCENE 1.   jetzt kommn ZWEI, eins auf der ERSTEN Rollbahn, 's andere is auf der zweiten, 's auf der zweiten biegt an der ersten Abzweigung .. will also auf die erste, bleibt kurz stehn, läßt das andere vorbeifahrn, das immer gerade weiterFÄHRT

Translation: now come TWO, one on the FIRST runway, the other is on the second, the one on the second turns off at the first junction .. wants onto the first, stands still briefly, lets the other one pass, which all the time MOVES straight ahead

✿ PARTICIPANT 2, SCENE 2.   'n Flugzeug kommt von LINKS auf Rollfeld EINS .. biegt nach RECHTS ab, 'n Flugzeug kommt von links auf Rollfeld ZWEI .. das erste Flugzeug läßt das auf Rollfeld zwei VORBEIFAHRN .. und das fährt gradeaus WEITER

Translation: a plane comes from the LEFT onto runway ONE .. turns off to the RIGHT, a plane comes from the left onto manoeuvring area [probably meaning: runway; the same in the following] TWO .. the first plane lets the one on manoeuvring area two PASS .. and that one CONTINUES to move straight ahead

✿ PARTICIPANT 3, SCENE 1.   auf dem Rollweg ZWEI kommt ein schnelles Flugzeug gefahrn, auf Rollweg eins ein .. laangsames, das auf Rollweg zwei biegt nach LINKS ab in die erste Abzweigung, das auf Rollweg eins fährt weider, das auff .. EBEN Abgebogene hält AN .. mm .. um das andere passieren zu lassen

Translation: on the taxiway [probably meaning: runway; the same in the following] TWO comes a plane moving fast, on taxiway one a .. slow, the one on taxiway two turns off to the LEFT into the first junction, the one on taxiway one moves on, the one on .. one that JUST turned off STOPS .. mm .. to let the other one pass

✿ PARTICIPANT 3, SCENE 2. ÄH, auf dem Rollweg eins kommt von LINKS das nächste Flugzeuch, biecht gleich nach RECHTS auf, äh, die Abzweigung rauf, auf, äh, Rollweg zwei kommt währenddessen auch ein Flugzeuch .. das von Rollweg eins abgebogene Flugzeuch hält an, um das auf Rollweg zwei fahrende Flugzeug passieren zu LASSENN .. das Roo .. auf Rollweg zwei pf .. fahrende Flugzeuch fährt immer gradeaus, das, ähm, abgebogene Flugzeuch von Rollweg eins hält seine Position

Translation: UHM, on the taxiway one [probably meaning: runway; the same in the following] comes from the LEFT the next plane, turns off immediately to the RIGHT on, uhm, up the junction, on, uhm, taxiway TWO meanwhile comes also a plane .. the plane that turned off from taxiway one stops, to let the plane moving on taxiway two PASS .. the taa .. on taxiway two pf .. moving plane goes on straight ahead all this time, the, uhm, turned-off plane of taxiway one holds its position

🔊 PARTICIPANT 4, SCENE 1.   is GRADEAUS übers Rollfeld, LINKS .. erstes Rollfeld und zweites Rollfeld .. obere, oben startet einer, fährt GRADEAUS, linke .. ZWEI-
TE Rollbahn .. is einer gestartet, LINKS abgebogen und biecht jetzt auf die .. erste
Rollbahn EIN und fährt .. hinter dem .. annern Flugzeug her, was sich auf der ersten Rollbahn befindet, weil .. das ff, erste VERSCHWINDET, das zweite, was dort
eingebogen is verschwindet jetzt auch .. gleich .. rechts
  Translation: is STRAIGHT across the maneuvering area [probably meaning:
runway; the same in the following], LEFT .. first maneuvering area and second
maneuvering area .. top, on the top starts one, moves STRAIGHT, left .. SECOND
runway .. one has started, turned off LEFT and now turns off onto the .. first runway
INTO [no English correlate for the German *ein* here] and moves .. after the .. other
plane, which is on the first runway, because .. the ff, first DISAPPEARS, the second,
which turned into there disappears as well .. soon .. right

🔊 PARTICIPANT 4, SCENE 2.   von links in Richtung rechts auf Rollfeld eins ..
erste Abzweigung RECHTS, von links auf Rollfeld ZWEI kommt ein zweites FLUCH-
ZEUCH, das erste WARTET .. an Roll, an der Abzweigung Rollfeld zwei, das zweite
bleibt immer noch auf Rollfeld zwei, fährt gradeaus in Richtung .. rechter Bildrand
  Translation: from the left toward the right on maneuvering area one[probably
meaning: runway; the same in the following] .. first junction to the RIGHT, from
the left onto maneuvering area TWO comes a second PLANE, the first WAITS .. at
run, at the junction maneuvering area two, the second stays still on maneuvering
area two, moves straight toward .. right border of the display

🔊 PARTICIPANT 5, SCENE 1.   ähm, zwei Flugzeuge bewegen sich jeweils auf Runway eins und ZWEI .. von Runway zwei biegt nach links AB und bewegt sich auf
Runway eins zu, STOPPT .. bevor es, äh, das Flugzeug auf Runway eins TRIFFT und
reiht sich dann hinter .. dem Flugzeug auf Runway eins ein ... beide bewegen sich
dann weiter .. nach RECHTS .. das erste ist verschwunden .. und das zweite folgt
nach .. und verschwindet jetzt auch .. am Bildschirmrand
  Translation: uhm, two planes move respectively on runway one and TWO .. from
runway two turns OFF to the left and moves toward runway one, STOPS .. before it,
uhm, HITS the plane on runway one and queues after .. the plane on runway one ...
both move then on .. to the RIGHT .. the first one has disappeared .. and the second
follows .. and disappears now as well .. at the border of the display

🔊 PARTICIPANT 5, SCENE 2.   ein Flugzeug kommt von der LINKEN Seite auf
Rollbahn eins, biegt RECHTS ab ... uund bewegt sich auf Rollbahn zwei zu, wo

grade ein WEITERES Flugzeugk, äh, von links nach rechts fährt, sch .. das erste
Flugzeug STOPPT .. läßt das zweite Flugzeug passiern auf Rollbahn zwei ... das
Flugzeug fährt weiter

Translation: a plane comes from the LEFT side on runway one, turns off to the
RIGHT aand moves towards runway two, where just ANOTHER plane, uhm, moves
from the left to the right, sh .. the first plane STOPS .. lets the second plane pass on
runway two ... the plane moves on

adaptation. The adjustment of the behavior of a computing device in a way that its available (allocated) resources suffice to accomplish a task.

agent. An agent has at least the following three properties: (1) It acquires knowledge by perceiving its environment, (2) it processes the perceived knowledge so as find a way to attain a goal, and (3) it executes actions to influence its environment so as to get closer to its goal or reach it. An agent typically has most of the following properties: reactivity, autonomy, collaborative behavior, communication ability, inferential capability, temporal continuity, personality, adaptivity, and mobility. Different types of agents can be distinguished: reactive (behaving according to stimulus–response pairs); deliberative (agent has plans, goals, intentions); situated (located in a dynamic environment); autonomous (self-starting behavior, often robots); rational (reflecting and evaluating own actions); and social (taking social goals into account) (Bradshaw, 1997; Strube, 1996).

algorithm. An algorithm is usually defined as having the following properties: (a) parameters/input (to specify a problem from the problem class described by the algorithm), (b) output, (c) determinate (same output for same input), (d) finite length (an algorithm is described by a finite number of instructions), (e) finiteness (an algorithm terminates after a finite number of steps), (f) determinism, definiteness (there is always a unique next step), and (g) effectiveness (it produces a result). Some of these properties may be missing, for example, in the context of operating systems, the property that an algorithm must terminate is usually dropped, because an operating system should run infinitely (Bibliographisches Institut, 1986; Knuth, 1973).

allocation. The allocation of a resource is the assignment of all or part of the resource to a task in order for the task to be carried out.

anytime algorithm. An anytime algorithm is an algorithm that refines its result over time so that it can produce a result at *any time*. The later the result is produced the more accurate it is. A subset consists of the algorithms that explicitly estimate the benefit of investing a required resource, especially time. Zilberstein (1996) lists seven properties anytime algorithms have:

> First is *measurable quality*: The quality of an approximate result can be determined precisely. ... Second is *recognizable quality*: The quality of an approximate result can easily be determined at run time ... Third is *mono-*

227

tonicity: The quality of the result is a nondecreasing function of time and input quality. Note that when quality is recognizable, the anytime algorithm can guarantee monotonicity by simply returning the best result generated so far rather than the last generated result. Fourth is *consistency*: The quality of the result is correlated with computation time and input quality. ... Fifth is *diminishing returns*: The improvement in solution quality is larger at the early stages of the computation, and it diminishes over time. Sixth is *interruptibility*: The algorithm can be stopped at any time and provide some answer. ... Seventh is *preemptability*: The algorithm can be suspended and resumed with minimal overhead (p. 74).

The output quality is determined by a metric. Zilberstein (1996) also gives three suitable metrics: "First is *certainty*, a measure of the degree of certainty that the result is correct. ... Second is *accuracy*, a measure of the degree of accuracy, or how close the approximate result is to the exact answer. ... Third is *specificity*, a metric of the level of detail of the result" (p. 74).

articulator. The component of the Levelt (1989) model that computes and controls articulatory movements on the basis of the phonetic plan.

AT **(activation threshold).** The activation threshold serves in determining whether an element (a refO or a designation in INC) is verbalized. If the activation of a designation is below the threshold, then it is only added to the preverbal message if it is semantically required.

available knowledge. The model knowledge that is accessible by an incremental process and its incremental algorithms.

best match. The concept in the CS that has the highest DOA with the candidate list.

blackboard. A common memory location for AI systems that holds intermediate results. Interdependent modules post data to the blackboard and use its data in new computations. The modules are sometimes seen as a group of colaborating experts. A blackboard can often be subdivided into two parts: the domain blackboard (reasoning about the domain) and the scheduling blackboard (reasoning about scheduling; Mercadal, 1990, p. 31).

candidate list. List of entities (refOs) from the CCR that is sent to the concept matcher by construction. The concept matcher matches its elements onto the concepts stored in the CS.

cascade. A cascade consists of incremental processes that work in parallel and that are arranged in a fixed, sequential order in such a way that each process has one preceding and one succeeding process. The incremental processes of a cascade are connected by increment streams and/orincrement buffers. A process reads input increments from its preceding process and sends output increments to its succeeding process. The first process of a cascade has no preceding process but reads input from the environment, and the last process has no succeeding process but sends its output to the environment.

category. A set of abstract or concrete entities that share a set of common properties. Their mental representations are concepts.

CCR (current conceptual representation). The internal representation of external states of affairs, realized as a referential net (Habel, 1986). It is a shared memory that is built up by construction and can be accessed by selection, linearization, and PVM-generation. Apart from PEs, it contains refOs that were computed by the concept matcher and the list of verbalization refOs, which constitute the traverse.

component. A part of a model or system that is independent of other parts. If a component is fully independent from others, it is a module. In contrast to a module, the informational encapsulation need not be absolute. The components of the conceptualizer are modelled by processes in INC.

concept. The mental representation of a category or an entity. Concepts are the symbolic elements from which a conceptual representation is constructed.

concept matcher. The process that matches the candidate list received from construction onto the entries in the CS. It determines the best match, the match list, and the DOA, which it returns to construction.

concurrency. Simulated parallelism. It is used for simulating the execution of multiple processes—in this context often called tasks—on one processor.

construction. The process of the conceptualizer that receives PEs from the PPU and builds up the hierarchical representation of the CCR from these PEs in cooperation with the concept matcher.

CS (concept storage). A referential net (Habel, 1986), which specifies the relations between simple and complex concepts. The hierarchical structure of an entry in the CS can be understood as a production rule: The simpler concepts are the guards; the more complex concepts and the relations between the concepts describe the action (and vice versa).

current preverbal message. The incremental preverbal message that is currently produced by PVM-generation. The increments contained in the current preverbal message are accessible by PVM-generation so that it can (a) keep track of still missing parts of the incremental preverbal message and (b) compute extensions, modifications, and self-corrections.

direction. A spatial entity that in standard mathematical terminology represents the orientation or sense of an entity. In this book, I use the more common word *direction*.

DOA (degree of agreement). A value between 0 and 1 computed by the concept matcher. It is a measure of the quality of the match between the candidate list and an entry in the CS.

DOAT (degree of agreement threshold). One of INC's parameters with values between 0 and 1. It is used by construction to decide whether a best match is good enough to be inserted into the CCR. If DOA $\geq$ DOAT the best match is inserted; if DOA $<$ DOAT the best match is ignored.

event. A situation type that consists of a change and at least one culmination point. In this book, it is mostly used synonymously to *situation*.

event thread. A sequence of events that have the same bearer.

Extended Wundt's Principle. Each processing component will be triggered into activity by a minimal amount of its characteristic input and produces characteristic output as soon as a minimal amount of output is available.

focused element. An element of the available knowledge. Each incremental process has one focused element. It is the entry point to the available knowledge of an incremental algorithm executed by the incremental process. An incremental algorithm starts evaluating the available knowledge from this element.

formulator. The formulator encodes a preverbal message linguistically and generates a phonetic plan.

frame problem. A problem first stated by McCarthy and Hayes (1969). In this book I, use it synonymously with the *persistence problem*, the problem to decide which facts (knowledge, part of the representation) are changed by an action and which are unaffected (persist).

head of traverse buffer. The first element in the traverse buffer. This element is the candidate for the next element that is verbalized. It is the only element of the traverse buffer seen by PVM-generation. When the LT of this element has expired, PVM-generation removes it from the traverse buffer and commences a new incremental preverbal message.

increment. A piece of information that is the input of an incremental process (*input increment*), the output of one (*output increment*), or both.

increment buffer. A buffer between two or more incremental processes. It can store a limited number of increments that cannot be processed further at the moment, because the reading process is not yet ready to take an increment from the buffer as input increment.

increment stream. An ordered sequence of increments that changes over time. Increments can be appended to and popped from the increment stream.

incremental algorithm. An algorithm that has the following properties: (a) It obtains a triple of focused element, local context, and available knowledge as input;

(b) it only considers the local context for its computations starting from the focused element; and (c) the output consists of modifications in the available knowledge, a new focused element, and an output increment.

incremental behavior. The *minimal* condition for calling the behavior of a model incremental is that it is capable of producing output before it has received all input possibly relevant for the correct and complete computation of the corresponding output. The *strong* condition for incremental behavior is that additionally input and output are read and written in parallel.

incremental model. A model that contains a cascade of incremental processes and a representation of the model knowledge. The incremental model manages (a) the views of the incremental processes on the model knowledge and (b) the access of the incremental processes to the model knowledge so that only one process has access to the representation at a given point in time.

incremental preverbal message. A preverbal message in Levelt's (1989) sense with the additional emphasis on the incremental way of production. Therefore, it is *a sequence of well-formed propositional structures on a subpropositional level.* Because complete preverbal messages are too big to constitute the increments between conceptualizer and formulator (they can be infinite in principle), the increments must be *sub*propositional. Nevertheless, increments themselves can be described by propositions.

incremental process. A process that behaves incrementally. It reads input from an increment stream, writes its output to another increment stream, and recursively executes the following two steps: (1) It determines a local context and (2) calls an incremental algorithm with respect to the available knowledge. The recursion ends if (a) a new input increment is available or (b) the result(s) cannot be improved. In the second case, the process suspends itself until a new input increment is available. An incremental process runs in an infinite loop until it is explicitly terminated from the outside.

incrementality. The property of a model, system, algorithm, or process to compute information in a piecemeal manner and the ability to produce output before all input is available.

indirect feedback. Feedback that is not realized as direct transmission of information. Instead, the component giving feedback alters a representation that the component receiving feedback is using as well. If the modification of the representation by the one component affects the operations of the other component, an indirect feedback has been given.

information. The difference between available knowledge and transferred knowledge.

internal speech. see phonetic plan.

knowledge. The facts and rules of a model or system. The major distinction is between declarative knowledge (fact knowledge, knowledge *what*) and procedural knowledge (rule knowledge, knowledge *how*).

linearization. The process of the conceptualizer that can reorder the elements of the traverse buffer. Its goal is to bring these elements into an appropriate order with respect to the current verbalization goal. The time it has available for doing this is the LT.

local context. The part (subset) of the available knowledge that is used by an incremental algorithm. It is a connected subpart of elements in the available knowledge around the focused element. In each recursion of the algorithm, the local context is different. It is determined by a heuristic that is specific to the incremental algorithm.

location. A spatial entity that represents a position of an object in space.

LOTB (length of traverse buffer). One of INC's parameters. It defines the number of elements that can be stored in the traverse buffer.

LT (latency). One of INC's parameters. It specifies the minimal time that a refO remains in the traverse buffer after selection inserted it and before it can be fetched by PVM-generation.

match list. The list returned by the concept matcher to the construction process that contains pairs as elements. Each pair assigns an element in the CS to an actual element in the CCR, if the CCR contains such an element.

metric. A metric determines the degree of usefulness of a resource for performing a task.

model. A textual and/or formal description of tasks and representations. Its implementation is a *system*.

model knowledge. The declarative knowledge of an incremental model.

module. A part of a model or system that is independent of other parts of the model or system. According to Fodor (1983), it has the following properties: (a) domain specificity, (b) mandatoriness, (c) limited central access to the mental representations, (d) fast speed, (e) informational encapsulation, (f) "shallow" outputs, (g) association with fixed neural architecture, (h) characteristic and specific breakdown patterns, and (i) the ontogeny exhibits a characteristic pace and sequencing.

monitor. The component of the conceptualizer that reads in the parsed speech from the speech comprehension system and compares it with the planned preverbal message. If it detects a deviation, it can generate a correction.

monitored traverse. The part of the CCR that contains the information that the monitor received from the language comprehension system. It is correlated with the information in the CCR and the traverse. In the ideal case, this is a one-to-one correspondence of refOs.

object. A concrete real-world entity.

parallelism. A mode of computation in which the overall process is subdivided into multiple subprocesses and in which these subprocesses are carried out on different processors simultaneously.

path. A spatial entity that represents the trajectory along which an object is moving or was moving.

PE (perceived entity). An increment that is the result of the perceptual preprocessing. It is the input to INC, where it is read by the construction process. They are perceptually unanalyzed and serve as the interface between perception and conceptualization.

phonetic plan. Also internal speech. In Levelt's (1989), model the output of the formulator and the input to the articulator.

PPU (preprocessing unit). The perceptual component that takes the perpetual, continuous perceptual input stream and segments it into PEs.

PVM-generation (preverbal-message generation). The process of the conceptualizer that polls the head of traverse buffer. When the LT of the head of traverse buffer has passed, PVM-generation starts to produce an incremental preverbal message, which it sends incrementally to the subsequent process, which is the first process of the formulator.

preprocessing. The computations necessary to get from different kinds of input to PES.

preverbal message. In Levelt's (1989) model, the propositions sent from the conceptualizer to the formulator. They correspond to semantic representations. In the context of INC, the notions incremental preverbal message and current preverbal message are particularly important.

process. Also called thread in the context of concurrency. A sequence of system of model states. It is a sequential program usually carried out in an infinite loop. A process executes a task that is part of the overall task of the system or model.

processor. A device that executes one or more processes.

resource. A material or immaterial auxiliary means required by a task in order to perform a function in achieving a goal. The performance or even the overall success of the task depends on allocation of the required resources or how much of the required resources are allocated to the task.

selection. The process of the conceptualizer that selects refOs for verbalization. Its local context is the traverse buffer, but it has access to the CCR and the traverse as well. It can change the traverse buffer by appending or replacing elements.

shared memory. A memory that is accessible by multiple processes. The processes do not partition the shared memory; that is, the shared memory does not consist of disjoint parts, each of which is accessed by only one process.

situation. An abstract concept representing a time interval or a point of time that relates an object and a spatial entity.

spatial entity. An abstract concept that represents spatial knowledge. In this book, it is one of path, location, or direction.

state. A set of variables with their assigned values of a system at a given point of time. In particular, it is the content of a knowledge representation at a given point of time.

symbol grounding problem. The problem that symbols—concepts in particular—cannot be defined exclusively by other concepts, because this results in circular definitions. To avoid circularity, concepts must be expressed in nonconceptual terms.

system. An implemented model. To build an implementation (an executable program) for a model, additional assumptions have to be made, whereas other issues can only be realized in a reduced version due to complexity.

thread. See process. The term *thread* is used especially in the context of concurrency.

traverse. The path through the CCR consisting of the verbalization refOs that were generated by PVM-generation during the production of incremental preverbal messages.

traverse buffer. An increment buffer that contains pointers to refOs in the CCR. These refOs were selected for verbalization but are not yet verbalized. The pointers in the traverse buffer can be manipulated by the processes selection and linearization until PVM-generation takes out the head of traverse buffer to start a new incremental preverbal message. If selection appends an element to the traverse buffer when it is filled, the head of traverse buffer is deleted.

update increment. An increment that updates an increment previously read or sent by an incremental process.

Wundt's Principle. Each processing component will be triggered into activity by a minimal amount of its characteristic input.

Adiwidjaja, A., & Gerhard, C. (2000). *VirtualDraw Version 2.3.* Documentation No. 6 of the project ConcEv. Hamburg, Germany: Universität Hamburg, Department of Informatics.

Albers, S. (1996). *Competitive online algorithms* (Tech. Rep. No. BRICS LS-96-2). Aarhus, Denmark: University of Aarhus, Department of Computer Science, BRICS.

Allen, J. F. (1983). Maintaining knowledge about temporal intervals. *Communications of the ACM, 26*(11), 832–843.

Allen, J. F. (1991). Time and time again: The many ways to represent time. *International Journal of Intelligent Systems, 6*(4), 341–355.

Altmann, G. T., & Kamide, Y. (1999). Incremental interpretation at verbs: Restricting the domain of subsequent reference. *Cognition, 73*(3), 247–264.

Amtrup, J. W. (1998). *Maschinelles Dolmetschen mit Mehr-Ebenen-Charts [Machine translation with multi-layer charts].* Unpublished doctoral dissertation, Universität Hamburg, Department of Informatics, Germany.

Anderson, J. R., & Lebiere, C. (1998). *The atomic components of thought.* Mahwah, NJ: Lawrence Erlbaum Associates.

Austin, J. L. (1962). *How to do things with words.* Oxford, England: Clarendon Press.

Avrahami, J., & Kareev, Y. (1994). The emergence of events. *Cognition, 53*(3), 239–261.

Bach, E. (1986). The algebra of events. *Linguistics and Philosophy, 9*(1), 5–16.

Baddeley, A. (1986). *Working memory.* Oxford, England: Oxford University Press.

Bard, E. G., Anderson, A. H., Sotillo, C., Aylett, M. P., Doherty-Sneddon, G., & Newlands, A. (2000). Controlling the intelligibility of referring expressions in dialogue. *Journal of Memory and Language, 42*(1), 1–22.

Bard, E. G., & Aylett, M. P. (2004). Referential form, word duration, and modeling the listener in spoken dialogue. In J. C. Trueswell & M. K. Tannenhaus (Eds.), *Approaches to studying world-situated language use: Bridging the language-as-product and language-as-action traditions* (pp. 173–192). Cambridge, MA: MIT Press.

Barsalou, L. W. (1999). Perceptual symbol systems. *Behavioral and Brain Sciences, 22*(4), 577–660.

Bibliographisches Institut. (1986). *Schülerduden Informatik [Students' dictionary Informatics].* Mannheim, Germany: Bibliographisches Institut.

Bic, L., & Shaw, A. C. (1988). *The logical design of operating systems* (2nd ed.). Englewood Cliffs, NJ: Prentice-Hall.

Bickhard, M. H. (2000). Dynamic representing and representational dynamics. In E. Dietrich & A. B. Markman (Eds.), *Cognitive dynamics: Conceptual and representational change in humans and machines* (pp. 31–50). Mahwah, NJ: Lawrence Erlbaum Associates.

Bierwisch, M., & Schreuder, R. (1992). From concepts to lexical items. *Cognition, 42*(1–3), 23–60.

Blumenthal, A. L. (1970). *Language and psychology: Historical aspects of psycholinguistics.* New York: Wiley.

Bock, K., Erwin, D. E., & Davidson, D. J. (2004). Putting first things first. In J. M. Henderson & F. Ferreira (Eds.), *The interface of language, vision, and action: What we can learn from free-viewing eyetracking* (pp. 249–278). New York: Psychology Press.

Bock, K., Irwin, D. E., Davidson, D. J., & Levelt, W. J. M. (2003). Minding the clock. *Journal of Memory and Language, 48*(4), 653–685.

Boddy, M., & Dean, T. (1994). Deliberation scheduling for problem solving in time-constrained environments. *Artificial Intelligence, 67*(2), 245–285.

Borodin, A., & El-Yaniv, R. (1998). *Online computation and competitive analysis.* Cambridge, England: Cambridge University Press.

Bradshaw, J. M. (1997). Introduction to software agents. In J. M. Bradshaw (Ed.), *Software agents* (pp. 2–46). Cambridge, MA: MIT Press.

Carroll, M. (1997). Changing place in English and German: Language-specific preferences in the conceptualization of spatial relations. In J. Nuyts & E. Pederson (Eds.), *Language and conceptualization* (pp. 137–161). Cambridge, England: Cambridge University Press.

Carstensen, K.-U., Ebert, C., Endriss, C., Jekat, S., Klabunde, R., & Langer, H. (Eds.). (2001). *Computerlinguistik und Sprachtechnologie: Eine Einführung [Computational linguistics and speech technology: An introduction].* Heidelberg: Spektrum Akademischer Verlag.

Chater, N., Pickering, M., & Milward, D. (1995). What is incremental interpretation? In D. Milward & P. Sturt (Eds.), *Incremental interpretation.* Edinburgh, Scotland: University of Edinburgh, Centre for Cognitive Science.

Clark, A. (2002). Local associations and global reason: Fodor's frame problem and second-order search. *Cognitive Science Quarterly, 2*(2), 115–140.

Clark, H. H. (1996). *Using language.* Cambridge, MA: Cambridge University Press.

Cooper, R., & Shallice, T. (1995). Soar and the case for unified theories of cognition. *Cognition, 55*(2), 115–149.

Crocker, M. W., & Brants, T. (2000). Wide-coverage probabilistic sentence processing. *Journal of Psycholinguistic Research, 29*(6), 647–669.

Dale, R., & Reiter, E. (1995). Computational interpretations of the Gricean maxims in the generation of referring expressions. *Cognitive Science, 19*(2), 233–263.

Davidson, D. (1967). The logical form of action sentences. In N. Rescher (Ed.), *The logic of decision and action* (pp. 81–95). Pittsburgh, PA: University of Pittsburgh Press.

Deacon, S. W. (1997). *The symbolic species.* London: Penguin.

Dean, S., & Boddy, M. (1988). An analysis of time-dependent planning. In *Proceedings of the 7th AAAI* (pp. 49–54). Cambridge, MA: MIT Press.

Dennett, D. C. (1996). Producing futures by telling stories. In K. M. Ford & Z. W. Pylyshyn (Eds.), *The robot's dilemma revisited: The frame problem in artificial intelligence* (pp. 1–7). Norwood, NJ: Ablex.

De Ruiter, J. P. (2000). The production of gesture and speech. In D. McNeill (Ed.), *Language and gesture* (pp. 284–311). Cambridge, MA: Cambridge University Press.

de Smedt, K. (1990a). *Incremental sentence generation: A computer model of grammatical encoding.* Unpublished doctoral dissertation, Nijmegen, The Netherlands: Katholieke Universiteit te Nijmegen. (NICI Tech. Rep. No. 90-01)

de Smedt, K. (1990b). IPF: An incremental parallel formulator. In R. Dale, C. Mellish, & M. Zock (Eds.), *Current research in natural language generation* (chap. 7). London: Academic Press.

de Smedt, K., Horacek, H., & Zock, M. (1996). Some problems with current architectures in natural language generation. In G. Adorni & M. Zock (Eds.), *Trends in natural language generation: An artificial intelligence perspective* (pp. 17–46). New York: Springer.

de Smedt, K., & Kempen, G. (1987). Incremental sentence production, self-correction and coordination. In G. Kempen (Ed.), *Natural language generation: New results in artificial intelligence, psychology and linguistics* (pp. 365–376). Dordrecht, The Netherlands: Martinus Nijhoff.

Dietrich, E. (2000). Analogy and conceptual change, or you can't step into the same mind twice. In E. Dietrich & A. B. Markman (Eds.), *Cognitive dynamics: Conceptual and representational change in humans and machines* (pp. 265–294). Mahwah, NJ: Lawrence Erlbaum Associates.

Dietrich, E., & Markman, A. B. (2000). Cognitive dynamics: Computation and representation regained. In E. Dietrich & A. B. Markman (Eds.), *Cognitive dynamics: Conceptual and representational change in humans and machines* (pp. 5–29). Mahwah, NJ: Lawrence Erlbaum Associates.

Dörner, D. (1999). *Bauplan für eine Seele [Blueprint for a soul].* Reinbeck: Rowohlt.

Egg, M., Koller, A., & Niehren, J. (2001). The constraint language for lambda structures. *Journal of Logic, Language, and Information, 10*(4), 457-485.

Erk, K. (2000). Die Verarbeitung von Parallelismus-Constraints. In *Informatik 2000 – 30. Jahrestagung der Gesellschaft für Informatik*. Berlin: Springer.

Eschenbach, C. (1988). *SRL als Rahmen eines textverarbeitenden Systems [SRL as framework for a text processing system* (Tech. Rep. GAP Arbeitspapiere 3). Hamburg, Germany: Universität Hamburg, Department of Informatics.

Eschenbach, C., Habel, C., & Kulik, L. (1999). Representing simple trajectories as oriented curves. In A. N. Kumar & I. Russell (Eds.), *FLAIRS-99. Proceedings of the 12th international Florida AI Research Society conference* (pp. 431–436). Orlando, FL: AAAI Press.

Eschenbach, C., Tschander, L., Habel, C., & Kulik, L. (2000). Lexical specification of paths. In C. Freksa, W. Brauer, C. Habel, & K. F. Wender (Eds.), *Spatial cognition II* (pp. 127–144). Berlin: Springer.

Eysenck, M. W., & Keane, M. T. (1995). *Cognitive psychology: A student's handbook* (3rd ed.). Hove, England: Psychology Press.

Finkler, W. (1997). *Automatische Selbstkorrektur bei der inkrementellen Generierung gesprochener Sprache unter Realzeitbedingungen [Automatic self-correction in incremental generation of spoken language under real-time conditions]*. Sankt Augustin, Germany: infix.

Fodor, J. A. (1975). *The language of thought*. New York: Crowell.

Fodor, J. A. (1983). *The modularity of mind*. Cambridge, MA: MIT Press.

Foth, K., Menzel, W., Pop, H. F., & Schröder, I. (2000). An experiment on incremental analysis using robust parsing techniques. In *Proceedings of the 18th International Conference on Computational Linguistics* (pp. 1026–1030). San Francisco, CA: Morgan Kaufmann.

Gärdenfors, P. (2000). *Conceptual spaces: The geometry of thought*. Cambridge, MA: MIT Press.

Gardent, C., & Thater, S. (2001). Generating with a grammar based on tree descriptions: A constraint-based approach. In *Proceedings of the 39th Annual Meeting of the ACL* (pp. 212–219). San Francisco, CA: Morgan Kaufmann.

Ghidini, C., & Giunchiglia, F. (2001). Local models semantics, or contextual reasoning = locality + compatibility. *Artificial Intelligence, 127*(2), 221–259.

Gigerenzer, G., Todd, P. M., & ABC Research Group. (1999). *Simple heuristics that make us smart*. Oxford, England: Oxford University Press.

Glenberg, A. M. (1997). What memory is for. *Behavioral and Brain Sciences, 20*(1), 1–55.

Glenberg, A. M., Robertson, D. A., Jansen, J. L., & Johnson-Glenberg, M. C. (1999). Not propositions. *Cognitive Systems Research, 1*(1), 19–33.

Goldstone, R. L. (1994). The role of similarity in categorization: Providing a groundwork. *Cognition, 52*(2), 125–157.

Grice, P. (1975). Logic and conversation. In P. Cole & J. L. Morgan (Eds.), *Speech acts* (pp. 41–58). New York: Academic Press. (Reprinted in: P. Grice, 1989, *Studies in the Way of Words*, Harvard, MA: Harvard University Press.)

Griffin, Z. M. (1998). *What the eyes say about sentence planning.* Unpublished doctoral dissertation, University of Illinois at Urbana-Champaign.

Griffin, Z. M., & Bock, K. (2000). What the eyes say about speaking. *Psychological Science, 11*(4), 274–279.

Guhe, M. (2003). Incremental preverbal messages. In H. Härtl & H. Tappe (Eds.), *Mediating between concepts and language* (pp. 119–140). Berlin: de Gruyter.

Guhe, M. (2006). Referential nets as ACT-R declarative memory representation. In D. Fum, F. Del Missier, & A. Stocco (Eds.), *Proceedings of the Seventh International Conference on Cognitive Modeling, Trieste, April 5–8, 2006* (pp. 363–364). Trieste: Edizioni Goliardiche.

Guhe, M., & Habel, C. (2001). The influence of resource parameters on incremental conceptualization. In E. M. Altmann, A. Cleeremans, C. D. Schunn, & W. D. Gray (Eds.), *Proceedings of the 2001 Fourth International Conference on Cognitive Modeling: July 26–28, 2001, George Mason University, Fairfax, VA* (pp. 103–108). Mahwah, NJ: Lawrence Erlbaum Associates.

Guhe, M., Habel, C., & Tappe, H. (2000). Incremental event conceptualization and natural language generation in monitoring environments. In *Proceedings of the First International Conference on Natural Language Generation (INLG), 12–16 June 2000* (pp. 85–92). Mitzpe Ramon, Israel: ACL.

Guhe, M., Habel, C., & Tschander, L. (2003a). Describing motion events: Incremental representations for incremental processing. In *Proceedings of the 5th International Workshop on Computational Semantics* (pp. 410–424). Tilburg, The Netherlands: Tilburg University.

Guhe, M., Habel, C., & Tschander, L. (2003b). Incremental production of preverbal messages with INC. In F. Detje, D. Dörner, & H. Schaub (Eds.), *The logic of cognitive systems. Proceedings of the 5th International Conference on Cognitive Modeling* (pp. 123–128). Bamberg, Germany: Universitäts-Verlag Bamberg.

Guhe, M., Habel, C., & Tschander, L. (2004). Incremental generation of interconnected preverbal messages. In T. Pechmann & C. Habel (Eds.), *Current research on language production in Germany* (pp. 7–52). Berlin: de Gruyter.

Guhe, M., & Huber, S. (1999). *Algorithmische Interpretation von Wegeskizzen: Segmentierung und Gruppierung 1 [Algorithmic interpretation of sketch maps: Segmentation and grouping 1].* (Tech. Rep. No. 2 of the project ConcEv). Hamburg, Germany: Universität Hamburg, Department of Informatics.

Guhe, M., & Huber, S. (2000). *Spezifikation des inkrementellen Konzeptualisierers INC [Specification of the incremental conceptualizer INC].* (Tech. Rep. No. 6 of the project ConcEv). Hamburg, Germany: Universität Hamburg, Department of Informatics.

Guhe, M., & Schilder, F. (2002a). Incremental generation of self-corrections using underspecification. In M. Theune, A. Nijholt, & H. Hondorp (Eds.), *Computational linguistics in the Netherlands 2001. Selected papers from the twelfth CLIN meeting.* (pp. 118–132). Amsterdam: Rodopi.

Guhe, M., & Schilder, F. (2002b). Underspecification for incremental generation. In *Proceedings of KONVENS 2002, 6. Konferenz zur Verarbeitung Natürlicher Sprache* (pp. 37–43). Saarbrücken, Germany: DFKI.

Günther, C., Schopp, A., & Ziesche, S. (1995). Incremental computation of information structure and its empirical foundation. In K. de Smedt, C. S. Mellish, & H.-J. Novak (Eds.), *5th European Language Generation Workshop* (pp. 181–205). Leiden, The Netherlands: Rijks University Leiden.

Habel, C. (1982). Referential nets with attributes. In *Proceedings of the Ninth International Conference on Computational Linguistics (COLING-82).* Amsterdam: North-Holland.

Habel, C. (1986). *Prinzipien der Referentialität: Untersuchungen zur propositionalen Repräsentation von Wissen [Principles of referentiality: Investigations on propositional representation of knowledge].* Berlin: Springer.

Habel, C. (1987). Cognitive linguistics: The processing of spatial concepts. *T. A. Informations (Bulletin semestriel de l'ATALA, Association pour le traitement automatique du langage), 28*, 21–56.

Habel, C. (1988). Prozedurale Aspekte der Wegplanung und Wegbeschreibung [Procedural aspects of route planning and route description]. In H. Schnelle & G. Rickheit (Eds.), *Sprache in Mensch und Computer* (pp. 107–133). Opladen, Germany: Westdeutscher Verlag.

Habel, C. (2003). Incremental generation of multimodal route instructions. In *Natural language generation in spoken and written dialogue. Papers from the 2003 AAAI spring symposium, TR SS-03-06* (pp. 44–51). Stanford, CA: AAAI Press.

Habel, C., & Tappe, H. (1999). Processes of segmentation and linearization in describing events. In R. Klabunde & C. von Stutterheim (Eds.), *Representations and processes in language production* (pp. 117–152). Wiesbaden, Germany: Deutscher Universitäts-Verlag.

Hampton, J. A. (1999). Concept. In R. A. Wilson & F. C. Keil (Eds.), *The MIT encyclopedia of the cognitive sciences* (pp. 176–179). Cambridge, MA: MIT Press.

Hansen, E. A., & Zilberstein, S. (2001). Monitoring and control of anytime algorithms: A dynamic programming approach. *Artificial Intelligence, 126*(1–2), 139–157.

Harley, T. A. (2001). *The psychology of language: From data to theory* (2nd ed.). Hove, England: Psychology Press.

Harnad, S. (1990). The symbol grounding problem. *Physica D*, 42(1–3), 335–346.

Hartsuiker, R. J., & Kolk, H. H. (2001). Error monitoring in speech production: A computational test of the perceptual loop theory. *Cognitive Psychology*, 42(2), 113–157.

Herrtwich, R. G., & Hommel, G. (1994). *Nebenläufige Programme [Cocurrent programs]* (2nd ed.). Berlin: Springer.

Hildebrandt, B., Eikmeyer, H.-J., Rickheit, G., & Weiß, P. (1999). Inkrementelle Sprachrezeption [Incremental language understanding]. In I. Wachsmuth & B. Jung (Eds.), *KogWis: Proceedings der 4. Fachtagung der Gesellschaft für Kognitionswissenschaft, Bielefeld, 28. September 1999 – 1. Oktober 1999* (pp. 19–24). Sankt Augustin, Germany: infix.

Hudson, R. (2003a). *An encyclopedia of English grammar and Word Grammar.* [Online encyclopedia]. Available at: http://www.phon.ucl.ac.uk/home/dick/enc-gen.htm.

Hudson, R. (2003b). Word Grammar. In K. Sugayama (Ed.), *Studies in word grammar* (pp. 7–32). Kobe, Japan: Kobe City University of Foreign Studies, Research Institute of Foreign Studies.

Jackendoff, R. (1987). *Consciousness and the computational mind.* Cambridge, MA: MIT Press.

Jackendoff, R. (1990). *Semantic structures.* Cambridge, MA: MIT Press.

Jackendoff, R. (1997). *The architecture of the language faculty.* Cambridge, MA: MIT Press.

Jackendoff, R. (2002). *Foundations of language: Brain, meaning, grammar, evolution.* Oxford, England: Oxford University Press.

Jameson, A. (1997). Modeling the user's processing resources: Pragmatic simplicity meets psychological complexity. In R. Schäfer & M. Bauer (Eds.), *ABIS-97, 5. GI-Workshop Adaptivität und Benutzermodellierung in interaktiven Softwaresystemen: Workshop-Beiträge* (pp. 149–160). Saarbrücken, Germany: Universität des Saarlandes.

Jameson, A., & Buchholz, K. (1998). Einleitung zum Themenheft "Ressourcen-adaptive kognitive Prozesse" [Introduction to special issue "resource-adaptive cognitive processes"]. *Kognitionswissenschaft*, 7(3), 95–100.

Jurafsky, D., & Martin, J. H. (2000). *Speech and language processing: An introduction to natural language processing, computational linguistics, and speech recognition.* Upper Saddle River, NJ: Prentice-Hall.

Kalish, D., & Montague, R. (1964). *Logic: Techniques of formal reasoning.* New York: Harcourt, Brace & World.

Kempen, G. (1997). *Grammatical performance in human sentence production and comprehension.* Unpublished manuscript, Leiden University, Department of Psychology, Experimental Psychology Unit.

Kempen, G., & Harbusch, K. (2002). Performance grammar: A declarative definition. In M. Theune, A. Nijholt, & H. Hondorp (Eds.), *Computational linguistics in the Netherlands 2001. Selected papers from the twelfth CLIN meeting* (pp. 148–162). Amsterdam: Rodopi.

Kempen, G., & Harbusch, K. (2003). Word order scrambling as a consequence of incremental sentence production. In H. Härtl & H. Tappe (Eds.), *Mediating between concepts and language* (pp. 141–164). Berlin: de Gruyter.

Kempen, G., & Hoenkamp, E. (1982). Incremental sentence generation: Implications for the structure of a syntactic processor. In *Proceedings of the Ninth International Conference on Computational Linguistics* (pp. 151–156). Prague, Czechoslovakia: ACADEMIA.

Kempen, G., & Hoenkamp, E. (1987). An incremental procedural grammar for sentence formulation. *Cognitive Science, 11*(2), 201–258.

Kempen, G., & Huijbers, P. (1983). The lexicalization process in sentence production and naming: Indirect selection of words. *Cognition, 14*(2), 185–209.

Kieras, D. E., & Meyer, D. E. (1997). An overview of the EPIC architecture for cognition and performance with application to human–computer interaction. *Human–Computer Interaction, 12*(4), 391–438.

Kilger, A., & Finkler, W. (1995). *Incremental generation for real-time applications* (Tech. Rep. No. RR–95–11). Saarbrücken, Germany: Deutsches Forschungszentrum für Künstliche Intelligenz.

Kleinberg, J. M. (1999). Authoritative sources in a hyperlinked environment. *Journal of the ACM, 46*(5), 604–632.

Knight, K., & Langkilde, I. (2000). Preserving ambiguities in generation via automata intersection. In *Proceedings of the American Association for Artificial Intelligence conference* (pp. 697–702). Menlo Park, CA: AAAI Press.

Knuth, D. E. (1973). *The art of computer programming: Vol. 1 Fundamental algorithms* (2nd ed.). Reading, MA: Addison-Wesley.

Kosslyn, S. M. (1994). *Image and brain: The resolution of the imagery debate.* Cambridge, MA: Cambridge University Press.

Kosslyn, S. M. (1995). Mental imagery. In S. M. Kosslyn & D. N. Osherson (Eds.), *Visual cognition* (2nd ed., pp. 267–296). Cambridge, MA: MIT Press.

Krahmer, E., & Theune, M. (2002). Efficient context-sensitive generation of referring expressions. In K. van Deemter & R. Kibble (Eds.), *Information sharing: Reference and presupposition in language generation and interpretation* (pp. 223–264). Stanford, CA: CSLI Publications.

Krahmer, E., van Erk, S., & Verleg, A. (2003). Graph-based generation of referring expressions. *Computational Linguistics, 29*(1), 53–72.

Krauss, R. M., Chen, Y., & Gottesman, R. F. (2000). Lexical gestures and lexical access: A process model. In D. McNeill (Ed.), *Language and gesture* (pp. 261–283). Cambridge, MA: Cambridge University Press.

Laird, J. E., Newell, A., & Rosenbloom, P. S. (1987). Soar: An architecture for general intelligence. *Artificial Intelligence, 33*(1), 1–64.

Lakoff, G. (1987). *Women, fire, and dangerous things: What categories reveal about the mind.* Chicago: University of Chicago Press.

Landau, B., & Jackendoff, R. (1993). "What" and "where" in spatial language and spatial cognition. *Behavioral and Brain Sciences, 16*(2), 217–265.

Langacker, R. W. (1987/1991). *Foundations of cognitive grammar.* Stanford, CA: Stanford University Press. (2 vols.)

Langacker, R. W. (2000). *Grammar and conceptualization.* Berlin: de Gruyter.

Larson, K., & Sandholm, T. (2001). Bargaining with limited computation: Deliberation equilibrium. *Artificial Intelligence, 133*(1–2), 183–217.

Levelt, W. J. M. (1983). Monitoring and self-repair in speech. *Cognition, 14*(1), 41–104.

Levelt, W. J. M. (1989). *Speaking: From intention to articulation.* Cambridge, MA: MIT Press.

Levelt, W. J. M. (1999). Producing spoken language: A blueprint of the speaker. In C. M. Brown & P. Hagoort (Eds.), *The neurocognition of language* (chap. 4). Oxford, England: Oxford University Press.

Levelt, W. J. M., Roelofs, A., & Meyer, A. S. (1999). A theory of lexical access in speech production. *Behavioral and Brain Sciences, 22*(1), 1–75.

Levinson, S. C. (1996). Relativity in spatial conception and description. In J. J. Gumperz & S. C. Levinson (Eds.), *Rethinking linguistic relativity* (pp. 177–202). Cambridge, England: Cambridge University Press.

Levinson, S. C. (1997). From outer to inner space: Linguistic categories and non-linguistic thinking. In J. Nuyts & E. Pederson (Eds.), *Language and conceptualization* (pp. 13–45). Cambridge, England: Cambridge University Press.

Lewis, R. L. (1996). Architecture matters: What Soar has to say about modularity. In D. M. Steier & T. Mitchell (Eds.), *Mind matters: Contributions to cognitive and computer science in honor of Allen Newell* (pp. 75–84). Hillsdale, NJ: Lawrence Erlbaum Associates.

Lewis, R. L. (1999). Cognitive modeling, symbolic. In R. A. Wilson & F. C. Keil (Eds.), *The MIT encyclopedia of the cognitive sciences* (pp. 141–143). Cambridge, MA: MIT Press.

Lewis, R. L. (2001). Cognitive theory, Soar. In N. J. Smelser & P. B. Baltes (Eds.), *International encyclopedia of the social and behavioral sciences.* Amsterdam: Pergamon.

Liu, Y. A. (2000). Efficiency by incrementalization: An introduction. *Higher-Order and Symbolic Computation, 13*(4), 289–313.

Lock, K. (1965). Structuring programs for multiprogram time-sharing on-line applications. In *American Federation of Information Processing Societies (AFIPS): Proceedings of the Fall Joint Computer Conference* (pp. 457–472). Montvale, NJ: AFIPS Press.

Luck, M., & d'Inverno, M. (2001). A conceptual framework for agent definition and development. *The Computer Journal, 44*(1), 1–20.

Marcus, M. P. (1980). *A theory of syntactic recognition for natural language*. Cambridge, MA: MIT Press.

Markman, A. B., & Gentner, D. (2001). Thinking. *Annual Review of Psychology, 52*, 223–247.

McCarthy, J., & Hayes, P. J. (1969). Some philosophical problems from the standpoint of artificial intelligence. In B. Meltzer & D. Michie (Eds.), *Machine intelligence* (Vol. 4, pp. 463–502). Edinburgh, Scotland: Edinburgh University Press.

McDonald, D. D. (1987). Natural language generation. In S. C. Shapiro (Ed.), *Encyclopedia of artificial intelligence* (pp. 642–655). New York: Wiley.

McNeill, D. (1992). *Hand and mind: What gestures reveal about thought*. Chicago: University of Chicago Press.

Medin, D. L., & Aguilar, C. (1999). Categorization. In R. A. Wilson & F. C. Keil (Eds.), *The MIT encyclopedia of the cognitive sciences* (pp. 104–106). Cambridge, MA: MIT Press.

Melinger, A., & Levelt, W. J. M. (2004). Gesture and the communicative intention of the speaker. *Gesture, 4*(2), 119–141.

Menzel, W. (1994). Parsing of spoken language under time constraints. In A. G. Cohn (Ed.), *Proceedings of the 11th European Conference on Artificial Intelligence* (pp. 560–564). New York: Wiley.

Mercadal, D. (1990). *Dictionary of artificial intelligence*. New York: Van Nostrand.

Meteer, M. W. (1990). *The "generation gap": The problem of expressibility in text planning*. Unpublished doctoral dissertation, University of Massachusetts, Amherst.

Meteer, M. W. (1991). Bridging the generation gap between text planning and linguistic realization. *Computational Intelligence, 7*, 296–304.

Meyer, D. E., & Kieras, D. E. (1997). A computational theory of executive control processes and human multiple-task performance: Part 1. Basic mechanisms. *Psychological Review, 104*(1), 3–65.

Miller, G. A. (1956). The magical number seven, plus or minus two: Some limits on our capacity for processing information. *Psychological Review, 63*(2), 81–96.

Morgenstern, L. (1996). The problem with solutions to the frame problem. In K. M. Ford & Z. W. Pylyshyn (Eds.), *The robot's dilemma revisited: The frame problem in artificial intelligence* (pp. 99–133). Norwood, NJ: Ablex.

Murphy, G. L. (2002). *The big book of concepts*. Cambridge, MA: MIT Press.

Newell, A. (1990). *Unified theories of cognition: The William James lectures, 1987.* Cambridge, MA: Harvard University Press.

Newell, A., & Simon, H. A. (1963). GPS: A program that simulates human thought. In E. A. Feigenbaum & J. Feldmann (Eds.), *Computers and thought* (pp. 279–293). New York: McGraw-Hill.

Newell, A., & Simon, H. A. (1972). *Human problem solving.* Englewood Cliffs, NJ: Prentice-Hall.

Nuyts, J. (2001). *Epistemic modality, language and conceptualization: A cognitive-pragmatic perspective.* Amsterdam: John Benjamins.

Pechmann, T. (1984). *Überspezifizierung und Betonung in referentieller Kommunikation [Overspecification and emphasis in referential communication].* Unpublished doctoral dissertation, Mannheim University, Germany.

Pianta, E., & Tovena, L. M. (1999). XIG: Generating from interchange format using mixed representations. In E. Lamma & P. Mello (Eds.), *Advances in Artificial Intelligence: 6th Congress of the Italian Association for Artificial Intelligence, Bologna, Italy, September 1999. Selected Papers.* Berlin: Springer.

Pinker, S. (1999). *How the mind works.* New York: Norton.

Prinz, J. J., & Barsalou, L. W. (2000). Steering a course for embodied representation. In E. Dietrich & A. B. Markman (Eds.), *Cognitive dynamics: Conceptual and representational change in humans and machines* (pp. 51–77). Mahwah, NJ: Lawrence Erlbaum Associates.

Pullum, G. K. (1991). *The great Eskimo vocabulary hoax and other irrelevant essays on the study of language.* Chicago: Chicago University Press.

Ramalingam, G., & Reps, T. (1993). A categorized bibliography on incremental computation. In *Conference Record of the Twentieth ACM Symposium on Principles of Programming Languages, Charleston, SC, Jan. 11–13, 1993* (pp. 502–510). New York: ACM.

Reiter, E. (1994). Has a consensus NL generation architecture appeared, and is it psycholinguistically plausible? In *Proceedings of the Seventh International Workshop on Natural Language Generation* (pp. 163–170). Kennebunkport, ME: ACL.

Reiter, E., & Dale, R. (1992). A fast algorithm for the generation of referring expressions. In *Proceedings of 14th International Conference on Computational Linguistics* (pp. 232–238). Cambridge, MA: MIT Press.

Reiter, E., & Dale, R. (2000). *Building natural language generation systems.* Cambridge, England: Cambridge University Press.

Reiter, R. (2001). *Knowledge in action: Logical foundations for specifying and implementing dynamical systems.* Cambridge, MA: MIT Press.

Reithinger, N. (1991). POPEL—A parallel and incremental natural language generation system. In C. L. Paris, W. R. Swartout, & W. C. Mann (Eds.), *Natural language generation in artificial intelligence and computational linguistics* (pp. 179–200). Boston: Kluwer Academic.

Reithinger, N. (1992). *Eine parallele Architektur zur inkrementellen Generierung multimodaler Dialogbeiträge [A parallel architecture for the incremental generation of multimodal dialog contributions]*. Sankt Augustin, Germany: infix.

Rieckmann, B. (2000). *Perspektivierung in der Sprachproduktion: Eine empirische Untersuchung zu Ereignisbeschreibungen im Englischen [Perpectivization in language production: An empirical study of event descriptions in English]*. (Tech. Rep. No. 7 of the project ConcEv) Hamburg, Germany: Universität Hamburg, Department of Informatics.

Roelofs, A. (1997). The WEAVER model of word-form encoding in speech production. *Cognition, 64*(3), 249–284.

Rosch, E., Mervis, C. B., Gray, W. D., Johnson, D. M., & Boyes-Braem, P. (1976). Basic objects and natural categories. *Cognitive Psychology, 8*(3), 382–439.

Rumelhart, D. E., & McClelland, J. L. (1986). *Parallel distributed processing: Explorations in the microstructure of cognition*. Cambridge, MA: MIT Press. (2 vols.)

Russell, S. J., & Norvig, P. (2003). *Artificial intelligence: A modern approach* (2nd ed.). Upper Saddle River, NJ: Prentice-Hall.

Ryan, J. L., Crandall, R. L., & Medwedeff, M. C. (1966). A conversational system for incremental compilation and execution in a time-sharing environment. In *American Federation of Information Processing Societies (AFIPS): Proceedings of the Fall Joint Computer Conference* (pp. 1–29). Montvale, NJ: AFIPS Press.

Schilder, F., & Guhe, M. (2002). Underspecified parallelism constraint. In *Proceedings of KONVENS 2002, 6. Konferenz zur Verarbeitung Natürlicher Sprache* (pp. 163–169). Saarbrücken, Germany: DFKI.

Searle, J. R. (1969). *Speech acts*. Cambridge, England: Cambridge University Press.

Searle, J. R. (1979). *Expression and meaning*. Cambridge, England: Cambridge University Press.

Shanahan, M. (1997). *Solving the frame problem: A mathematical investigation of the common sense law of inertia*. Cambridge, MA: MIT Press.

Simon, H. A. (1955). A behavioral model of rational choice. *Quarterly Journal of Economics, 69*(1), 99–118.

Simon, H. A. (1982). *Models of bounded rationality*. Cambridge, MA: MIT Press. (2 vols.)

Simon, H. A. (1996). *The sciences of the artificial* (3rd ed.). Cambridge, MA: MIT Press.

Slobin, D. I. (1996). From "thought and language" to "thinking for speaking". In J. J. Gumperz & S. C. Levinson (Eds.), *Rethinking linguistic relativity* (pp. 70–96). Cambridge, England: Cambridge University Press.

Smith, E. E. (1995). Concepts and categorization. In E. E. Smith & D. N. Osherson (Eds.), *Thinking* (pp. 3–33). Cambridge, MA: MIT Press.

Smith, E. E. (1999). Working memory. In R. A. Wilson & F. C. Keil (Eds.), *The MIT encyclopedia of the cognitive sciences* (pp. 888–890). Cambridge, MA: MIT Press.

Smith, N. (1999). *Chomsky: Ideas and ideals.* Cambridge, England: Cambridge University Press.

Smith, N., & Tsimpli, I.-M. (1995). *The mind of a savant.* Oxford, England: Blackwell.

Smith, N., & Tsimpli, I.-M. (1996). Modules and quasi-modules: Language and theory of mind in a polyglott savant. *UCL Working Papers in Linguistics, 8,* 1–18.

Strube, G. (Ed.). (1996). *Wörterbuch der Kognitionswissenschaft [Dictionary of cognitive science].* Stuttgart: Klett-Cotta.

Tannenbaum, A. S. (1987). *Operating systems: Design and implementation.* Englewood Cliffs, NJ: Prentice-Hall.

Tappe, H., & Habel, C. (1998). *Verbalization of dynamic sketch maps: Layers of representation and their interaction.* Full version of one-page abstract/poster presented at Cognitive Science Conference; Madison, WI, August 1–4, 1998. ftp://ftp.informatik.uni-hamburg.de/pub/unihh/informatik/ WSV/TappeHabel_CogSci_1998.pdf.

Todd, P. M., & Gigerenzer, G. (2000). Précis of "Simple heuristics that make us smart". *Behavioral and Brain Sciences, 23*(5), 727–780.

Tomlin, R. S. (1997). Mapping conceptual representations into linguistic representations: The role of attention in grammar. In J. Nuyts & E. Pederson (Eds.), *Language and conceptualization* (pp. 162–189). Cambridge, England: Cambridge University Press.

Tulving, E. (1999). Episodic vs. semantic memory. In R. A. Wilson & F. C. Keil (Eds.), *The MIT encyclopedia of the cognitive sciences* (pp. 278–280). Cambridge, MA: MIT Press.

Turhan, A.-Y., & Erichsen, M. (1998). *The Sketch Program "Zeichnung": Documentation of Zeichnung, Version 2.2.* Documentation No. 2 of the project ConcEv. Hamburg, Germany: Universität Hamburg, Department of Informatics.

van Benthem, J. (1990). *The logic of time* (2nd ed.). Dordrecht, The Netherlands: Kluwer Academic.

van Deemter, K. (2002). Generating referring expressions: Boolean extensions of the incremental. *Computational Linguistics, 28*(1), 37–52.

van der Sluis, I., & Krahmer, E. (2001). Generating referring expressions in a multimodal context. In W. Daelemans, K. Sima'an, J. Veenstra, & J. Zavrel (Eds.), *Computational linguistics in the Netherlands 2000. Selected papers from the eleventh CLIN meeting* (pp. 158–176). Amsterdam: Rodopi.

van der Sluis, I. (2005). *Multimodal reference: Studies in automatic generation of multimodal referring expressions*. Unpublished doctoral dissertation, Tilburg University, The Netherlands.

Vilain, M. B. (1982). A system for reasoning about time. In *Proceedings of AAAI-82* (pp. 197–201). Pittsburgh, PA: AAAI Press.

von Kleist, H. (1985). Über die allmähliche Verfertigung der Gedanken beim Reden [On the gradual production of thoughts when speaking]. In H. Brandt (Ed.), *Kleists Werke in zwei Bänden*. Berlin: Aufbau Verlag. (Original work published in 1805.)

von Stutterheim, C. (1999). How language specific are processes in the conceptualizer? In R. Klabunde & C. von Stutterheim (Eds.), *Representations and processes in language production* (pp. 153–179). Wiesbaden, Germany: Deutscher Universitäts-Verlag.

Wahlster, W. (Ed.). (2000). *Verbmobil: Foundations of speech-to-speech translation*. Berlin: Springer.

Wiese, H. (2003a). Are hedgehogs like pigs, or tortoises like toads? Language-specific effects of compound structure on conceptualisation. In F. Schmalhofer, R. M. Young, & G. Katz (Eds.), *Proceedings of EuroCogSci 2003: The European Cognitive Science Conference 2003* (p. 448). Mahwah, NJ: Lawrence Erlbaum Associates.

Wiese, H. (2003b). Semantics as a gateway to language. In H. Härtl & H. Tappe (Eds.), *Mediating between concepts and language* (pp. 197–222). Berlin: de Gruyter.

Wirén, M. (1992). *Studies in incremental natural-language analysis*. Unpublished doctoral dissertation, Linköping University, Sweden.

Wundt, W. (1900). *Völkerpsychologie: Vol. 1. Die Sprache [Psychology of peoples: Vol. 1. Language]*. Leipzig: Engelmann.

Ziesche, S. (1997). *Perspektivierungsprozesse in der Sprachproduktion [Perspectivization processes in language production]*. Unpublished doctoral dissertation, Universität Hamburg, Germany.

Zilberstein, S. (1996). Using anytime algorithms in intelligent systems. *Artificial Intelligence Magazine, 17*(3), 73–83.

Milton Keynes UK
Ingram Content Group UK Ltd.
UKHW022105141024
449569UK00031B/1790

9 781138 972506